How to Say It®

from
The Heart

JACK GRIFFIN

Prentice
Hall Press

Library of Congress Cataloging-in-Publication Data

Griffin, Jack.
   How to say it® from the heart : communicating with those who matter
in your personal and professional life / by Jack Griffin.
      p. cm.
   ISBN 0-7352-0162-5
   1. Interpersonal communication.   I. Title.

P94.7.G75 2001
153.6—dc21   00-051591

Acquisitions Editor: *Tom Power*
Production Editor: *Jacqueline Roulette*
Page Layout: *Dee Coroneos*
Designer: *Sue Behnke*

Copyright © 2001 by Jack Griffin

Printed in the United States of America

10 9 8 7 6 5 4 3 2 1

ISBN 0-7352-0162-5

ATTENTION: CORPORATIONS AND SCHOOLS

Prentice Hall Press books are available at quantity discounts with bulk purchase
for educational, business, or sales promotional use. For information, please
write to: Prentice Hall, Special Sales, 240 Frisch Court, Paramus, NJ 07652.
Please supply: title of book, ISBN, quantity, how the book will be used, date
needed.

 Paramus, NJ 07652

http://www.phdirect.com

Dedication

For Anita—from the heart.

Contents

v

Part 2
Among Family and Friends   47

7 *Appreciation and Thanks* **76**

8 *Cheers and Encouragement* **87**

9 *Celebration and Congratulation* **102**

10 ***Asking Favors*** ***113***

11 ***Invitation and Welcome*** ***126***

Part 3
Talking with Children About . . .   169

18 *Sex* *207*

Part 4
The Languages of Love   217

19 *Getting Acquainted* *219*

20 *The Body Language of Love* *233*

Part 5
On the Job   271

Why This Book Is for You

"The heart has its reasons, which reason does not know."

—*Blaise Pascal (1623–1662)*

"Say what you mean and mean what you say."

How often have you been given that advice? Probably about as often as you have given it yourself. And why not? Advice just doesn't get much better than this. Saying what you mean and meaning what you say is all about saying it from the heart. Simple, yes?

You bet.

But, like most truly simple concepts, putting it into practice is, for most of us, devilishly difficult.

The Head-Heart Disconnect

We all believe that sincerity, genuine expression, and emotional truth are vital to our relationships with family, friends, loved ones, and also with the people with whom we work. Yet if you have trouble connecting heart with head with words, you are not alone. Getting these three variables to come out equal is the great equation of life. It is an equation we try each and every day to solve. For most of us, the calculation is hit-or-miss. For some of us, the results just never balance out. For the truly successful among us—those who get full pleasure and satisfaction from living and working with and among families, friends, colleagues, customers, subordinates, and bosses—the equation almost always comes out just right. For these fortunate folk, the line from heart to head to words runs straight and true and sure.

But what about the rest of us?

- We want to say what we mean, but we sometimes speak before we know what we mean.

- We mean one thing but end up saying another.

xvi

- The "right" words just don't come.
- The "right" words come—but much too late.
- We feel strong emotion, which we cannot put into words.
- Words just get in the way of what we feel.
- What we feel just gets in the way of words.
- We feel the "right" things, but we say the "wrong" things.

Love, anger, fear: No emotions are more basic or more universal—more heartfelt—than these. Yet no emotions are more difficult to communicate, to manage, to put into words. This book will show you how.

More Words for More Feelings

If love, anger, and fear are not major problems for you, that still leaves plenty of other challenging matters of the heart to tackle. For example:

- Making meaningful announcements
- Apologizing from the heart
- Expressing heartfelt thanks and appreciation
- Providing real encouragement
- Extending congratulations from the heart
- Asking favors
- Making invitations more inviting
- Making a persuasive case
- Providing genuine sympathy
- And just keeping in touch

Saying It from the Heart—to Your Kids

You'll also find helpful how-to advice on talking with children about such emotionally difficult subjects as

- Anger
- Caring

- Death
- Divorce
- Drugs
- Feelings
- Manners
- Sex

Learning the Language of Love

Then there's the life arena in which absolutely nothing is more important than saying it from the heart: love.

In love, we find it most essential—and most difficult—to say what we mean and mean what we say. This book will help you identify and overcome the obstacles that stubbornly interfere with heartfelt expression just when we need it most.

- You'll learn about the body language of love, about what to say when you want to get acquainted, and about what to say on a date.

- A special chapter is devoted to the enduring romance of the love letter in the 21st century.

- There are chapters on getting a date, on what to say during a date, on writing love letters via e-mail, and on how to use words to patch up the rough patches in any relationship.

The Heart of the Job

Anybody who thinks saying it from the heart has nothing to do with saying it on the job must be in a pretty dreary line of work. The truth is that the workplace is filled with intense emotion and populated by fragile egos. As for the stakes, they are the very highest—your future and that of your firm. Work time is the right time to say it from the heart. You'll find guidance on:

- Making announcements
- Turning occasions of apology into opportunities for strengthening business relationships

- Expressing thanks with sincerity
- Creating inclusive celebrations and congratulations
- Criticizing creatively, precisely, and without leaving scars
- Complaining effectively
- Reaching out with sympathy and condolence
- Motivating from the heart
- Asking favors
- Making invitations more inviting
- Promoting yourself and promoting your projects

The Heartline Concept

If all this information in one book seems a bit overwhelming, the fact is that saying it from the heart is saying it from the heart, regardless of whom you're communicating with. The concept that unifies the approach to all of the diverse people and situations included in this book is what we call the heartline: the most direct route from heart to head to words. Truly effective communication begins with discovering the heartline for a particular time, place, and person.

> Each situation we explore in *How to Say It® from the Heart* identifies the heartline for that particular situation and tells you how to get onto it and use it to journey to your goal without detours, without stalling, and without getting lost.

Learning Your Lines

It is natural to think the following:

1. My feelings are unique. No one can know what I'm really feeling.

2. Feelings in general are unpredictable; therefore, speaking from the heart has to be spontaneous. It either happens, or it doesn't. Hit or miss. Lucky or unlucky.

It is natural to think this way, but it is neither accurate nor useful. Sure, your feelings are your feelings, but that doesn't mean you are alone in having them. This book will help you identify your feelings with those of others, and, once you do that, we'll look together for the words that connect you most directly not only with what your heart says, but what the hearts of others need and want to hear.

And you'll learn something else, too: Saying it from the heart is too important to leave to chance. In any important communication, the last thing you want to do is wing it. This book will show you how to rehearse and prepare for meaningful emotional communication.

Keys to Understanding

"The heart," the great French philosopher Pascal wrote, "has its reasons, which reason cannot know." Learning to say it from the heart will help you to know those reasons, to understand them, and to communicate them. I promise you this: *How to Say It® from the Heart* will help you to communicate effectively, powerfully, and successfully, to the people and in the situations that matter most to you.

Part 1

Getting Ready
to Say It
from the Heart

This part introduces you to the concepts
and techniques of communicating from the heart.

1

Find Your *Heartline*

*J*ust be yourself! Don't think so much! Just say whatever comes into your head! Let it all hang out! Don't censor yourself! Let your feelings be your guide! When the time comes, the words will come to you!

Our world is filled with bad advice, and this is some of the worst. Not that it is motivated by anything malicious; all of these pronouncements are founded on the belief that our society and our culture value spontaneity above all else. We take it for granted that spontaneous expression is the most direct form of communication and that the most direct communication is necessarily the most honest. In effect, we equate thoughtless speech with honest speech. If we take this to the next step, that the most honest speech is necessarily the best speech, then we must conclude that the best speech is the least thoughtful speech—and, indeed, the less thought given to what we say, the better!

Language, many biologists, anthropologists, and philosophers tell us, is what finally distinguishes human beings from the other subjects of the animal kingdom. Language is certainly the medium through which we make most of our needs known and, largely, through which we obtain satisfaction of those needs. Language, any way we look at it, is central to everything we are and hope to be. Should we, then, be so willing to disavow responsibility for it and control over it?

There is no need to waste your time answering what is obviously a rhetorical question. The point is this: Honest, effective language—speaking from the heart—does not require abandonment of thought. Quite the contrary: The more thought, the more imagination that goes into what you say, the more honest, effective, and heartfelt it can be.

What Is the Heartline, Anyway?

But why should we have to give more than a passing thought to expressing what we feel? Shouldn't this just come naturally?

Maybe it should. It would be nice if it did. But, then, it would also be nice if we all played golf like Tiger Woods, played guitar like Eric Clapton, and played the stock market like Warren Buffett.

The Declaration of Independence notwithstanding, we aren't all created equal, and life ain't necessarily fair. To a Woods, a Clapton, or a Buffett, excellence in their particular fields seems natural. We know, however, that their skills are not simply inborn, but are a combination of natural ability, hard work, and, probably, some other elements thrown in along the way. Yet when we listen to an eloquent, persuasive speaker, we assume that the right words just come naturally to her, and we bemoan the fact that we don't share her eloquence.

The *bad* news is that sports prowess, musical virtuosity, and financial genius are not birthrights. Nor is the ability to speak from the heart. Like a skillful golf swing, a perfect command of the guitar, or an insightful grasp of investment strategy, creating honest, clear, persuasive speech is too complex a process to be entirely natural and native to us. The *good* news is that all of us, if we want, can learn to play golf or play it better, pick out a chord or two on the guitar, and even invest with a degree of sound judgment. We can also learn to speak from the heart. The steps in this learning process follow.

Step One. Give up the notion that speaking from the heart is speaking without thought. This entails abandoning the lie that motives of the heart and the head are incompatible and necessarily in conflict.

Step Two. Give up the notion that spontaneous speech is the best speech. Not only is it okay to prepare, it is the best way to ensure that you really will. And, above all else, speaking from the heart is saying what you want to say.

Step Three. Give up the notion that you naturally know what you want to say, but just have trouble putting it into words. The fact is that an important initial process in speaking from the heart is to determine just what it is you need to say. Often, we have to devote some time and thought to figuring out what is in our hearts. Just because something is important to us, we can't assume that we are fully aware of it. You need to determine what you want to express before you begin to put it into words.

Step Four. Give up the notion that once you know what you want and need to say, the words will just come. It doesn't necessarily work that way. Certainly, you can't count on it. How many times have you felt strong, urgent emotion—only to find yourself tongue tied: so angry you couldn't speak, so happy you couldn't speak, so sad, so moved, so frustrated? As often as strong emotion drives speech, it also inhibits it or trips it up. Motivated by powerful feelings, we all too often say things we later—or even instantly—regret.

Now, having abandoned the preceding four obstacles to speaking from the heart, you can take the following positive steps:

Step Five. Discover what is in your heart. Determine what you want and what you need to say. We begin to discuss this step in detail in Chapter 3, but it is also a theme throughout the book.

Step Six. Find your *heartline*—the most direct route from heart to head to words. Not only do you need to determine what it is you want and need to say, you need to say it most efficiently and directly. Communication, like a radio or television signal, is subject to interference from various sources. Some of the most common sources of interference include:

- Conflicting emotions, competing motives. We aren't always single-minded. Sometimes we feel more than one strong emotion about a given issue.
- Fear of embarrassment
- Fear of causing embarrassment
- Fear of incurring criticism
- Fear of what the other person will think or feel
- Imperfect understanding of the situation at issue
- Inadequate command of the range of language options available

Many of the chapters in this book will help you focus on overcoming interference, the obstacles that sometimes block the heartline, the route from heart to head to expression.

All About Janus

The heartline is not a bodily organ or physiological structure. It is, rather, a strategy for communication. As such, it changes, depending on the time, place, and people involved. By definition, communication cannot be a solo endeavor. At minimum, it is a dialogue. "If a tree falls in the forest," the familiar philosophical question goes, "and no one is there to hear, does it make a sound?" Similarly, without someone with whom to communicate, is there communication? The search for the heartline in any given instance depends as much on who the other person is as it does on your own feelings, needs, and desires.

The communication strategies presented in this book always look two ways, toward yourself and toward others. Think of the Roman god Janus, the mythic guardian of gates. He is a god with two faces, one that looks inward, to the space within the gate, and one that looks outward, beyond the gate. Keep the image of Janus in mind when you set out to say it from the heart. Your task is to focus on yourself and your needs while simultaneously directing your attention to the recipient of your communication—to what you know about him, about his interests, his needs, his concerns. Saying it from the heart is as much about other people as it is about you.

Imagination Is the Key

It doesn't take the genius of a rocket scientist to figure out that those we celebrate as the great users of language—the famous poets and novelists, the great historians and orators—are also great users of the imagination. Indeed, it is the imagination that we most treasure in our great writers. But why reserve this faculty for the great writers? What about us more ordinary folk?

Whether you set out to write the great American novel or a note of congratulations to a friend who's just gotten a plum job, an exercise of imagination will make the communication more effective.

- Never try to communicate to a void. Use your imagination to visualize your audience, your reader, your conversation partner, the recipient of your message. Imagine writing as conversation, face to face.

- Imagine how the other person feels *now* and how you would like him to feel *after* he reads or listens to your message.

- Imagine yourself out of yourself. That is, focus on the other person.

- Imagine the dialogue before you even utter a word. When you have something really important to say, preview the conversation in your imagination. Rehearse it. Play the scene for yourself, like a movie.

- Imagine the outcome of the communication. What issues will it resolve? What will things be like *after* you've written that all-important letter or had the conversation you know is necessary but you've been dreading?

The Best Policy

It's been said many times: *Honesty is the best policy*. But it is also true that honesty is not the *only* policy—just the best.

If you can communicate with absolute truthfulness and objectivity, you are in the best possible position. Take that as your starting point. Begin with the truth, the whole truth, and nothing but the truth.

But honesty is not always simply equivalent to the truth. Your best friend is a Sunday painter, an art amateur who takes a lot of pleasure in the little canvases he creates. He's modest about them, but it's clear to you that he is very proud of his work. He's just completed a new portrait of his son and daughter, a picture he's been laboring at, off and on, for months now. He shows it to you . . . and it's a dreadful mess. The poor kids look like they've been playing in heavy traffic.

You gaze, slack-jawed, at the painting. Your friend beams.

Is honesty the best policy here?

Yes—but not the truth. In this case, an honest response takes into account the following:

- *What you feel about your friend.* You like him, and you don't want to hurt him. These are the feelings and this is the goal closest to your heart.

- *How you imagine your friend feels.* In this case, only a very slight exercise of the imagination is required. Obviously, he's proud of what he has done. He wants you to share his opinion of the painting.

- *The purpose—the objective—of this communication*. You are not an art critic, and, although you have been asked your opinion of this painting, the true purpose of this conversation is not art criticism. It is letting your friend feel good about what he has done.

The response that is most honest in this case, truest to your feelings, truest to what you conceive as your friend's feelings, and truest to the purpose of this particular communication, does not fully adhere to what you perceive as absolute, objective truth.

"You really see your kids in a unique, loving way. That certainly shows in this portrait!"

It is an honest, if not fully truthful, response.

15 Ways to Begin to Say It from the Heart

Every fugitive from high school physics is familiar with the principle of inertia: the tendency of a body in motion to remain in motion or a body at rest to remain at rest unless acted upon by an external force. This law of physics also translates nicely into a law of human psychology. Many of us just naturally have trouble getting started. The first words are the hardest to get out, and sometimes the prospect of communication seems just too daunting even to begin. Here are some tactics for overcoming the inertia that may keep us from saying it from the heart.

1. *What's your hurry?* There is no law against thinking before you speak or write. Take the time to sort out your thoughts, to identify the purpose of your communication. Think about what you are feeling, and what you want to accomplish by communicating on this occasion.

2. *Don't put yourself on the hot seat.* We are conditioned to believe that dialogue or conversation should be a rapid-fire give and take. Many of us are made uncomfortable by silences of even a few seconds between question and response. Don't feel obliged to come back with a fast answer. Take the time you need. If necessary, buy time with phrases such as, "That's an important question. Give me a moment to think about that."

3. *Mentally review what you feel, think, and want.* Then formulate what to say.

4. *Rehearse spontaneity.* If you envy the quick, suave wit of Hollywood leading men and ladies, just remember: They're all following scripts. But be aware that real life can be scripted, too. It is not dishonest to plan what you are going to say in a particular situation, and it is also a good idea to exercise your imagination in order to anticipate what the others involved in the situation are likely to say. Mentally rehearse all important upcoming exchanges.

5. *Do your homework.* The most convincing, persuasive communication is not filled with flowery phrases and lovely language, but with useful, relevant facts. If you feel strongly about a certain issue, learn all you can about it before you sit down to write or get up to speak.

6. *Select your audience.* Be certain that you direct your important communications to the right people. Often, this is obvious—but not always. For example, if you have prepared a heartfelt appeal in an effort to get hired for a new job, be sure that you identify the person who has the power to hire you. Talk to her, rather than to her assistant or associate.

7. *Communicate at the right time.* Too many of us speak up whenever the spirit moves us. Sometimes this is necessary; but whenever possible, give careful consideration to selecting the most advantageous time to speak or write. For example:

   * You really want a raise. Bring up the subject after you have successfully completed a project, not following some disappointing result.

   * You know that your spouse has good and bad days, or that he/she is most decidedly not a morning person. Broach critical subjects on the good days and never in the morning.

   * Your workplace has a rhythm all its own. Mornings are hectic, afternoons generally quiet. Bring up important issues when they are likely to receive extended, cool, calm attention.

   * In any workplace, Mondays are typically bad days to raise issues that can be put off until Tuesday.

   * At work, come Friday, many people find it difficult to focus.

- All other things being equal, the high-energy time for most people is late in the morning, between about ten and eleven. A high energy level typically correlates with positive emotions and higher levels of optimism. Often, this is a good time to present issues that matter to you.

- For most people, late afternoon is a dull, low-energy time, especially between two and four.

8. *Give up the idea that there are "good" versus "bad" feelings.* Accept the idea that there are "right" and "wrong" feelings. This distinction has nothing to do with morality. "Right" feelings are those you want your listener or reader to have as a result of your communication. In contrast, "wrong" feelings are those that will prompt your listener or reader to act in a way contrary to what you want. Exercise your imagination to determine which feelings are the "right" ones in a given situation, and shape your communication in ways you believe will produce those feelings.

9. *Don't ask for what you want.* Instead, go into the communication focused on what the other person wants. This does not require you to commit to a life of ceaseless self-denial and self-sacrifice. It does require a change of perspective. Let's say you are an auto salesperson. What you want is to sell the customer a car. You want this not so much because you have a strong desire to see the customer happily driving a car, but because you need to earn this month's mortgage money. If you were absolutely honest, you might approach the customer in the showroom with a remark like this: "You really *have* to buy this car. If you do, I won't have to worry about this month's mortgage payment." Of course, this approach is not likely to produce a sale. Instead, try focusing not on your needs and wants, but on those of the customer: "This car is a great value because . . ."

10. *Deal with your fears.* Fear—anxiety about potential embarrassment, about eliciting an angry response, about possible rejection, and so on—can certainly block or distort important communication. Don't try to ignore your anxious feelings. The surest way to intensify a negative emotion is to *try* to ignore it. This only forces you to focus on the feeling. Instead, try the following:

* Recognize and acknowledge the negative feelings that you have. Don't try to ignore or run away from them.

* Deliberately try to imagine the worst things that can happen to you as a result of the communication you are about to make. Develop a full scenario. Play it out. Experience the emotions *before* the conversation or before you send the letter; don't wait for the fears to sneak up on you.

* Having played out the worst that can happen, imagine the best outcome. How will you feel? What will it be like to succeed in this encounter? Play out this scenario, too. Will this exercise cure your case of nerves? Probably not, but it will make the emotions associated with a high-stakes communication more familiar and, therefore, less threatening. To this extent, it *will* reduce your anxiety and help you get in touch with your heart-line in this particular situation.

11. *Look like you're saying it from the heart.* Chapter 2 is all about how you can use body language to communicate persuasively.

12. *Don't just "speak" effective body language, learn how to "read" it, too.* Chapter 2 will also help you to become sensitive to the body language cues your listener gives you. Observe the effect of your words on the other person.

13. *Persuade with your ears.* Those who speak most successfully from the heart are those who listen most acutely and sensitively. Chapter 4 will help you become the best listener you can be.

14. *Never beg, but be prepared to bargain.* Persuasive speech establishes a certain rhythm of give and take. You can create this rhythm by not *asking* for what you want but by negotiating for it instead. What's the difference? Asking is taking; negotiating is trading one valuable commodity for another. It is taking *and* giving. Most persuasive communication is based on negotiation. For one thing, negotiation keeps issues alive. If you simply ask, "Can I get a raise?" and the answer is "No," the conversation grinds to a dead halt. If, however, you approach this issue as a negotiation, it tends to become a living thing—or at least a request that invites a creative response. For instance:

- Since I took over management of Project X, we've seen a 15 percent increase in profit margin, and we've added two new territories. Best of all, the year's not over. You've given me a lot of creative freedom, for which I'm grateful. However, I now feel that it is time for my salary level to catch up to the level of my responsibilities, qualifications, and, most of all, achievements.

15. *Create a pleasant climate.* It is easier to speak sincerely and persuasively in a friendly, receptive context than in a climate that feels cold or even hostile. Among family and friends or in the workplace, cultivate the habit of creative small talk. Not all communication needs to be profoundly heartfelt. Get into the habit of asking people how their day is going, or how they enjoyed that recent vacation, or how that new car is working out. Ask your kid what kind of day he had at school. Ask your friend for recommendations of must-see movies. Whatever you ask, focus on the interests of the other person—but keep it light and good natured.

Here's a final tip for overcoming the inertia that holds you back from saying it from the heart: Dig into the rest of this book. You'll get the most out of it if you read all the chapters in Part 1 and consult the rest as your needs dictate.

2

Not Another Word!

$\mathcal{I}$n 1971, psychologist Albert Mehrabian concluded a study of the nature of persuasion. He found that when listeners judge the emotional content of a speech, they give the most weight to the speaker's facial expressions and body movement—his "body language." Mehrabian was able to quantify just how much weight: 55 percent. That is, he found that 55 percent of a speech's power of persuasion—its effectiveness—depends on visual, not verbal, cues.

This is a powerful conclusion. So we find that only 45 percent of the effectiveness of a speech comes from the words?

No.

Actually, Mehrabian found that the *next* most important factors in determining the persuasive power of a speech, after visual cues, were "vocal qualities"—not words, but tone of voice, voice pitch, and the pace of delivery. These accounted for 38 percent of the speech's effectiveness. Adding 55 and 38 percent gives us 93 percent. According to Mehrabian's study, 93 percent of the effectiveness of a speech—ostensibly a *verbal* presentation—has nothing to do with the meaning of the words used. The words themselves account for a mere 7 percent of the effectiveness of a speech.

The Body's Language

The lesson of Mehrabian's study is that anyone who would communicate from the heart—convey important matters in a sincere and persuasive way—must always address the nonverbal aspects of verbal

13

communication. Movement, expression, and tone speak volumes, regardless of the words that are used or not used.

Space Invaders

In his popular 1970 classic, *Body Language,* Julius Fast explains that human beings, like other animals, stake out and defend a certain territory, or personal space. Among nonhuman animals, defense of territory is carried out through a combination of symbolic gestures—a cat will arch its back, a dog will snarl and bare its teeth—and out-and-out violence. Among people, however, the defenses are purely symbolic. They are sufficiently subtle that we aren't always consciously aware of the defensive gestures and postures, but they are effective nonetheless.

The Masking Defense

Fast speaks of our masking behavior, the face we present to the outer world, which is rarely our real face. Indeed, it is often considered inappropriate, even outrageous and "antisocial" to allow our face to express what we really feel. From a very early age, we are conditioned to mask our feelings through certain facial expressions and other bodily gestures. In effect, we are taught to employ a body language that lies and that, most of the time, disguises more than it reveals about what we have in our hearts. The ultimate motive of this masking behavior, Fast argues, is the defense of personal space. The trouble is, however, that such a defense not only is often unnecessary—a kind of outmoded artifact of our biological and cultural evolution—but can be downright destructive. It can make us appear insincere, nervous, afraid, evasive, or even treacherous. It blocks the heartline, and it often contradicts visually and subconsciously what we are saying verbally and deliberately.

Some of the common masks include the following:

- *The forced smile.* The smile can be one of the most powerful means of nonverbal communication. It can be the ultimate ice-breaker, a surefire messenger of sincerity, pleasure, trust, and good humor. Yet it can also be a powerful mask. We smile when we are happy, to be sure, but also when we are embarrassed, when we apologize, and when we suffer a minor mishap. Often the smile masks annoyance, impatience, even anger.

- *The forced scowl.* The great World War II general George S. Patton spoke of putting on his "war face," a stern scowl, rigid and immobile, which he used to practice daily in front of a mirror. Many of us adopt similar masks.

- *Closed gestures.* The way we fold our arms across our chest or cross our legs is often a defense against the invasion of our space.

These and similar masks are not all bad. In crowded urban societies we couldn't get along without them. They make day-to-day casual contact with any number of strangers and near-strangers easier. Doubtless, they avert much unpleasantness, ranging from harsh words to fistfights. We do not want to let the whole world into our most intimate range. Our social, cultural, and psychological well-being demands the maintenance of a certain zone of personal space.

But the masks we wear can also interfere with important communication, sabotaging the messages we want to convey.

- We may subconsciously telegraph unfriendliness.

- We may subconsciously tell the world we are insincere, uncertain, fearful, or out-and-out lying.

- We may convey anger and impatience.

- We may convey boredom.

Is there any way to control when and where we put on our masks? And is there any way to shed the masks we don't want?

Body language is truly a language in that it is a symbolic means of communication and it can be learned. Because it can be learned, we can control and regulate the way we use it. We can indeed become aware of the language we use in given situations, and we can alter it to a significant degree. The next section has some suggestions for how to do this.

Body Language: 15 Key "Phrases"

1. *Make a forthright entrance.* We've all known a man or a woman on whom all eyes focus when he or she enters a room. It is not necessarily that this person is particularly attractive, but, as the cliché goes, he or she "really knows how to make an entrance."

The problem with clichés is that we become so familiar with them that we stop thinking about what they really mean. The fact is that how you enter a room makes a very powerful statement about who you are and, perhaps even more important, who you think you are. To some lucky people, making a powerful positive first impression comes naturally and easily. For others, hard work and practice are required to overcome a natural tendency to awkwardness. Even if you are one of the latter, the extra effort is worth it. Why? Uncomfortable though it may be, it's a lot easier to put the effort into a positive first impression than it is to attempt to undo the negative effects of an unfavorable impression. Sometimes, you never get the opportunity even to try.

2. *Walk tall.* Life, our parents tell us and tell us more than once, ain't always fair. If you're on the short side, you won't like to hear that tall people have a built-in body language advantage. We tend naturally to invest more authority in tall people. We find them "naturally" more commanding, maybe we even think they are more sincere or trustworthy. The good news is that, even if you aren't tall, you can *walk tall*. Begin by dressing in ways that emphasize whatever height you have.

- Avoid boxy-looking tailoring.
- Avoid horizontally striped patterns.
- Shorter men should avoid baggy, loosely cut pants, and shorter women should favor longer hemlines.

Even more important than dressing to accent stature is to avoid entering a room or approaching another person in a cringing, stooped, or slouching manner. Concentrate on maintaining an erect posture as you make your entrance, and do so forthrightly, without hesitation, and with a purposeful stride.

How do you acquire a "purposeful stride"? Move with a purpose, and know where you are going.

- Try always to approach any communication situation having already formulated the purpose and the objective of the communication.
- If you have to do your thinking as you make your entrance, chances are that you'll appear hesitant or absent-minded. Work out as much as you can beforehand.

3. *Show a sincere smile.* Have you ever had the misfortune to face a grim, closed-mouthed loan officer? It gives you a sinking feeling, with cartoon visions of winged money bags flying anywhere but toward you. A scowling negotiator won't cut you much slack, you believe, just as a frowning salesperson probably won't make the sale. In contrast, a sincere smile is an invitation. Anything less than this sends the message that you intend to offer little or nothing and that you are receptive to little or nothing. If you come on like a tough nut to crack, many of the people you approach will decide that you just aren't worth dealing with.

If you find it easy and natural to smile, good for you! But some of us have to work harder at it.

- Begin by relaxing. Before you make your entrance, glance downward, move your jaw around, then move your tongue around the inside of your mouth. Inhale deeply, hold it, then let out your breath forcefully. Repeat this exercise a few times.

- When your facial muscles feel relaxed, think about something, someone, or some place you enjoy. Imagine pleasurable times, people, and places. Chances are that the combination of facial relaxation and a pleasant frame of mind will bring the easy, welcoming smile that is a tremendous communication facilitator.

4. *Make and maintain eye contact.* The one body language "phrase" that just about everyone knows about is *eye contact.* We all know and accept that looking someone in the eye conveys openness and honesty. It also transmits powerful energy. We've all heard people speak about the "sparkle" in someone's eye, as if that sparkle were an unusual thing, a thing that made the person in question seem special. Actually, *all* of us have a sparkle in our eyes, but it is rarely noticed. Why? Because, even though we all recognize the importance of eye contact, few of us actually make full eye contact when we meet or speak.

To exploit the sparkle in your eyes, to convey honesty and transmit energy, make eye contact—immediately, before the first words are spoken. For some people, this is not easy. Many of us learn to be shy. We are afraid of seeming to stare. We are, in fact, fearful of "invading" another person's space with our gaze. Working to overcome these inhibitions, these obstacles to making and maintaining eye contact, is well worth the effort of practice. Eye contact is a highly charged form of communication.

5. *Develop a memorable handshake.* Back in that amorphously undefined time known only as the good old days, diligent fathers took their sons aside and solemnly explained the great importance of a good, solid handshake. The handshake was seen as the deal maker and the deal closer. It conveyed a world of confidence, trust, and strength. The power of a hearty handshake was regarded as very nearly mystical.

Maybe this seems corny nowadays, but the fact remains that physical touch and physical warmth cut through the veneer of techno-sophistication and antiseptic business practices to make a compelling *human* impression.

And it is an impression that lasts far longer than the moment occupied by the gesture. A warm, hearty handshake not only conveys openness and a willingness to communicate, it creates a physical association with your presence that tends to fix you that much more vividly in the other person's memory.

Here are the steps to a memorable handshake:

First: Deliver a dry-palm handshake. Keep a handkerchief with you to wipe your hands dry before entering a meeting or conference where there will be handshakes all around. A sweaty, clammy palm is physically unpleasant—and it conveys your anxiety rather than your confidence and the pleasure you take in this meeting.

Second: Grasp the other person's hand fully, at the palm rather than by the fingers.

Third: Deliver a *moderately* tight grip. A firm handshake does not require a bone-crushing grip, but you should not offer a passive dead fish, either.

Fourth: Hold the other person's hand a few fractions of a second longer than you are naturally inclined to do. This conveys additional sincerity and truly "holds" the other person's attention while greetings are exchanged.

Fifth: While giving the handshake, resist the urge to look down at the clasped hands. Instead, look into the other person's eyes.

Sixth: Be sure to start talking *before* you let go. A simple phrase like "It's great to meet you" or "Glad to be here," spoken while hands are still clasped, becomes a powerfully effective greeting.

6. *Don't rush to take a seat.* You enter a room. What comes next? Often, the next action is taking a seat in an office, at a conference table, or in a living room. How you do this tells those present something about your attitude and approach to them. You need to be aware that the people already in the room cannot help but watch you sit. We always tend to look intently at anyone who enters "our" territory. When you enter the room and take a seat, you are—at least for the moment—the center of attention.

- Don't rush to sit. Doing so will make you appear anxious. More important, if others in the room are already seated, your standing will give you a few moments to be looked up to. Remember: Height has its advantages. If everyone in the room is sitting and you are standing, then you are the tallest person in the room—at least for the time being. This gives you an aura of authority, however temporary.

- Think about where you will sit. If you have a choice, choose a firm chair rather than a sofa or a very soft chair. You want a chair that keeps you upright and that allows you to maintain an erect posture, not a chair that swallows you whole.

- If you are to be seated at a table, it is not appropriate for you to usurp the seat at the head of the table—unless, of course, you are running the meeting. Beyond this, be aware that there is a psychological power geography at work around any conference table. The greatest power position is at the head of the table. The second most dominant position is at the other end of the table. Perhaps surprisingly, the seats to either side of the head of the table are the weakest positions at the table and should be avoided, if possible.

7. *Transmit a feeling of relaxed energy.* Personal energy is a positive quality conveyed largely through nonverbal signals. Avoid confusing energy with restlessness or nervousness; instead, strive to convey a feeling of relaxed energy, a combination of enthusiasm and confidence that may be summed up in the word *poise.*

8. *Breathing is an important aspect of nonverbal communication.* Obviously, you don't need a book to teach you how to breathe—but by becoming conscious of how you breathe, you can gain a further measure of control over your body language. Most of the time, we give no thought to how we breathe. The process is, as it should be, completely automatic. However, when you become upset, nervous, or scared, breathing typically becomes shallower, shorter, and faster. Under these circumstances you probably become quite conscious of the change in breathing pattern. More important, the change is also noticeable to others who observe you.

Being perceived as short of breath and anxious is not a positive body language message. Fortunately, it is possible to train yourself to breathe slowly and deeply, even when you are nervous. This requires some thought, but it can be done, and doing so will benefit you in two ways. Learning to control your breathing will not only keep your nervousness from being communicated, it will also actually cause you to feel less nervous. Fear creates certain physical sensations and symptoms; then, as we become aware of these sensations and symptoms, we become even more anxious, which, in turn, intensifies the sensations and symptoms. It is an all-too-familiar vicious cycle.

When you feel anxious, focus on your breathing. Force yourself to slow down, to breathe deeply and regularly. The task of directing your attention to your breathing will, in and of itself, help reduce your anxiety. Regulating your breathing will reduce anxiety as well.

9. *Nothing "speaks" body language more eloquently than the head and face.* The head tilted to one side indicates interest and close listening. This is a positive, desirable gesture, which always engages your conversation counterpart. Just make certain to vary the gesture. No body language gesture is positive if it is held statically.

10. *A* slightly *out-thrust chin conveys confidence.* Be careful with this one, however. Don't exaggerate. Boldly thrust out your chin, and you will probably be perceived as arrogant—or as someone with a most peculiar knack for impersonating Mussolini.

11. *Nodding the head up and down conveys agreement, while shaking the head from side to side conveys disagreement.* This is obvious, of course. But it is quite common to fall into the trap of sending mixed signals. We've all talked with people who *say* yes even as

they—ever so slightly—shake their head *no*. It is very important to become sufficiently conscious of your body language to prevent garbled transmissions such as this.

12. *Use your hands.* Next to the head and face, the hands are the most fluent speakers of body language; however, many people worry about "what to do with" their hands. Stop worrying. Instead, feel free to gesture with your hands to help drive home your verbal points. Here are some tips:

* Open hands, palms up, suggest honesty and openness.
* Rubbing the hands together communicates positive expectancy.
* Putting the fingertips together steeple-fashion conveys confidence.

13. *When you're on stage . . .* The body-language basics that apply in everyday communications are also useful in more formal public speaking situations. Here are some ideas:

* Maintain eye contact with your audience. This is not always easy when you have to look down at your typescript; therefore, rehearse the speech and practice looking up frequently. Each time you look up from your typescript, try to make contact with a specific person in the audience. Don't stare out blankly. Vary the targets of your gaze, but do pick a specific target each time.
* Insofar as it is appropriate to your subject matter, smile as often as possible.
* Use hand gestures to underscore key points. Choreograph and practice useful, expressive gestures as required.
* Adopt a firm, upright, but comfortable stance at the podium. Soldiers required to stand at attention for extended periods quickly learn to appear rigid without actually standing rigidly. Do not lock your knees, but, instead, flex them slightly. This will have the effect of relaxing you without leading to a slouch position.

14. *Extend your nonverbal message with the clothes you wear.* You don't need this book to tell you how important clothing is in our culture. Here are some general rules for achieving solid, positive nonverbal communication through clothing:

- Be sensitive to the manner of dress that prevails in the group you work with. Dress appropriately for this context.

- Among sales professionals, a rule of thumb is to dress "a notch above" the customer. This is a safe, conservative guideline for most business situations.

   15. *Adjust your tone of voice.* Remember, Albert Mehrabian's study of the sources of the persuasiveness of a speech concluded that 38 percent of the power of a speech is the result of "vocal qualities," especially tone of voice. Here are some suggestions for developing vocal qualities that help you to speak from the heart:

- Much as tall people tend to command more authority than shorter folk, people with deep voices are generally perceived as more persuasive than those whose voices are relatively high pitched. This is true of women as well as men. If your voice is pitched in the higher registers, consider consciously trying to speak in a lower pitch. Practice until you are comfortable with the level you have achieved.

- Consciously pitching your voice lower has the added benefit of slowing you down, which enhances the articulation of each word. Slower, more precise speech tends to add value to each word. Whether in conversation or in a formal speaking situation, most speakers can benefit from making a deliberate effort to slow down. For public speakers, the rule of thumb is not to exceed 150 words per minute, which means that it should take you a full two minutes to read a double-spaced, typewritten page of text. The 150 WPM rule is too slow for most casual conversation, which usually proceeds at about 200 words per minute.

- Lowering pitch also tends to minimize any nasal vocal quality, which many listeners find annoying. (If you suffer from persistent allergies or chronic breathing problems, the state of your health as well as the effectiveness of your communication may benefit from a visit to the doctor.)

- Especially in formal speaking situations, be sure to speak loudly enough. Don't strain, but be aware that a speaker can do absolutely nothing more annoying than fail to make herself heard.

25 Moves to Avoid

Just as body language can be an asset to effective, persuasive communication, it can also undercut and sabotage your message. Many conversations are compromised before a single word is spoken. Here are some moves to become aware of and to avoid:

1. *Avoid the tentative entrance.* When you decide to enter a room, a meeting, a conference, or even when you approach someone with whom you want to speak, carry the action through smoothly and forthrightly. Approach with the knowledge of what it is you want. This will help you move with confidence.

2. *Do not fail to establish eye contact.* Avoidance of eye contact will be interpreted as fear, indecisiveness, weakness, dishonesty, or any number of other negative things.

3. *Avoid the "dead fish" handshake.* A weak, limp handshake is an instant disappointment. People anticipate pleasure in a warm, firm grip. If you fail to deliver this, you will begin communications with a failure of expectation.

4. *Avoid the bone-crushing handshake.* You don't have to prove your strength or assert your dominance by making someone else uncomfortable. This is not impressive. It kicks off communication with resentment.

5. *Men should avoid offering women a loose, overly delicate handshake.* Men should use the same *moderately* firm grip they would deliver to another man.

6. *Avoid displaying what is generally called "nervous energy."* Remember, your object is to convey relaxed energy. This is *not* transmitted through tapping feet, darting eyes, drumming fingers, and fingers that fiddle with necktie, jewelry, or hair.

7. *Don't lose control of your breathing.* The rapid, shallow breathing associated with anxiety will only increase your anxiety—thereby creating a vicious cycle that will tend to make your breathing even more rapid and shallow—and will communicate nervousness to others. This will compromise your credibility. Practice breathing deeply and regularly.

8. *Avoid sighing.* This is a bad habit in most communication contexts because it is usually interpreted either as a sign of distress or of boredom.

9. *Avoid yawning.* If you must yawn—and, after all, you're only human—disguise it best you can. If the yawn becomes obvious, apologize and explain: "Please excuse me. My neighbor pulled in the driveway at three this morning, his car alarm went off, and I just couldn't get back to sleep."

10. *Avoid scratching your head.* This is a classic signal of confusion or disbelief.

11. *Don't bite your lip.* People who are scared chew their lip. Don't transmit this signal.

12. *Keep your hands away from the back of your head or neck.* People often rub the back of the head or neck when they are frustrated or feeling impatient.

13. *Don't let your chin hang down.* The familiar expression "keep your chin up" is good advice in most communication situations. A lowered chin conveys defensiveness or insecurity.

14. *Don't squint.* Narrowing the eyes communicates disagreement, resentment, anger, or disapproval. A pronounced squint suggests utter puzzlement.

15. *Don't look down or otherwise avoid eye contact.* If you can't look the other person in the eye, she will assume that you are hiding something.

16. *Don't stare.* Eye contact is crucial, but a steady stare suggests at the very least an arrogant need to control, intimidate, and dominate. At its worst, vacant staring just seems weird and will alienate the person or persons with whom you are speaking.

17. *Be careful about raising your eyebrows.* Raising the eyebrows indicates surprise. Nothing wrong with that, if you want to communicate surprise, but, in some contexts, raised eyebrows suggest disbelief. You may inadvertently offend the speaker.

18. *If you wear eyeglasses, look through them, not over the top of them.* This gesture communicates doubt and disbelief. It may also be interpreted as a not-so-subtle put-down.

19. *Don't cross your arms.* Crossing your arms in front of your chest is a powerful signal of defiance, defensiveness, resistance, aggressiveness, or a closed mind.

20. *Don't rub your eyes, ears, or the side of your nose.* These gestures always communicate a degree of doubt that can seriously sabotage your verbal message.

21. *Get out of the habit of wringing your hands.* Few gestures more strongly communicate anxiety—even something verging on terror.

22. *Avoid holding head position and facial expressions for a long time or repeating any single gesture over and over.* Look alive and lively, not embalmed.

23. *Avoid assorted tics and nervous habits.* Here's what to watch for and avoid: continuous hand motions, rubbing your face, putting your hands anywhere near your mouth, repeatedly shrugging your shoulders. If you do such things, work to wean yourself away from them. The first step is awareness.

24. *In formal speaking situations, beware of nervously shifting your weight from side to side.* This is highly distracting to your listeners.

25. *Avoid ending declarative sentences on a rising note.* This is a verbal habit more common to women than men. It makes a statement sound tentative, even doubtful, as if the speaker were continually seeking approval.

Simple awareness of the positive and negative nonverbal body language "phrases" we all use is a major step toward taking control of these gestures and using them to advantage.

3

Plain Talk

On November 19, 1863, the president of the United States delivered a speech at the dedication of the Soldiers' National Cemetery at Gettysburg, the scene of what, even in the midst of the bloody conflict, seemed the turning-point battle of the Civil War. Abraham Lincoln had been invited to speak at the last minute. His appearance was an afterthought; for the *featured* speaker of the afternoon was Edward Everett, widely regarded as the greatest orator of his age. Indeed, Everett's ringing remarks consumed a full two hours, whereas Lincoln's speech was concluded in two minutes. Today, no one remembers a word of Everett's flowery oration, but the brief, simple, straightforward utterance of Lincoln, *The Gettysburg Address,* is beyond doubt the most profound verbal monument ever erected to military achievement and human sacrifice.

If ever a political leader spoke from the heart, it was Lincoln at Gettysburg. At 271 words, it takes little enough space to reproduce here:

Fourscore and seven years ago our fathers brought forth on this continent a new nation, conceived in Liberty, and dedicated to the proposition that all men are created equal.

Now we are engaged in a great civil war, testing whether that nation or any nation so conceived and so dedicated, can long endure. We are met on a great battle-field of that war. We have come to dedicate a portion of that field, as a final resting place for those who here gave their lives that that nation might live. It is altogether fitting and proper that we should do this.

But, in a larger sense, we can not dedicate—we can not consecrate—we can not hallow—this ground. The brave men, living and dead, who struggled

> here, have consecrated it, far above our poor power to add or detract. The world will little note, nor long remember what we say here, but it can never forget what they did here. It is for us the living, rather, to be dedicated here to the unfinished work which they who fought here have thus far so nobly advanced. It is rather for us to be here dedicated to the great task remaining before us—that from these honored dead we take increased devotion to that cause for which they gave the last full measure of devotion—that we here highly resolve that these dead shall not have died in vain—that this nation, under God, shall have a new birth of freedom—and that government of the people, by the people, for the people, shall not perish from the earth.

Don't skip over it. Do yourself the favor of reading once again these very familiar words. What is so moving about this speech?

- The language is elegant, to be sure, but hardly ornate or flowery—certainly not by the leaden Victorian oratorical standards of the day.

- The language is straightforward, with a preponderance of nouns and verbs rather than adjectives and adverbs.

- The speech concerns certain abstract principles such as liberty and equality, but it focuses on concrete manifestations of those principles: the sacrifice of those who fought and fell at Gettysburg.

- The speech is not a lecture. It is a kind of conversation. That is, Lincoln emphasizes communion with his audience. He does not say "I" or "you," but "we." He focuses on what "we" are doing, here at this new cemetery at Gettysburg, and in this "great civil war."

- The speech has vigorous, very clear direction. It begins by evoking the American Revolution, which created a nation conceived in liberty and dedicated to the proposition that all men are created equal. It then explains that we are engaged in a civil war to test whether a nation so conceived and so dedicated can endure. It then explains what the dedication of the cemetery has to do with this struggle. But then it concludes by magnifying the achievement of those who fought and died at Gettysburg. The movement is simple, direct, and swift. The result is that both the battle and the ceremony are given the greatest possible meaning, and the audience is swept up in that meaning.

Lincoln wasn't just a gifted orator. He was a man who knew what he had to say, and then he found the most direct, most sincere way to say it. At Gettysburg in particular, he found his heartline. There are no oratorical tricks; no fancy metaphors; no evasions. There is a thorough understanding of the facts, a firm grasp of what this speech must accomplish, and an unwavering drive to accomplish it.

Many of the most profound, most consequential of human utterances are the simplest. It takes work and hard thought to achieve this level of *effective* simplicity. The architect Ludwig Mies Van Der Rohe understood this when he summed up his aesthetic philosophy in the famous phrase "Less is more." Or just consider one of the most advanced expressions of human thought ever produced, Einstein's statement of the equivalence of mass and energy. An expression of the foundation of reality itself, it consists of only three terms: $E = mc^2$. The income tax return that the most humble earner among us files yearly is far more complex than this—but hardly of equivalent consequence.

The real work of Einstein's equation was not in the writing of an E, an equals sign, an m, a c, and a superscript 2. As with Lincoln's speech—so brief that it was written on the back of an envelope—the real work was in all the preparation toward knowing what to say, then distilling that information to its most direct form. The major work of saying it from the heart begins before a word is said or written.

Finding Out What You *Really* Want to Say

Fans of the original 1960s television show *Star Trek* are familiar with the pointy-eared Vulcan, Mr. Spock. The product of a mixed marriage—Vulcan father, earthling mother—Spock was perpetually torn between his thoroughly logical Vulcan heritage and his highly emotional earthling heritage. Viewers had no difficulty accepting this conflict, since they took for granted that logic and emotion are naturally and inevitably incompatible.

This, in fact, is one of the many myths that guide our lives. For the purpose of persuasive communication, it is not a useful myth and should be discarded. Communicating on an emotionally effective level requires thoughtful preparation and logical presentation. Think about *The Gettysburg Address*. Certainly, it is an example of emotionally powerful communication. In its directness, simplicity, and utter clarity, it is also a model of logical presentation.

Your first step, then, in preparing to speak or write from the heart is to discard the erroneous notion that the heart and the head are incompatible. On the contrary, determining the logic of what you *want* to say will make communication on an emotionally potent level possible.

Once you accept this, you can proceed to the next step: the Inventory.

THE INVENTORY METHOD

This can be as simple as drawing up a list of the points you wish to make about a particular subject, issue, or problem:

Point A

Point B

Point C

Then take a sheet of paper and write your Point A on the top. Below this, make another heading: *What I know.* Now list the facts you know about Point A. When you have finished this, make another heading: *What I need to know.* Write down the items you need to learn more about in order to discuss Point A more effectively.

Repeat this procedure for each of the points you have listed in your inventory. When this is completed, take out another piece of paper and head it, *Objections.* Here you may jot down arguments against any or all of the points you intend to make. Study this list, then head another piece of paper, *Answers.* Sketch out responses to the items you have listed on your *Objections* page.

Once this inventory is complete, you will find that you have a blueprint from which you can construct your speech, your letter, your memo—whatever item of communication you are creating. In short, you will know what it is you *want* to say, as well as what it is you *need* to say.

The inventory method works well when you need to focus on some particular subject or set of issues that you wish to discuss or write about. This is not particularly surprising. You can also use a version of the inventory method to help plan your workday so that you can employ the time more effectively as a period in which your communications will be meaningful and most effective.

Try thinking of your workday in an entirely new way—not as a series of hours or a series of projects, customers, or tasks, but as a series of equations.

Let's hold on to this idea for a moment or two.

Equations consist of known and unknown variables. The fewer unknowns, the easier it is to solve the equation. From the perspective of six o'clock in the morning, as you turn on the tap of the shower, the impending workday seems to be filled with variables. After all, you're not a soothsayer who sees into the future. But consider this: However many other variables there may be in a particular workday equation, *you* are always one of them. And you have a choice: You can enter the equation as a known or an unknown variable.

It's easy to nail yourself down.

Before you leave for the office, jot down a short list of objectives and issues for that day: things you want to accomplish and issues or problems that you believe you will confront. Once you've made this list, your next step is to review it, item by item, and ask yourself what your position is relative to each item:

- How you feel about the item
- What kind of outcome you want to obtain in dealing with the item
- What the item means to you
- What you need to do in order to deal with the item
- What you need from others in order to deal with it

Here's an example of a list of items a person might address on a certain day:

1. Estimate costs for Smith project.
2. Speak to boss about the Jones & Jones proposal.
3. Talk to Claire about expediting shipments to Mr. Barney, one of our top customers.

Next, take these one by one and jot down what they mean to you:

1. *Estimate costs for Smith project.* I'll need to talk to Pete to get figures. I need for him to make this a priority. If I can get these costs estimated today, I can get to my customer before the competition does. It's important to me to make this sale.

2. *Speak to boss about Jones & Jones proposal.* She's resistant to this, but I think this is a good idea, and it would do my career good to take charge of a project like this—if it works. I think this is a

good idea, but I'm not sure. I need more information on the demographics of the proposed territory.

3. *Barney is giving me hell about shipping delays.* I'm worried about losing this customer. It is important that this issue get resolved. How can I motivate Claire?

Now you have outlined not only your objectives for the day, but also what each one means to you, and, at least in a general way, what you have to do to achieve them.

The second objective, talking to your boss about the Jones & Jones proposal, looks like it needs to be put on hold so that you can get more information. No use talking about it today, then. So you reduce its priority to last place. Although the original objective number 3 is pressing, number 1 probably needs to get underway first. So, now you have your day's priorities mapped out:

1. *Estimate costs for Smith project.* I'll need to talk to Pete to get figures. I need him to make this a high priority, because, if I can get these costs estimated today, I can get to my customer before the competition does. It's important to me to make this sale.

2. *Mr. Barney is giving me hell about shipping delays.* It makes me look bad—makes the company look bad, too. It is important that this issue get resolved. How can I motivate Claire to expedite?

3. *Get more information on the demographics* of the proposed territory for the Jones & Jones proposal before talking to the boss about it.

THE K.I.S.S. FORMULA

Many people who are fond of acronyms reserve particular affection for this rather rude one: *K.I.S.S.*—Keep It Simple, Stupid. It's just abrasive enough to be memorable, and the advice it embodies is valuable, if we add to it a dash of thought.

As you outline just what it is you want to say, keep the outline as simple as possible. The "as possible" part is important. What you *decide* to say should be no more complicated than what you *have* to say—but it shouldn't be any simpler, either. Both complicating and oversimplifying distort expression. Keep it as simple as it can be, but no simpler than that.

You can apply the K.I.S.S. formula to specific subjects, problems, and issues, of course, but you can also apply it more generally to your workday.

If you've ever envied the way a Hollywood star walks through a film role, knowing how it will all turn out, knowing just what to do and just what to say, consider giving yourself the Hollywood advantage: a script.

Terrific idea! The only problem is that this is *real* life. Real life doesn't come with a script.

True enough. But this doesn't mean you can't create one.

- Focus on the most important and difficult of your day's objectives, and plot out your approaches to them. This might take the form of a few quick notes, or it might be a genuine script, with your lines written out.

- Look at what is now your number-one objective for the day: Estimate costs for the Smith project. I'll need to talk to Pete to get figures. I need for him to make this a priority. If I can get these costs estimated today, I can get to my customer before the competition does.

How will you go about motivating Pete? Give some thought to this now, before you approach him. You decide that you know two important facts:

1. The most powerful motive is self-interest.
2. Pete takes pride in doing the best job he knows how.

The first fact, while not specific to Pete, is certainly a safe assumption. The second, which relates more directly to what you happen to know about Pete, is also important. Now, write a script that exploits both of these facts about what motivates Pete.

You: Pete, can I speak with you a moment? We have an opportunity to hook up with a very major customer. To do this, we'll need to give him the most competitive bid possible—our very best shot. And you, my friend, are the only one who can get us the figures we need to present our leanest and meanest bid.

You've sketched out an opening that plays on Pete's self-interest (he'll be given a key role in this big deal) and on his pride in workmanship (he's the only one who can furnish what's needed). But you're not home yet. Having scripted a good approach, keep preparing. The next step is to anticipate potential resistance:

Pete: I'll get to it just as soon as I can, but I'm swamped right now.

Don't back down. Your mission is to keep your project on the front burner.

You: I sure know that feeling! The thing is, this is such a high-profile deal that I'm sure you'll want to be part of it. And, right now, our priority has to be to take an aggressive stance. We don't want to let it slip.

Here is a secret of saying it from the heart, which you will encounter repeatedly in this book: Never *tell* the other person what to do. Telling is not persuasive. Instead, arrange reality so that he'll decide for himself to do what you want him to do.

How do you pull this off?

The easiest way is to imitate what top-notch sales professionals do. Focus on the "customer's" needs, not on yours. How will complying with your request benefit Pete? That is the question you must answer. Remember, the car salesman is almost certainly more concerned about making his next mortgage payment than he is about seeing to it that you drive away happy. The benefit he derives from selling you a car is the ability to pay his mortgage this month. Nevertheless, he makes no mention of his mortgage payment. To make the sale, he focuses on the benefits you will derive from the purchase.

Having prepared a script for your number-one priority, you can go on to sketch out another script for the number-two priority: motivating Claire in Shipping to expedite shipments to your customer, Mr. Barney.

You understand what you need from Claire, but you also understand that, for the purposes of persuading her, you must focus on her needs. There is nothing wrong about beginning with the assumption of her self-interest. But what else do you know about Claire, more specifically? From past experience, you've found that she's a bit touchy, defensive about her turf. This is important to know, because you realize that she isn't likely to respond positively if you imply that her department is not up to snuff where Mr. Barney's shipments are concerned. So, you decide not to go there. A better strategy is to paint her a picture.

You: Claire, I've been getting some flak from one of our major cus-
             tomers, Barney. You know him, don't you?

Claire: Yes, sure. I know Mr. Barney.

Put the burden on Mr. Barney, not on yourself and not on Claire.
Start to define the problem not as *yours* or *hers,* but *ours:* "one of our
major customers."

You: Well, Barney's been complaining about lead times for shipping.
             Now, my first reaction to this is, well, everybody's worried about
             shipping time. But take a look at this . . .

You decide that you'll show Claire log entries that demonstrate the
gap between request date and ship date. Let her draw her own conclusions. Let the decision to improve be *her* decision, *her* idea, not *yours.*

10 SIMPLE GADGETS OF PLAIN TALK

Gadgets are simple devices to make work a little easier. Here are some
gadgets to help you to speak plainly, directly, and as simply as the subject and issues will allow:

1. Ask yourself what you want.

2. Ask yourself what you need.

3. Ask yourself how you feel.

4. Sketch a verbal plan to help you communicate with others to
    achieve your objectives.

5. Use words that unite (*we, us, our*) rather than divide (*I, you*).

6. Beware of setting *I* against *you.*

7. Focus on how what you want will benefit the other person.

8. Avoid defining a winner versus a loser.

9. Use language that emphasizes potential rather than limits.

10. Use many nouns and verbs, but few adjectives and adverbs.

50 Words from the Heart

One of the many advantages of living in modern times is indoor
plumbing. Turn a tap, and water flows. In the old days, people resort-

ed to a pump, and to get the pump working, you often had to prime it by adding a bit of water from a bucket. Modern water delivery systems have improved, but our verbal pumps can still benefit from priming. Here are some words and phrases that will help you get started speaking from the heart:

admire	extraordinary	learning
advice	foundation	love
advise	generous	loyalty
benefit	genius	marvel
best	grateful	mentor
celebrate	guidance	model
congratulate	guide	perform
contribute	help	praise
create	honor	progress
dedicate	hope	resourceful
enhance	humanity	succeed
enterprise	improve	thanks
ethics	ingenious	understanding
example	innovative	valuable
excellence	inspiration	willingness
exceptional	invaluable	wisdom
experience	inventive	

50 Words to Avoid

Try to avoid these downers. They tend to cast activity and enterprise in a negative light:

absolute	bitter	dead
accident	cheated	dire
against	clueless	disaster
angry	company policy	doom
annihilate	cornered	dreary
beat	crush	dumb

escape

exclude

exhausted

exploit

fail

gut

hardship

hopeless

humiliate

luck

maul

mediocre

minor

mistake

must

obey

obligatory

quit

retire

retreat

retrench

rid

robbed

shocked

showdown

status quo

strict

tired

trouble

ultimatum

unchanging

unfair

Speaking with
Your Ears

$\mathcal{I}$n the previous chapter, we talked about actually scripting your key verbal encounters as a way of ensuring that you deliver your message as simply, directly, and fully as possible. Thinking about speaking from the heart as a kind of scripted performance is a good thing.

At least, mostly.

The benefits such an approach offers include giving you a feeling of greater control and permitting you to prepare, to rehearse, and to set specific goals concerning just what it is you wish to communicate. Nevertheless, it is not useful to carry the idea of performance to the extreme, causing you to neglect the interactive aspect of all meaningful communication.

Perhaps we just need to think about the idea of performance more deeply. The great stage actors do not simply follow a script, "broadcasting" their part to the audience. Instead, they learn to "read the house," to pick up on the signals the audience sends their way. For them, a performance is, in large measure, a give-and-take proposition. For the actor, this faculty of give and take is an extraordinary skill, a kind of sixth sense. For those of us, however, who just want to speak persuasively, sincerely, and effectively, it is a much simpler matter. The skill we must develop is the ability to listen and to hear. Do you want to persuade others? Use your ears.

The Two-Way Street

When you enter into a conversation or rise to speak, you naturally feel a certain burden. You take upon your shoulders the responsibility for creating meaning, for putting yourself across. This is an important responsibility, and it can be a weighty burden. It is easy to forget that it is actually a shared burden. Your listener also has a responsibility to interpret what you say, to listen to it, to hear it, to understand it. If you've ever spoken to someone who refuses to hear—or who is simply, well, rather dense—you know how much heavier your load becomes. Communication is like moving a massive piece of furniture. It really is a two-person job. If one of the people gets lazy or just isn't strong enough, more of the burden falls on the other. Sometimes, the load is just too great, and the piece tumbles to the ground. The coffee table is broken; the message fails to get across.

Carrying your heavy load, you are grateful for all the help you get. You are resentful if that help isn't there.

Communication is much the same. If you are blessed with a good listener, your task is easier and much more gratifying. You feel good about yourself, and you naturally feel grateful to the other person.

Now, you can't always choose your listeners. With luck, you'll find yourself communicating with someone who hears you, who understands you, who carries her share of the load. Then, again, you might not be so fortunate. What you *can* control, however, is your own ability to listen. The benefits of this are great:

- The mere presence of a listener helps the speaker direct his communication toward a goal.

- The more effectively the speaker communicates, the greater value you *and* the speaker receive from the communication.

- The more effectively the speaker communicates, the more positive will be his feelings about you.

- The more positive the other person feels toward you, the more readily you'll be able to put your message across when it is your turn to speak. You will be more persuasive.

Many people needlessly mystify communication, seeing it as a kind of black art practiced most effectively by people with a special gift for spellbinding genius. Actually, the essence of effective communication is information. The more useful information you load into a package of communication, the more effective, persuasive, and dynamic that communication will be.

There are, of course, many sources of useful information. But one of the richest—a surefire source, in fact—is the person with whom you are speaking. The more you know about what that person feels, thinks, wants, and needs, the more background you will have at your disposal to help you pack your words with information that is useful to him.

How do you gather this information? You listen. You listen to the other person.

The Pronoun Equation

You enter a conversation as the personal pronoun "I" confronting another personal pronoun, "you." How can you tell if the conversation is successful, the communication effective? The sum of "I" and "you" comes to equal "we." This is the equation of persuasion. There is no winner or loser. Neither the "I" nor the "you" is greater. Together, however, they come out as "we." This will not happen without effective speaking as well as listening. Do not focus so intensely on the one that you neglect the other.

10 Ways to Become a Better Listener

1. *Practice creative self-restraint.* Remember the kid in the fifth grade who somehow couldn't resist raising her hand to answer each and every question? When you are in an intense conversation, a high-stakes exchange, it is very easy to start acting like that fifth grader. In your eagerness to keep the conversation going, to parade before the other person everything you know, to answer questions before the other person's mouth is even closed, you may well find yourself nearly unable to sit still, be quiet, and just listen. Be careful not to hog the conversation. *Listen.*

2. *Make a conscious effort to appear as if you are enjoying the conversation.* The message you want to convey is that you are intensely interested in what the other person is saying to you. Keep your self-restraint lively. Smile. Nod when appropriate. React.

3. *Use verbal mirrors: echoing.* Let the other person know that you are hearing and understanding her. You may do this by repeating—echoing—key phrases she uses.

Other person:	I need to get this project moving.
You:	I understand. It's critical for you to get the project moving.

4. *Use verbal mirrors: rephrasing.* Another way to reassure the other person that you understand what she is telling you is to rephrase key points of her message:

Other person:	I need to get this project moving.
You:	You want to get off the dime on this project.

5. *Tell the other person that you understand.* This is obvious, but often neglected:

Other person:	I need to get this project moving.
You:	I understand you.

6. *Don't neglect your response, but suspend it long enough to hear out the other person.* Be sure to learn what interests and concerns the other person, what he needs and what he wants, before responding by introducing your opinions, ideas, and needs. To the extent possible, create a foundation of common interest before offering any differing opinion or point of view.

Let's say you enter a conversation believing that Task A is important and that the best approach to Task A is through Methods 1 and 2. The conversation turns to Task A. Like you, the other person thinks this task is highly important; however, she believes that the best approach to it is through Methods 2 and 3. Now, what's your best move?

* Choose not to express your opinion, but just agree.
* Choose to disagree.
* Choose to agree as much as possible, then, taking off from this common ground, explain how and where your opinions differ.

The last alternative is probably the most productive.

Other person:	Task A is crucial to our operation. The approach I favor is Methods 2 and 3.
You:	I certainly agree with you that Task A is extremely important to achieving our goals, and I also like Method 2, but have you considered using Method 1 instead of Method 3?

Other person: Why should I?

You: Well, these are the benefits I've found . . .

7. *Listen, so that you can focus on the other person's needs.* The goal of a conversation is not to come off as mindless and selfless, but always to express yourself in a way that exhibits your interest in the other person—*his* needs, *his* concerns—even when you are discussing your own point of view. Listening is a gift you exchange with the other person in the conversation. It provides benefits to both of you. By listening carefully, you ensure that the ideas and opinions you express are relevant to the needs and concerns the other person expresses.

8. *Stalk the main thought.* Think back to how your high school English teacher struggled to get you to put some focus and direction in the essays you wrote. "Begin with a topic sentence!" she'd plead. "State your theme and develop it."

This is simple, sound advice. Starting with a clear, strong statement of theme keeps your writing focused and makes your essay far more persuasive. Nobody enjoys reading a pointless, meandering essay. It's frustrating and a waste of time.

You can apply the same principle to verbal communication. State your topic clearly. You can also apply the principle to *listening* to someone else's verbal communication. Try to identify the "topic sentence" in what the other person says, then underscore it verbally. For example, your friend John, who is struggling with the decision over which new car to buy, is meandering generally about automobiles. Suddenly, he remarks that "Safety is my biggest concern." You recognize this as a "topic sentence." Don't let it pass you by. "John, it sounds to me like you really want to begin your shopping around by focusing on the cars with the best safety features. Maybe that will help you narrow down the field." Now the conversation will have a sharper, more definite direction.

9. *Pounce on and develop what interests you.* Perhaps this has happened to you: You're riding to work on the same old bus or commuter train. The man seated beside you strikes up a conversation. You'd just as soon keep reading your paper, but, to be polite, you respond. Suddenly, he says something that actually interests you. Suddenly, the conversation takes on direction and purpose. It has acquired a theme, a main thought, and you're almost sorry when your stop rolls by.

Be on the alert for anything that strikes a chord. Stay alert for a main thought that sparks and fuels the conversation. When you find it, jump on board.

10. *Connect with your own interests.* Focus on the other person's needs, feelings, and interests, but bring them home to yourself. When the other person expresses the need to "move the project along," think about how that need feels to you. Get in touch with the feeling created by a sense of urgency. Strong feelings are the basis not just of a conversation, but of a relationship. Connect with those feelings and let them drive your remarks.

You: I know what it's like to get excited about the possibilities of a project. You really want to move it along, keep that energy flowing, and maintain the momentum.

Other person: Exactly. That's exactly how I feel.

Body Language:
How to Hear More Than Words

One of the most excruciating spectacles one may witness is the agony of a failed stand-up comic. He drops joke after joke, punch line after punch line, only to be met by silence.

"I *died* up there tonight," the poor man moans to the bartender after his performance. "I just *died*."

You probably can sympathize with this feeling. All of us have, from time to time, said something in the anticipation of eliciting a certain response, only to receive nothing but a stone face and silence. Imagine, then, how your partner in conversation will feel if you fail to react to what he says. Don't let him die.

Of course, you should avoid phonying up an exaggerated response to each and everything said. But do demonstrate that you are listening—listening with interest, comprehension, and pleasure—by mirroring the speaker's message:

- If the speaker is excited about something, get excited, too.

- If the speaker expresses delight, smile in return.

- If the speaker raises an issue that is clearly of critical importance to him, narrow your gaze, bring your hand thoughtfully to your chin—*show* that the subject is of critical importance to you, too.

Body language works two ways. You can broadcast it, and you can receive it. The more sensitive your "receiver," the more fully you will comprehend the other person and the more accurately and effectively you will be able to tailor your remarks to the needs, desires, and interests of the other person. Look for the following signals from your conversation partner:

- *Head tilted to one side.* Assume that she is listening intently to what you are saying and is interested. Astute sales professionals call such a gesture a "buy signal." It is a nonverbal cue that the other person is intrigued by what you are offering. Keep going. Pursue this line of conversation.

- *Scratches head.* A signal of confusion or disbelief. Don't panic when you encounter this. Instead, pause, and ask a question: "Am I making myself clear enough here?" Or: "I'm not sure I'm making myself clear. Let me put it another way. . . ." Respond to the need that is being transmitted to you.

- *Lip biting.* An indication of anxiety. This may suggest that an issue you've brought up has touched a nerve. It may also signal concern about something that has come up in the conversation. If you are aware that an area is sensitive, you will have to exercise judgment as to whether to move on quickly to another topic or express your understanding of the sensitive nature of the issue: "I realize that this is an area that causes anxiety, but I think it's an important issue to explore."

- *Rubbing the back of the head or neck.* A signal of frustration and impatience. When you pick up on this cue, it is probably best to move on to another topic. Practice a graceful transition: "But, of course, that's not nearly so important as XYZ." Alternatively, you can pause and ask the interviewer where *he* wants to go: "Maybe you'd rather talk about ABC."

- *Chin lowers markedly.* This is a token of defensiveness. It is possible that something you've said has been interpreted as a criticism. Insert a soothing remark: "Of course, I recognize that each department has its own management style. I am wide open and prepared to be flexible."

- *Nodding up and down.* A major buy signal. Keep the conversation going in the current vein. You are eliciting agreement.

- *Shaking head from side to side.* What you have said is being rejected. Respond directly. "It seems that you don't agree with me on this point. What part of my position gives you trouble?" Don't offer a challenge. Instead, ask a question like this, which will keep the conversation from grinding to a halt.

- *Eyes narrow.* Much like a head shake from side to side, this indicates rejection of what you have said. Respond directly: "I feel that we're not in agreement on this point. Can you tell me what disturbs you about what I've said?"

- *Squinting or very marked narrowing of the eyes.* This does not signal rejection so much as puzzlement. Pause, take a breath, then offer: "I want to be very clear on this point. Let me put what I've said another way."

- *Raised eyebrows.* A signal of surprise or disbelief. Meet this situation head on: "I know this is hard to believe, but . . ."

- *Peers over the top of his/her glasses.* Another signal of disbelief.

- *Avoidance of eye contact.* If eye contact has been tenuous or nonexistent from the start of the conversation, it is likely that you are simply speaking with a shy person. Go out of your way to be friendly. Take the lead in this dance. Note, however, that if eye contact drops off during the interview, you may be losing the interviewer's interest. Move quickly in response: "Shall we move on to a different topic?"

A more subtle nonverbal signal to look for is the way the other person breathes. Don't strain yourself looking for this sign. If you notice nothing unusual, there is no message being conveyed. However, if the other person's breathing pattern changes noticeably, you can assume that something you have said has struck a chord.

- *Breathlessness or shallow, rapid breathing.* This indicates anxiety. Respond with reassurance: "Well, don't worry. This is a problem we can certainly solve."

- *Sudden intake of breath.* Indicates the eagerness to say something. Pause. Let the other person speak—now.

- *Sigh.* This is a powerful indication of frustration or boredom. It is a signal that you should move on to another topic.

Words and Phrases to Promote Active Listening

Don't become so focused on listening that you let your end of the conversation lapse. This might well kill the conversation. Punctuate your listening with words and phrases such as the following. These are calculated to keep the conversation moving as well as on track:

accurate	extraordinary	positive
additional	fertile	productive
agree	further	right
Can you explain that further?	I agree	take into account
	I appreciate that	tell me more
Can we pursue that further?	I hadn't thought about it that way	that's a concern of mine, too
consider	I see	that's interesting
correct	I understand	thought
discuss further	It's an issue we face	we should discuss
evaluate	opportunity	yes

Just as certain words and phrases can keep things lively, others tend to bring the dialogue to a premature halt. Avoid such negative expressions as the following:

absolutely not	that can't be done	wrongheaded
couldn't possibly	that's not the way I do it	you're mistaken
no		you're wrong
no way	that's settled	

Part 2

Among Family and Friends

*N*owhere is saying it from the heart more important than when you speak or write to family and friends.

5

Announcements

Shakespeare's Macbeth expresses what is perhaps the most chilling, dismal view of life to be found in all literature. "Tomorrow, and tomorrow, and tomorrow," he says,

> Creeps in this petty pace from day to day,
> To the last syllable of recorded time;
> And all our yesterdays have lighted fools
> The way to dusty death. . . .

Macbeth goes on to conclude that life is "a tale / Told by an idiot, full of sound and fury, / Signifying nothing."

Fortunately, most of us don't feel quite this low. We see our lives as meaningful, filled with friends and family; filled, too, with events that are milestones, crossroads, and turning points, which make life no tedious, idiotic tale, but an exciting story to be shared with those who matter to us. That's where announcements come in. They are a sharing of the news—good, bad, and always important.

Finding the Heartline

The essence of the announcement is news, and the essence of news is fact. If you were ever on the staff of your high school newspaper, you doubtless recall the faculty adviser drumming the "five *W's*" into your head. Every good news story answers these five questions: Who? What? When? Where? Why?

While all good announcements should incorporate the five *W's*, you'll want to move beyond the facts to the feelings. In doing so, recall that the announcement may be about you and your family, but its purpose is to include others in the recognition and celebration of the event.

49

Sidestepping the Pitfalls

Announcements typically risk problems in three areas:

1. They fail to be sufficiently inclusive.
2. They fail to convey your feelings.
3. They fail to include all of the relevant facts.

1. Keep your audience in mind when you compose an announcement. How much does the reader or listener know about you and your family? Obviously, if you are speaking or writing to a close friend or family member, you don't have to fill in a lot of background information. But if you are sending an announcement to your outer circle of acquaintances, the reader may need more background material: names, dates, occupations, activities, achievements, and so on.

2. For certain events and to certain people, you may want to send a simple commercial card to carry your announcement. There's nothing wrong with that, but when you want to say it from the heart, take the time and effort to express your feelings—not just about the event, but about sharing the news of the event with the other person.

3. Double check to make certain that your announcement is a good "news story" in that it includes the five *W's.*

Saying It: To Family

A BIRTH—PHONE CALL TO THE NEW GRANDPARENTS

Hi, Mom and Dad. It's finally happened! Three-thirty-five this morning. She's a girl, Claire Rose, beautiful of course, 8 pounds, 4 ounces, head full of jet black hair. Sally and I are both tired, but incredibly happy. It all went so well that we'll be coming home tomorrow. So, congratulations, Grandma and Grandpa!

It's okay to sound excited about exciting things! Just remember to pack in all the essential data.

CAREER MOVE—PHONE CALL TO SISTER

Hey, sis. I've got big news, and I wanted you to be the first to know. I'm leaving Ajax and moving to Smith and Johnson. I'll be an account executive—a big move up from account associate—and while the money is good, $7,500 more per year, it's the opportunity that I'm really excited about. I'll be handling at least three major accounts myself and filling in on others as needed. This will be what I've always wanted: a chance to develop business from the ground up.

Let me give you my new address, phone, fax, and e-mail. All of this is effective on May 15.

The key phrase here is "I wanted you to be the first to know." Those closest to you get a substantial kick from the knowledge that you thought of them first. Be sure to let this fact be known.

If you feel comfortable discussing money with the person on the other end of the phone, there is nothing wrong with doing so. It's an important component of the news. Note here, however, that the speaker is careful to distinguish the money from what excites him most about the new job. This information also provides material for the other person to respond to. The subject of money does not open up the conversation as the subject of opportunity does.

AN ENGAGEMENT—PHONE CALL TO PARENTS

Mom, Dad, there's one less question you'll have to ask me: "When are you two going to tie the knot?" We're looking at June! Bill proposed yesterday—at dinner—with the most beautiful ring I've ever seen. Right before the dessert course!

I suppose you're wondering where we're planning to live. Bill's been offered a terrific job in Hendersonville. So we'll be no more than an hour from you guys.

A person certainly can be forgiven a self-centered focus in an announcement like this one, but note that this daughter makes the effort to shift the focus to her folks, telling them, with delight, that she and her husband plan to live nearby.

DIVORCE—PHONE CALL TO BROTHER

Well, Ted, I'm sorry to have to tell you that it's final. Sheila and I signed the divorce papers this morning. I know this disappoints you and hurts you, because you always worked so hard to help us try to patch things up. Both Sheila and I appreciate that, you know, but we just couldn't make it work.

Ted, both of us feel this is best for us, and I know Sheila will be giving you a call soon. She loves you like a brother, and she doesn't want to lose your affection or drift out of touch.

I'm sure you understand this is hard for us, but we're both going to be okay.

Even if it's not entirely unexpected, an announcement like this is bound to come as something of a shock. It is a mistake to attempt to sugarcoat bad news or hard truth, but that doesn't mean you can't present it in its best light and with whatever reassurances are possible under the circumstances. A divorce affects more than the two people most directly involved. It sends ripples through a whole matrix of relationships. Here the speaker does his best to contain the damage by reassuring his brother that no one is falling apart—life will go on—and that the brother's relationship with his sister-in-law does not have to end.

Saying It: To Friends

A BIRTH—PHONE CALL TO A CLOSE FRIEND

Hi, Sweetie. Congratulations! You are an aunt!

He's a boy, Thomas William, 9 pounds, 4 ounces, and he came into the world at 9:44 this morning. And he is a real loud one!

I feel terrific—tired, but very happy. Bill took it all harder than I did. He's sound asleep!

Look, you can come by the hospital tonight, if you want. We plan to be home day after tomorrow.

The best "news stories" are those that hit home. This new mother focuses her announcement on her friend—a brand-new honorary "aunt"—before going on to the all-important details concerning the baby, herself, and her husband.

CAREER MOVE—PHONE CALL TO A BUSINESS ACQUAINTANCE

Mr. Mackinson, this is Ed Walters. I'm calling to thank you for our conversation two months ago, in which you gave me some very helpful advice and information concerning positions at Smith and Johnson. I followed up on our conversation, applied, and interviewed, and, as of March 3, I'll be working at Smith and Johnson as a sales associate in aftermarket services.

This is an exciting opportunity for me, and I just wanted to share the news with you—since you were so instrumental in helping me to make the move. I would like to stay in touch. My new phone number is 555-555-1234 and the e-mail is edwalters@internet.com.

It is important to keep your acquaintances and business associates informed of career moves you make. In this case, the speaker also wants to acknowledge the role his acquaintance played in landing him a new job. Those who help you deserve to be thanked, of course, but putting it in the form of an announcement call adds an additional dimension to the thanks. It gives the other person a certain proprietary stake in the caller's success. Thus the caller has added to his network of business contacts—an important step in a developing career.

AN ENGAGEMENT—PHONE CALL TO A FRIEND

> Ellie, I hope you're sitting down. Big news. The biggest. As of yesterday, I am engaged to Howard Wallace. You met him last year, at Cindy's party. Tall, very good looking, works as a financial analyst, drives a '57 Chevy. You remember him, right?
>
> We haven't set the date yet, but it looks like no more than six months. We don't want to wait forever.

Gauge your audience. In this case, the speaker is not certain that her friend remembers her fiancé, so she is careful to jog her memory, to give his full name, some background, then place him in time. Finally, she asks for feedback: "You remember him, right?" Sharing exciting news is not fun if you leave the other person in the dark.

DIVORCE—PHONE CALL TO A FRIEND

> Helen, I'm sorry to have to tell you that Bob and I are now divorced. It is official as of Friday. It's really hard for me to give you this news, because I know how much effort you put into helping us try to work things out. Bob and I are both very grateful, and you certainly enabled us to go through this with a lot more civility and understanding than would have been the case without your concern and help.
>
> Bob, I know, is very worried that our split up will end his friendship with you and Clark. I hope that isn't the case. I hope that we will all be able to maintain our friendship. You mean a lot to me—and to Bob, too. I really need your support.

The speaker fully understands and appreciates that her divorce has effects that reach beyond her and her former husband. This announcement takes her friend's feelings into account and serves to reassure her that the divorce does not include divorce from the friends she and her former husband have in common. An announcement should convey more than completed fact. It is also an opportunity to look toward the future.

Writing It: To Family

A BIRTH—NOTE TO A BROTHER WHO LIVES FAR AWAY

Hey, Bro—

You're always on my case about never writing to you. Well, now I've actually got something to write about. You now have a nephew, Sean Graham, 8 pounds, 11 ounces. He came into this world at precisely 5:45 this morning—a regular little commuter! Sally, Sean, and I are doing just fine, and we'll all be home by the time you get this.

I'm going to try to get some sleep now—while I can. Next letter will include some snapshots.

All the best,

Pete

Strike a tone appropriate to the person you're writing to. The kind of banter present here conveys the warmth of an easy, loving relationship. Writing a letter like this is easier if you visualize your correspondent. Think of the letter as a conversation, face to face, except that the face is in your mind's eye.

AN ENGAGEMENT—A NOTE HOME

Dear Mom, Dad, and Sis,

If my handwriting is hard to read, I apologize. I'm writing as fast as I can to keep up with my excitement. I'm getting married!

Her name is Cheryl Young. We met just a month ago, and, well, it's just one of those things, as they say. Everything about us just clicks. We know we're made for each other. We met at an environmental rally—like me, Cheryl's a believer in living in harmony with the planet—and we just can't get enough of each other.

I can't say that *I* asked her to marry me. The subject came up, we talked, and we came out wanting to get married. So there we are.

We haven't set a date yet, but Cheryl and I will be coming home for the Christmas holiday, and we'll all have a chance to sit down and make our plans. See you in a few weeks.

Can't wait to see you,

Simon

Sudden announcements can be fun—or more than a trifle terrifying. The writer acknowledges the suddenness of the decision to get married, and he explains the circumstances as best he can. Recognizing that the surprise announcement may make some family members feel as if they've been left out of a crucial life decision, the writer is especially careful to ensure that the family is included in the planning for the wedding. To the degree that it is possible to do so, an announcement from the heart should reach out to others and draw them into the impending event.

CAREER MOVE—LETTER TO DAD

Dear Dad,

As of June 5, you may address your daughter as Marybeth Koslow, Branch Manager, Garner and Yost.

You know that promotion I'd been waiting for? It never came. So I made a move to a firm that agreed to hire me at the level I was bidding for at Smith and Johnson. I'll be leaving a lot of great people, but I just couldn't keep my career on hold any longer.

My new firm is Garner and Yost, at 1234 West Peter Lane, same Zip as the old place, 00056. The phone number there is 555-000-9999. I'll call you with my direct line as soon as I get started there.

Dad, I'm very excited by the new responsibility. The pay raise is welcome, too, although it is about 10 percent less than I would have gotten at Smith and Johnson. But, then, that promotion seemed to be a ship that just wasn't coming in—and you know what 10 percent of nothing is. I'm just proud of myself that I was able to make this move and get what I wanted. You, Dad, taught me that—to decide on what you want, then aim for it and don't give up until you've reached your target. That's what I was thinking about when I made the move. Thanks. Thanks for everything.

Love,

Marybeth

This announcement does double duty as a heartfelt expression of gratitude. Always look for ways to include your correspondent in your message. Sometimes, you have news to share that is all about you, period. That's fine. But, often, you will discover that you can expand *your* news to take in others, including the person to whom you are writing. If you can do this, you ensure a meaningful communication that will generate much warmth.

DIVORCE—A LETTER HOME

Mom, Dad—

This is the hardest letter I've ever had to write. Carla and I finalized our divorce Tuesday. The papers are all signed.

Hard as it has been on us, I know it is, in many ways, even harder on you. You were always so hopeful that things would work out, and you were helpful, too, in trying to guide us through these past several months. From the bottom of my heart, I thank you for your support and kindness. It's just that Carla and I both realized that our marriage had gone beyond fixing. We are both convinced that the divorce, hard as it is, is for the best.

Mom, Dad, I'll be home for the Thanksgiving holiday. I really look forward to seeing you both. I need to spend some time with you—at home.

Love,

George

The letter does not ask for sympathy but, instead, offers it. Here is a good example of a writer getting his message across without dwelling on himself. Note also that while the subject of the letter concerns the severing of one bond, it closes by reaffirming another: the bond between a child and his parents.

Writing It: To Friends

A BIRTH—LETTER TO MULTIPLE FRIENDS

Dear Friends:

Ken and I are thrilled to announce the arrival of our first baby, Cindy Marie, who made her debut on April 15, at 3:55 p.m. She's a perfect 10. (Actually, she weighs 8 pounds, 3 ounces, and measures 21 inches long.)

All three of us are healthy and happy—though two of us are pretty tired just now!

Please give us a call at 555-453-9000, and we'll fill you in some more.

Love,

Ken and Patty

Many announcements can be more or less mass produced and sent out in multiple copies to your friends. If you want to use the news as an occasion to get in touch, why not invite a phone call? Such an invitation is particularly important here, since some people might assume that the new parents are too busy to be bothered. If you want to invite contact, do so.

AN ENGAGEMENT—NOTE TO A GROUP OF FRIENDS

Dear Sally, Penny, Gina, and Brenda:

Roger and I are engaged!

It took place Friday at Chez Maurice.

"I know you don't usually have dessert," he said, "but after a meal that good, I thought you should have *something.*"

And he takes this gorgeous diamond ring out of his pocket. He didn't even say anything. I just looked at the ring, and I said, "Yes. Yes, I will."

We haven't set an exact date yet, but June has always looked good to me. I'm counting on you guys as bridesmaids. I'll let you know as soon as we've set a date.

Love to all of you,

Patti

In these days of word processing, there is nothing wrong with sending out multiple copies of the same announcement. The letter can still be personalized, like this one to a group of friends. There is also no rule dictating that a letter can do nothing more than report and describe. When you have an exciting event to talk about, consider giving your account more immediate impact by including actual dialogue. Step into the role of novelist—even if only for a moment or two.

CAREER MOVE—NOTE TO A FRIEND WHO HAS BEEN OUT OF TOUCH

Dear Fred:

How long has it been since we were last in touch? Two years? Three? Anyway, I've got big news, and it seemed that sharing it was a really good excuse to write.

As you know, I've been with Stein Company for years now, working in Customer Service. Recently, I started investigating another track, in sales, and found a position with Youngblood, here in Dayton. I'll be starting on March 3 as an account executive. It's a major move for me—and I have to tell you that your advice and support when I was just starting out helped me get to this position.

Fred, thanks, and I hope that we can get together next time you come through Dayton. Or why not give me a call at 555-555-0003. We have a lot of catching up to do. What's up with your life and work?

All the best,

Frank

Sharing news makes an excellent occasion for reestablishing old connections and getting back in touch with old friends.

A DIVORCE—LETTER TO A FRIEND

Dear Meg,

I am sorry to have to tell you that Ben and I are now divorced. The decree became final last week. As you can imagine, it's been a rough several months, but, finally, it is what both Ben and I want and need, and it is for the best—hard as it is.

I am writing to you in particular to tell you how much I have come to value your friendship over the years. Ben gave me many wonderful things during our marriage, and your friendship is one of these. I truly hope that, even though Ben and I are no longer together, you and I can stay in touch and remain friends.

Meg, I'll call in a few days. I'm still at the old address and number.

Hoping you will understand,

Emma

Divorce is painful for the couple directly involved, of course, but it is also awkward and difficult for others, especially friends of the couple. This announcement also serves as an opportunity for the writer to express her wish that the change in her circumstances does not end a friendship. Look for opportunities to leverage your communications, to make letters and conversations serve multiple purposes.

E-Mailing It: To Family

A BIRTH—E-MAIL SENT TO MULTIPLE FAMILY MEMBERS

Hi, Everybody!

With all of us online these days, e-mail seems the fastest way to get the big news out. The big news? We have a boy! He came into this world at 2:19 on the morning of December 3 after a wonderful natural childbirth delivery—well, wonderful for me, since it was Sarah who did most of the work! Little Sam—Samuel Patrick—was 8 pounds, 4 ounces, and he measured just over 20 inches in length. All of us are happy and healthy and eager to get out of this hospital and back home.

As you can appreciate, we're all a bit exhausted just now, but we'd love to hear from all of you, at our home number (555-009-3492) anytime after Saturday.

Gary and Sarah

E-mail is the perfect tool for sending quick, informal announcements to groups of family, friends, and others. A big part of communicating from the heart includes inviting further contact—but be sure to make it convenient for you. This new family wants some time to itself before fielding a lot of phone calls.

ENGAGEMENT—E-MAIL TO THE FAMILY CIRCLE

Attention all!

Well, I've finally gone and done it. I asked Carol to marry me—and, shocking though it may be, she said yes. We haven't set the date yet, but stay tuned.

Mom, Dad—Carol and I plan to visit you for the holidays. I'll call with the details.

This quick, lighthearted announcement was sent to the family members who are online. Because it was sent to multiple recipients, the sender is careful to address a special aside to his mother and father, who are just two of many recipients.

CAREER MOVE—E-MAIL TO DAD

Dad:

I wanted you to know right away that I am leaving Acme Tire for a new position in sales at Supreme Automotive. The money's quite a bit better—25 percent increase—but it's the increased opportunity and challenge that really excite me, Dad. I have a half dozen salespeople reporting to me.

I start on the 15th, and I'll call you then from my new office to give you my new numbers and fill you in on all the details.

Best to Mom,

Jerry

The writer understands what his father wants to hear: an increase in salary and responsibility. The other details are secondary and can wait for a subsequent phone conversation.

E-Mailing It: To Friends

A BIRTH—E-MAIL TO MULTIPLE RECIPIENTS

Howdy, Friends:

Please join Carol and me in welcoming John Peter into our family and into this world. He arrived—three weeks early, I might add—at 6:30 p.m. yesterday, and despite the early arrival, he's just fine, perfect in every way. Birth weight was 7 pounds, 2 ounces, and he's almost 20 inches long. Carol is tired and very, very happy.

We'll be sticking around the hospital through today and tomorrow, but we expect to be home by Friday. We'd welcome your calls on the weekend.

Ed Porter

25 Words and Phrases to Use

announcement	friends	please call
big news	get together	proud
delighted	gratitude	share
event	happy	stay in touch
excited	include you	thanks
exciting news for you	major change	thrilled
first to know	milestone	understanding
for the best	news	your help
	opportunity	

15 Words and Phrases to Avoid

bad news	no time	regret
bore you	nothing much to say	same old routine
bored	nothing new	too busy
disaster	nothing exciting	won't want to hear this
dull	owe you an explanation	
I won't go into that		

Apology and Forgiveness

$\mathcal{M}$ost of us look at apologizing as an act of damage control. We don't like to do it, but we all know it's sometimes necessary. That's a pretty dreary way to look at the subject, so maybe it's high time to change our thinking about apology.

Recall the last time you were on the receiving end of somebody's error. Absent an apology, it was undoubtedly a completely negative experience. But what happened when an effective apology followed?

Some months ago I purchased an attaché case. Within days, the latch on the right side broke. I trotted it back to the store, and they gave me a new case. Less than a week later, the latch broke off that one as well.

This time, I was pretty steamed. I didn't just go back to the store, I called the manufacturer.

> "Mr. Griffin," the customer service person I spoke with began, "I am very sorry to hear about the problem you've had—not once, but twice. The fact is that we have recently become aware of a manufacturing defect in some of our units. We'll make it right. You don't need to go back to the store a second time. We'll send you an improved attaché, and you can return the defective one in the same shipping carton. You won't have a problem with the new case—but if you do have any questions, please call. We are very sorry for the inconvenience we caused you, and we want you to be delighted with our product."

I can't say that this phone call made me deliriously happy about my purchase, but I did feel pretty good about the manufacturer. They hadn't left me hanging, they took responsibility, they expressed concern, and I believed that they were determined to make things right.

But there was more to how I felt. After this apology, I was willing to forgive—and that felt good.

I'm no saint, but my feeling of forgiveness and even gratitude was not unusual. It does feel good to be able to forgive. In forgiveness we have the power to relieve someone of bad feelings, perhaps even of anxiety. Forgiveness empowers us.

So try thinking of the apology you have to say or write not as an onerous chore, an embarrassment, and a grim necessity, but as an opportunity to empower someone, to make someone feel good. Think of the act of apology in a positive light, as an opportunity to please and to create satisfaction, to give somebody an occasion for good feelings.

Finding the Heartline

Before you embark on an apology, it is important to address an area of frequent misunderstanding.

We apologize because we feel bad. This is normal; however, it is not a motive that makes for a truly effective apology. Instead of apologizing because you feel bad, consider apologizing to make the other person feel good—or, at least, better. As always, a crucial step toward effective communication is moving the focus from yourself and training it on the other person. This does not mean that you must deny your needs or your objectives; rather, it implies that the most effective way of getting what you want is to focus on what the other person needs. You apologize because you feel bad and want to feel better. In order to feel better, communicate in a way that addresses the other person's feelings, that makes him feel good. The effect your communication has on him will work wonders on you.

The heartline here—the most direct route from your feelings to effective expression—is via your sympathetic imagination of how the other person feels now, how you would like him to feel after you have apologized, and what you can say to create that feeling. Imagine beyond yourself.

Sidestepping the Pitfalls

Apologies tend to falter and fail for one or more of the following three reasons:

1. *The speaker/writer focuses on himself rather than on the feelings and needs of the other person.* As just stated, the most effective apologies are those that remove the focus from your own feelings and address the feelings, needs, and concerns of the other person. Insofar as the apology succeeds in making the other person feel better, it will succeed in making you feel better as well.

2. *The speaker/writer mistakes excuse for apology.* It is all too natural to become defensive when we apologize and offer excuses in the guise of apology. There is nothing wrong with a valid excuse; that is, a *valid* excuse is an explanation—information—and information is almost always valuable and helpful. The problem is when we set out to apologize and end up offering excuses instead. This creates disappointment, augmenting the bad feelings created by the error in the first place. Separate the apology from the explanation or excuse. You may deliver both, but, whatever you do, do not fail to deliver the apology— and deliver it first.

3. *The speaker/writer tells the other person how to feel.* "You must hate me for this," one mortified soul exclaims. Or: "You must think I'm a real idiot."

Statements such as these do not make anyone feel better about whatever problem has occurred. By making such declarations, you are telling the other person that he *should* hate you and he *should* think you are an idiot. You are prompting, even daring, him to think as poorly of you as possible.

A dependable rule of thumb in offering any apology is never to tell the other person what to think or how to feel.

Saying It: To Family

TARDINESS OR MISSED APPOINTMENT

Dad, I'm sorry I'm late. I really appreciate your having waited. I got caught in traffic, and my cell phone wouldn't work. I kept expecting the traffic to open up, but it just got worse and worse. I hope this hasn't put too big a dent in your day. Anyway, I can drop you off at the store when we're finished here, so that should save you some time.

The speaker knows his father well, and nothing formal or elaborate is required by way of apology. He begins, as most apologies should begin, by saying that he is sorry, then goes on to express appreciation for his father's patience. Only after apologizing and expressing appreciation does the speaker offer an explanation. He then expresses the hope that his tardiness has not wasted too much of his father's time; again, note that the emphasis is on the other person's needs. Finally, the speaker finishes the apology by offering something in the way of reparation. No matter how sincerely and persuasively you express your regrets, the most effective part of any apology is the offer of a solution—of some act or gesture or step to make the situation better.

MISINFORMATION—TO A SON

A 12-year-old boy has been told by his mother that the video store down the block is having a big sale on video games today. The boy took some allowance he had saved and went to the store, only to discover that his mother had given him the wrong information. The sale was yesterday. He returns angry and disappointed.

> Billy, I'm very sorry I gave you the wrong information. I don't know how I made that mistake. I must have misread the ad in the newspaper. I wish I could undo it. Maybe we can make some phone calls together and see if other shops have on sale any of the games you are interested in.

The parent should not dismiss the child's anger and disappointment, but she needn't make lavish amends, either. It would certainly be possible for the mother to give her son enough cash to buy what he wants, even if it isn't at a sale price. But, in the so-called real world, it is seldom possible to undo mistakes in this fashion. Instead, the mother thinks of another alternative, which more realistically reflects the way things occur in the adult world.

BAD BEHAVIOR/RUDE TREATMENT—BROTHER TO SISTER

> Sis, I'm sorry I teased you yesterday. I was in a bad mood, and I acted like a jerk. I'll do the dishes tonight—if you say you forgive me.

Minor friction is part of everyday family life. Acknowledging it, apologizing for it, then offering a modest penance is usually all that's required to clear the air.

CARELESS REMARK—APOLOGY TO WIFE

> Sweetheart, I'm sorry I let the cat out of the bag with Mark and Terri. I should have known you wanted to surprise them with the news, and I went ahead and spoiled it. I know that disappointed you—but at least I've learned my lesson. Next time, I'll think before I start running my mouth.

Most acts that merit apology are the product of a moment's thoughtlessness. Apologize, express understanding of the thoughtless mistake you made, empathize with the other person's feelings, promise it won't happen again—then move on.

Acknowledge your errors, but don't dwell on them or blow them out of proportion. Remember, you do not want to tell the other person how to feel—especially if your message is that she should feel worse than she does.

DELAYED THANK YOU—FOR A BIRTHDAY GIFT

> Tom, I don't deserve such a thoughtful brother as you are. Your wonderful gift arrived almost a week ago, and here I am just picking up the phone now. Things have been incredibly hectic around here, with the children home from school. But that, of course, is no excuse. I really love the gift, and I use it all the time. Thanks so much for it!

With a close family member, a sentence like the one that begins this apology is appropriate. Be careful, however, about delivering such stern self-criticism to friends or acquaintances. Note that, after the opening sentence, the speaker does not dwell on her sin of omission but instead focuses on the "wonderful gift" and how much she enjoys it. The point of the apology is not to demonstrate how bad you feel about your own oversight, but how grateful you are for the other person's thoughtfulness—even though your expression of gratitude is tardy.

ACCIDENT—BROKEN HEIRLOOM

> Mom, I just wanted to tell you again how sorry I am about the figurine. I know how much that piece meant to you. I am happy I found a place that can repair it, but I also know that it just won't be quite the same. I wish I could undo my clumsiness, but, instead, I'd like to take you out to dinner this evening. Maybe you can watch me knock over the dessert trolley at Chez Pierre.

Accidents happen, and it won't do anybody any good if you beat yourself up over a relatively minor mishap. Make your first priority damage control. What can be done? What can be fixed? Attend to that first, rather than lavish a lot of words on regret. A little self-deprecating humor, as in the closing line of this example, may lighten the tone of the episode. Just make certain that you don't make light of the other person's feelings or imply that she has no right to be upset.

Saying It: To Friends

TARDINESS OR MISSED APPOINTMENT—PHONE CALL: RUNNING LATE

> John, this is Ted. I'm very sorry, but I just got out of a client meeting that ran late. Can you stand to wait for me another twenty minutes? With crosstown traffic, it will take me at least that long. I really appreciate it. Thanks, buddy.

The best time for an apology is before the harm is done. Try to inform the other person of a problem either before it occurs or even while it is occurring. Provide the essential information only. Note that the speaker does not waste time with excuses. After first apologizing, he gives a simple explanation. It is always best to *ask* the other person for patience, not demand patience of him. There is a big difference between "Can you stand to wait for me another twenty minutes?" and "You'll have to wait twenty minutes." You have already inconvenienced the other person; now is not the time to back him into a corner, too.

Do not make promises you can't keep. If you know it will take you 40 minutes to get where you are going, don't promise 20. Note here that the speaker provides a basis for his estimate of 20 minutes—crosstown traffic—and mentions this figure as a base ("at least").

End by thanking the other person for his understanding.

MISINFORMATION—WRONG PHONE NUMBER GIVEN

> Hi, Tom. I heard from Ed that the phone number I gave you for that customer was wrong. I am very sorry. I double-checked the number I have, and I just must have written down the wrong number. I hope my mistake didn't mess you up too badly. Were you able to get all the contact numbers you need?

This is what might be called a preemptive apology. Tom didn't call the speaker to tell him about the error; the speaker heard about it from Ed, a third party. To salvage some part of an impression that, despite the mistake, he's on top of the situation, the speaker did not wait for Tom to complain, nor did he just let the incident pass. Instead, he took the initiative and called Tom to apologize.

Don't make trouble for yourself, but it is generally a useful move to go out of your way to own up to your errors. Note here that, besides the apology, the speaker takes the opportunity to ask Tom if he needs any more information.

BAD BEHAVIOR/RUDE TREATMENT—TOO MUCH TO DRINK

> Mary, I am very sorry if I was out of line last night. I want you to know that being boorish like that is just not my style—at least not without three martinis in me. I used just terrible judgment, and I value your friendship and opinion so much that—well, I just want to say I'm sorry. I hope I didn't cause you any embarrassment. If I did, I hope that you will be frank with me, and I hope that you will let me try to make it right.

Apologies for irresponsible behavior are difficult to make, because we—quite appropriately—feel ashamed. The best approach is to own up to what you did, apologize for it, and invite a response from the other person. Do not carry on about the incident, however, accusing yourself of a multitude of sins. Do not burden the other person with your guilt. Your object is not to make the other person feel sorry for you or feel that *she* has caused *you* embarrassment. Your object is to take responsibility for your actions and to apologize for them, period.

CARELESS REMARK—REVEALED PRIVILEGED INFORMATION

> Patti, I hope my remark to Darren at lunch today hasn't put you in hot water. I should *not* have mentioned those wholesale figures. Of course, I wouldn't have, had I known that Darren is a client of yours. But, in any case, I shouldn't have been broadcasting that kind of information indiscriminately. I am truly sorry. Is there anything I can do that would help with damage control?

Making a careless remark is like breaking an egg. Once it's done, it's done. All that's left for you to do is apologize sincerely, express the hope that you have not caused much harm, and ask if there is anything you can do to repair the situation. If you have any suggestions for a remedy, you should mention them. If not, just offer your help. Do not, however, make any promises you cannot keep.

DELAYED THANK YOU

> Harry, I have been meaning to thank you for putting me in touch with Max Goberman. He and I talked, and it looks like we'll be doing some business together. I should have called you right away to thank you, but—well, I have no excuse. I was just thoughtless. So, better late than never. I'd like to take you to lunch, if you're free later in the week or next.

Sometimes we slight our friends or commit a minor sin of omission without any good reason at all. In these cases, don't fabricate an excuse. Just deliver the apology and, if possible, make amends—here, a lunch invitation.

ACCIDENT—CONVERSATION WITH A NEIGHBOR

> Molly, I can't tell you how sorry I am about what our dog did to your rose bed. This isn't like her at all, but let me assure you that she'll be confined to our yard from now on. I just won't let something like this happen again, and I really do appreciate your being so understanding and forgiving. I know how much your beautiful roses mean to you. Now, what can I do to help you get your roses back in order?

The principal object of an effective apology is not to let the other person know that you are sorry—although you should make that clear. Instead, your primary object should be to assure the other person that you will act responsibly and that you will do whatever can be done to make things right. In this case, two courses of action are called for: First, something to ensure that the accident won't be repeated and, second, an offer to help repair the present damage.

Note that the speaker does not blame his dog, but takes the responsibility on himself. Note also, that he does not go overboard and wallow in self-castigation; however, he does sympathize with the other person, letting her know that he understands how important the roses are to her. Someone who has suffered a loss or injury because of your error or oversight not only wants the damage repaired, but also has the need for understanding. Feelings are very much involved.

A very effective way to salvage something quite positive from an accident is to praise and thank the other person for her patience, understanding, and generosity. Yes, it would be better if the accident hadn't happened, but the aftermath of the accident does give the injured party an opportunity to be magnanimous and forgiving. Acknowledging such emotional generosity builds good feelings.

Writing It: To Family

TARDINESS OR MISSED APPOINTMENT—ARRIVED LATE AT BROTHER'S GRADUATION CEREMONY

Dear Gary,

Thank you for being so understanding about my late arrival on your big day. I felt terrible about being so late, but your understanding made me feel much better. I guess my little brother really has grown up—and grown up to be just a great guy.

Anyway, late or not, I was thrilled by the ceremony, and I had a great time at your party. I'll see you at the Fourth of July get-together!

Love,

Mary

Some of life's most significant moments come once and once only. It is very appropriate to make a big deal about them. The writer had certainly apologized on the occasion of her lateness, but she feels that an event so important merits a follow-up letter to underscore just how proud she is of her brother. The writer goes out of her way to praise, admire, and thank her brother for his understanding. The goal of a good apology is to create positive feelings, not just to patch up hurt ones.

MISINFORMATION—WRONG DIRECTIONS

Dear Mom and Dad,

Little brother let the cat out of the bag and told me what you were too polite and considerate to tell me: that the directions I had given you to the big outlet mall were all wrong and that the two of you drove all over Creation for two hours before finally calling it quits and coming back home.

Your patience and understanding amaze me. *I* would have been on the phone the minute I got home. Thanks for going so easy on me.

I am very sorry I steered you wrong. I don't know how I got the wrong directions, but I wish I hadn't passed them on to you. I called my friend Elise, who gave me the *right* directions (she swears it!), and I'd like to drive you guys out to the mall on the weekend of the 23rd. I'll be able to get into town then. Please call if it's a date.

Love and apologies,

Cindy

With family members, a lighthearted but sincere tone is often best. You want to affirm the bond between you by showing that, where your loving and understanding family is concerned, you do not live in fear of the consequences of a mistake. At the same time, you do not want to make too light of the inconvenience your error has caused.

The two positive steps taken here include praise for the kindly, loving character of the parents and an offer to turn this frustrating incident into an occasion for a family excursion.

BAD BEHAVIOR/RUDE TREATMENT—LOST TEMPER

Dear Dad:

I'd give anything if I could take back the harsh words I spoke yesterday. I know I apologized over the phone earlier, but I wanted you to have something in writing, something you could look at to see how I really feel.

I've been under a lot of pressure on the job. That's not an excuse for my outburst, but it is an explanation. I'm just sorry you got in the way of my temporary seizure of immaturity. I am happy, though, that you did not return my angry tone in kind and that, as always, you were the voice of sanity, wisdom, and love.

Sorry, Dad.

Love,

Ned

A note of apology following up on a verbal apology underscores your earnest desire to patch things up. Often, we can say more emotionally meaningful things in writing than in speaking. That is the case here. Note, by the way, how the writer shifts the focus from himself to his father in the closing sentence. The best apologies do not dwell on oneself.

CARELESS REMARK—NOTE TO BROTHER-IN-LAW

Dear Bob,

I hope my remark didn't get you in trouble with June. My sister and I are accustomed to speaking frankly, but then it occurred to me that you might not have wanted to share all that information with her at this time. Of course, this fit of discretion came upon me only *after* I had opened my big mouth.

Please let me know if my remarks have upset anything, and, if you wish, I will have a talk with June.

Regards,

Clyde

If you are not sure that you have done something wrong, it may still be a good idea to write a note that clears the air. Just be careful not to create trouble unnecessarily.

DELAYED THANK YOU

Dear Aunt Beth:

I have been wearing the wonderful sweater you sent me for three days straight, and it suddenly occurs to me that I haven't so much as thanked you for it. What a thoughtful gift! And how thoughtless of me not to have thanked you the moment I had unwrapped it.

I love the sweater. The very best thing about it is that, every time I wear it, I think of my favorite aunt.

Love,

Louisa

Never write a belated thank-you note that reads as if it were the product of a painful sense of duty. This one looks as if it had been a heartfelt pleasure to write. Certainly, it would be a delight to read.

ACCIDENT

Dear Dad:

I am very relieved that insurance will cover the damage I did to your car. Thanks for letting me know. Again, I can't tell you how sorry I am for my carelessness. If there is anything the insurance doesn't cover, please, please, *please* let me know, so that I can take care of the shortfall. My reason is selfish: It would make me feel better.

Love—and thanks for your understanding,

Danny

This note addresses the aftermath of a minor fender bender. Despite the insurance payment, it accepts continued responsibility for the accident—without, however, magnifying the incident out of proportion.

Writing It: To Friends

TARDINESS OR MISSED APPOINTMENT

Dear Martha and Crawford:

Sam and I are so very sorry that we missed your party. We had been looking forward to it for weeks, but a family emergency came up at the last minute, and we really had no choice—nor did we have any time to get word to you.

I'm sure the evening was a tremendous success and great delight. Please keep us in mind for next time!

Sincerely,

May Morgan

You owe some acknowledgment and an expression of regret when you fail to attend a party after having accepted the invitation. You need not, however, go into a detailed explanation of what prevented your attending. "Family emergency" communicates urgency without compromising your privacy.

MISINFORMATION

Dear Roy:

You're right: I was wrong. The information I had received concerning the availability of the new equipment was not accurate. I am very happy that you chose not to act on what I insisted was correct, but I certainly regret having given you a hard time about it. It *must* have been very frustrating for you—but you certainly had the great good grace not to show it.

Next time, I'll try to keep a more open mind. I apologize for trying your patience.

Yours,

Ed

When you're right, you're right, and when you're wrong—well, don't evade it. Step up to the plate and acknowledge your error. In this case, no lasting harm was done, but the writer does not emphasize this or use it to excuse himself. Instead, he expresses gratitude that the other person did not lose his temper, despite being put in a frustrating situation.

BAD BEHAVIOR/RUDE TREATMENT

Dear Mary:

Something's been bothering me since Friday. You came into the store and were looking for something special for your friend. I was so busy—so rushed—that I just did not treat you very politely. Certainly, I did not offer you the time and courtesy that you deserve.

I regret this very much, and I hope that you can see your way clear to forgiving me for this lapse. Next time you come in, please expect the kind of treatment you certainly deserve.

Sincerely,

Martin Overman

A timely note can do much to repair an oversight or lapse in courtesy. In situations such as this, a written note is more effective than a phone call because it suggests that you have devoted more time and effort to the gesture of apology.

E-Mailing It: To Family

CARELESS REMARK

Max:

I just realized that I mentioned to Mom that she would be seeing you in May. Of course, she doesn't know about the surprise anniversary party you're planning for her and Dad. I don't think I spilled the beans—or that she suspects anything. But she may mention you're coming out in May, so be prepared with an alibi.

I'm sorry I put my foot in it, Max. But I think we'll be all right.

A quick attempt at damage control can often minimize the consequences of a careless remark.

DELAYED THANK YOU

Hey, Cuz—

E-mail seemed the quickest, surest way to get hold of you. I forgot to thank you over the phone yesterday for the help you gave my friend Ted in putting together his resume. He was just full of praise for everything you did. He's a good guy, who deserves all the breaks he can get. Thanks—and sorry for the delay in acknowledging your timely help.

E-mail is such an easy, ready-to-hand, casual medium of communication that it sometimes seems necessary to justify using it in place of a letter or phone call. Don't apologize for sending an e-mail. This suggests that you are knowingly doing something inappropriate or taking the easy way out. However, if you feel you need to explain your choice of medium, do so.

E-Mailing It: To Friends

TARDINESS OR MISSED APPOINTMENT—TO A WORKGROUP

Everyone:

I've decided that the two saddest words in the English language are "flight" and "cancelled." Imagine my surprise when I got to the airport yesterday morning and found that my flight had dematerialized. Next one was a three-hour wait—and even that was delayed on the ground. So my absence yesterday was not due to lack of interest or will—just the whim of the airlines. Please accept my apologies.

Folks, can we get together Wednesday at 8:30 for a quick fill-in session for yours truly?

If you've got an ironclad, bullet-proof excuse, use it. Note that this explanation/apology ends not with a "too bad," but a proposal for positive action.

BAD BEHAVIOR/RUDE TREATMENT

Al:

I'm sitting at my keyboard feeling like a real jerk. I wish I could just rewind the tape and erase the rude remark I made to you this morning. I was way out of line. I have absolutely no excuse to offer, but will you accept my sincere apology?

In the heat of the moment, we sometimes say things we instantly regret. E-mail is a handy means of instant communication and can be the best route to a quick apology. Note the frank, straightforward approach here—an appeal to accept the offered apology.

ACCIDENT—TO CO-WORKERS IN AN OFFICE

To the Person With the Broken Souvenir Mug:

You know who you are. Now I'll own up to who I am. I am the person who broke your 1965 New York World's Fair souvenir mug. I was admiring it in the coffee room, and it slipped out of my hand. I left the pieces there, but, alas, it looks to me beyond repair.

I am very sorry for this accident, and I hope that the owner of the mug will approach me—kindly and gently—to discuss some form of reparation.

Ed McGraw

This is lighthearted, but it does not make light of the loss. It is also an opportunity for the writer to demonstrate to the entire office his willingness to take responsibility for what he has accidentally done.

25 Words to Use

accept	discuss	negotiate
acknowledge	effective	plan
agree	generous	prepared
apologize	goodwill	resolve
appreciate	help	responsibility
appropriate	hope	thank
care	improve	willing
concerned	investigate	
correct	judgment	

25 Words and Phrases to Avoid

afraid	fault	refuse
blame	hopeless	reject
can't do anymore	impossible	too late
cannot	incapable	unfair
catastrophe	insist	unworkable
crisis	mess	waste
demand	nonnegotiable	worthless
disaster	not my fault	
fail	panic	

7

Appreciation and Thanks

*C*ommunicating thanks and appreciation should be easy. For one thing, it is an inherently pleasant task. We enjoy expressing gratitude, and we enjoy receiving such expressions. It is pretty hard to go seriously wrong when you thank someone. Just uttering the word "thanks" does wonders. Yet, like almost any other communication endeavor, this one can be improved on. There are three potential problems with communicating thanks:

1. *Failure to do it at all*. This is the most serious problem. In the rush of our day-to-day affairs, we often fail to take the time to thank others for what they have done. Get into the habit of expressing gratitude. Everyone wants to be appreciated. Everyone wants to have their work recognized.

2. *Failure to do it in a timely fashion*. It is important to communicate your thanks as soon as possible. Don't put off that thank-you note you've been meaning to write.

3. *Failure to be specific*. This last point deserves further discussion. Many expressions of thanks seem insincere or, at least, unsatisfying, not because the person expressing gratitude is actually ungrateful, but because the expression is vague, general, and abstract. There is a big difference between saying "Thanks very much" and "Thank you very much for mailing those letters. It saved me enough time to get to the drugstore before it closed, and my poor kid really needed his cough syrup."

To be sure, the short expression is much better than none at all, but the longer, highly specific expression is far more valuable.

- It fully acknowledges the favor or service that was done.

- It lets the other person know the beneficial effect of what he has done.

We all like acknowledgment—the more specific, the better. Even more, we derive satisfaction from seeing the impact of our work. This, at minimum, is what a fully developed thank-you communication should furnish: specific acknowledgment and an assessment of impact. You don't need flowery adjectives and adverbs to do this. You don't need blissful outcries of eternal gratitude. What you need are the facts, nouns and verbs mostly, simply and straightforwardly expressed.

Finding the Heartline

Take two preliminary steps:

1. Identify the person or persons to thank. This may be self-evident, but if it requires asking some questions, take the time to do so.

2. Put aside what you are doing and make the thank-you call, write the thank-you note, or send the thank-you e-mail. Do it now.

A note on the second step. Be prepared to follow up with additional thanks once the full impact of the favor or service performed is known. For example, you ask a friend for permission to be listed as a credit reference on a loan application. He says yes, and you thank him, explaining what this loan will enable you to do. A few days later you get word that the loan has come through. You call your friend to tell him the news, to thank him, and to let him know that the full amount was approved and at a favorable rate. "Thanks. I know that including your name as a reference really helped."

Beyond these preliminaries, energize your thank you by getting in touch with your gratitude. Take the time to appreciate what is being done for you. Next, assess the effect of the favor or service and communicate that effect to the other person. Remember, if he cares enough to do what you ask, he cares enough to want to know the beneficial effect of the effort he is making. It really is that simple.

Sidestepping the Pitfalls

Avoid lavish, but hollow expressions of thanks. You don't have to repeat the thanks. Just make it specific. If appropriate, follow up your initial thanks with a report on results, but don't drown the other person in your gratitude. In and of itself, this is annoying. Beyond this, it also suggests your disbelief that this person could act decently.

Avoid tardy expressions of thanks. To be effective, a thank you should be timely.

Avoid ill-advised attempts at wit that make light of the service or favor that is being performed. Bantering when sincere gratitude is called for can be highly damaging to a relationship:

"I was able to get you 25 cents more per hour," said the assistant manager.

"Great! Now I can buy that yacht I've had my eye on," quips the grocery clerk.

"Go to hell," concludes the assistant manager.

Saying It: To Family

FOR A GIFT—PHONE CALL FROM A COLLEGE STUDENT

Hi, Dad. The Super-X Calculator just arrived today. What a fabulous tool! It is just what I need. I mean this is really a thoughtful gift. The best thing about it is that I can take it with me to the lab. I don't have to drag out the laptop. This is faster, more efficient. Just what I need. Thanks.

This is a good example of a thank you with a high degree of specificity. The speaker vividly explains the benefit he will derive from the gift.

FOR A FAVOR—PHONE CALL FROM SISTER TO BROTHER

Bob, hi. I just wanted to thank you, Big Brother, for taking my car to the mechanic. I know I'm supposed to be a liberated woman and all, but I'm convinced that mechanics take men more seriously than women, and, anyway, I've been all over the place with that car, trying to find someone who'll believe me about the squeaks and rattles. I don't know what you said to this mechanic, but I just picked up the car—and it runs perfectly. No squeaks. Not a single rattle. Whatever you did really produced results. I knew I could depend on you—as always. Thanks, Bob.

Share the successful outcome. Did the brother's intervention really help to resolve the problem? Who knows? The point is that he did what his sister asked and the result was positive. She doesn't speculate in her thanks, but simply gives him credit for the good work.

FOR FINANCIAL SUPPORT—PHONE CALL FROM A STRUGGLING STUDENT

Aunt Esther, hi. I just picked up the money you wired. You are a real lifesaver! What a time for my computer to go down! I have reports due in three classes, and these professors are not kindhearted like you. Tell them your computer's on the fritz, and you might as well tell them the dog ate your homework.

This cash will get me up and running right away. My grades are saved—and so is my scholarship. I just can't thank you enough for being there when I really needed you.

In part, this phone call lets the student's aunt know that the money has been wired safely and successfully. Beyond this, she is treated to a vivid picture of what her generosity has accomplished: nothing less than the salvation of her nephew!

FOR ENCOURAGEMENT

Mom, Dad, I just got word. The job is mine! I still can't believe it. But the important thing is that *you* both believed it, from the beginning, and your encouragement was really important to me—especially, Dad, when you told me about your experience with the architectural firm. That helped me hold my head up high and make a good impression. Thanks for everything you've done and said.

Letting loved ones share in a victory is an intense experience. What makes this a moment to remember is the degree to which the caller is specific, citing a particular episode his father shared with him.

Saying It: To Friends

FOR A GIFT

Martin, I've just begun reading the novel you gave me. It really is beautiful—and I just laid it aside long enough to call you to tell you what a thoughtful gift it is. Thanks. It means a lot to me.

The sooner you convey your thanks the better. You don't wait to finish the dinner before you begin to compliment your host. So why wait until you're through with the novel?

FOR A FAVOR

Dan, just calling to thank you for the loan of the pickup truck. I couldn't have rented anything in time, and, without the truck, I would have been late on this contract. And this was one customer I didn't want to tick off. Thanks to you, he's happy. Great truck you've got there, too!

The added compliment sweetens the thanks.

FOR FINANCIAL SUPPORT

Ellen, your check just arrived in the mail. I can't tell you how much I appreciate this loan. It will get me through until my internship kicks in. I really don't know what I would have done without your help. This goes above and beyond friendship. Thanks so much.

In addition to letting the lender know how much her generosity means, the speaker offers a gauge of the magnitude of the good deed: something "above and beyond."

FOR ENCOURAGEMENT

Tom, thanks for putting up with me yesterday. I know I was pretty down in the mouth—and certainly no fun to be around. Your kind words were just what I needed. I can always count on you to provide perspective on the hardest problems. Thanks to you and our talk, I feel much better, and I will proceed with the plan we discussed.

Advice and encouragement are delicate commodities. Those who offer them are rarely 100 percent sure of their effectiveness. Positive feedback, in the form of heartfelt thanks, is most welcome.

Writing It: To Family

FOR ADVICE

Dear Dad,

I am now 15 percent richer than I was yesterday. I got the raise you and I talked about. And I sure am glad we talked about it. Your advice about letting

Mr. Perkins be the first to mention an actual figure was perfect. I would have angled for 7 percent, 10 at the most. By doing what you suggested and letting him propose a number, I did much better. He offered 12, I countered with 18, and we settled on 15. I couldn't have done it without you, Dad. Thanks.

Best to Mom,

Sandy

The more you can tell the advice giver about the successful effect of his advice, the more delighted he will be. Here the writer provides a concise blow-by-blow description. She's careful also to compare and contrast what she would have done without the advice versus what she did armed with it.

FOR FINANCIAL SUPPORT

Dear Mom and Dad:

Your wonderful check arrived today. Thanks so much. I know it is a sacrifice for you both, and Sally and I deeply appreciate it. This will get us over the hump until my first paycheck from the new job. Most of all, it represents relief from worry. That's the greatest gift of all, and I am very, very thankful for it.

Love,

Eddy

Demonstrate that you take no gift for granted; however, do not dwell on any hardship you may be causing. Acknowledge the sacrifice, but don't rub it in!

FOR A GET TOGETHER—NOTE TO BROTHER AND SISTER-IN-LAW

Dear Ken and Lynn,

It was just great seeing you again—and the food, well, it's hard for a Texan to vote for a Georgia barbecue, but you've won me over. It was sloppy and delicious. Just the way it should be.

The talk was equally appetizing and satisfying. I haven't had an opportunity to relive old times like that since the old times weren't that old! The occasion has given me wonderful memories, more than enough to last until the next time we're together.

All my love,

Jake

Hit the highlights. Choose a detail or two to throw into relief. This will reawaken some of the original pleasure of the event itself.

Writing It: To Friends

FOR FRIENDSHIP

Dear Clark,

Like most other reasonably happy people, I take a lot for granted. One thing I do not want to take for granted is your friendship. I've been around long enough to have learned that it is rare to find a friend as loyal, entertaining, and kind as you. True, we've been out of touch from time to time, but, mostly, we've shared a lot of key life experiences—and we also shared our notes to American History 101 way back when, which was my only A that semester.

Clark, you are a wonderful friend. I want you to know that. And I want you to know that *I* know it, too.

All the best,

Phil

You don't have to restrict your thank-you correspondence to notes in acknowledgment of some particular gift, favor, or service. Why not thank a friend for being a friend? This kind of letter makes both the writer and the recipient feel great, and it is the kind of letter that is saved and treasured for years—a cherished gift.

FOR A GIFT

Dear Mary:

I could begin, "How did you know I wanted a toaster oven?" But the fact that I've been talking about buying one for the past, oh, three or four years probably makes the question unnecessary. You *knew* it was just what I wanted, and I am so thrilled that you bought it for me. I love it!

Your friend,

Selma

A little humor at your own expense is always welcome. Do be careful with humor in letters of thanks, however. Humor should never be allowed to undercut the sincerity of the sentiment. It should certainly not belittle the gift or the deed.

FOR A BUSINESS REFERRAL

Dear Perry:

Many thanks for referring Mr. Thornton to me. We had a meeting yesterday, and we will be doing business together. He is a delightful person, which comes as no surprise inasmuch as he is a good friend of yours.

Perry, I not only appreciate the business you have sent my way, but, even more, the vote of confidence you have given me in making the referral. Your good opinion means the world to me.

Thank you, my friend,

Ben

Acknowledging and giving thanks for all business referrals is an absolute must, and it should be done promptly. It is also highly effective to put such thanks in the form of a letter, rather than with a phone call or even an e-mail. The traditional formality of a letter underscores the value you place on the referral.

Go beyond thanks. The essence of a referral is a vote of confidence for you. Acknowledge this by saying how much you value your friend's good opinion of you.

E-Mailing It: To Family

FOR BIRTHDAY GIFT—E-MAIL TO BROTHER

Frank:

The golf clubs just arrived. I can't believe it! These aren't golf clubs. They're monuments to engineering. Just beautiful. I will use them, and I will treasure them.

Why did I say "I can't believe it"? I should have expected nothing less than first-class, top-drawer thoughtfulness from you.

Love,

Max

Ideally, an e-mail message to family or friends should embody a feeling of spontaneous intimacy and informality. In a thank you for a gift, try to set down your initial reactions to the gift. The use of e-mail suggests immediacy, even urgency. It shows how impatient you were to convey your gratitude. Take advantage of this by sending e-mail thanks without delay.

FOR ADVICE

> Mom: Thanks for the advice on what to serve at my dinner party. I intend to follow it to the letter. With a menu like the one you've laid out, I don't see how I can miss. I was very nervous when I spoke to you about this. Thanks to you, I am confidently looking forward to the evening. I'll give you a full report.

You don't have to wait for final results to express your thanks for advice. Even without the *final* results, however, note that the writer does communicate *a* result: Thanks to her mother's help, she no longer feels anxious about the impending dinner party, but is looking forward to it with pleasure. Moreover, she ends by promising to keep her mother in the loop.

FOR UNDERSTANDING

> Dear Mom and Dad:
>
> A quick e-mail to thank you for your understanding. I was looking forward to seeing you both for dinner—but I couldn't say no to this client. And much as it hurt me to change our plans, I just knew that you would understand and forgive me. Thanks for making my life easier!
>
> Can we reset the date for next Saturday?

This is a follow-up e-mail message to reinforce an expression of gratitude for understanding in a difficult situation. Thanking people for understanding in such situations reassures them that they are not taken for granted or relegated to a secondary priority.

E-Mailing It: To Friends

FOR HOSPITALITY

> Dear Martha:
>
> What a pleasure—what a kick—it was, staying with you! And I can't tell you how grateful I am that you were able to put me up on such short notice. My trip was so sudden that a hotel was out of the question. I don't know what I would have done without your wonderful hospitality.

Please take this as an open invitation to stay with me next time you get up to Baltimore. I don't know that I dare claim that I will be as gracious a hostess to you as you were to me, but I'll sure give it my best.

Thanks again, Martha.

Love,

Cindy

The best hospitality thank you's include a reciprocal invitation. If you make the invitation, be absolutely prepared to make good on it.

Note that the writer emphasizes two principal points: the pleasure of the stay, and the fact that her friend responded so generously on short notice. A thank you is most effective if the writer identifies one or two specific highlights. This keeps the message from sounding "canned."

FOR A FAVOR

John:

Thanks for covering for me yesterday. You were a real lifesaver! It was the first time I ever made conflicting appointments—and, boy, I sure picked two top-drawer clients to double book like that. Thanks to you, I didn't end up disappointing and alienating one of them.

Thanks, Buddy. I knew I could count on you, and I owe you one.

And I *mean* it, too. Just ask whenever you need this favor returned. Consider it done.

Best,

RJ

"A friend in need . . ." It is a great feeling when your friend proves his friendship by bailing you out of a tight spot. Render recognition and thanks as soon as possible. Put muscle behind the thank you by promising a quid pro quo—and make certain to live up to what you promise.

FOR A DINNER INVITATION

Dear Edna—

I wanted to thank you again for thinking of me and including me among the guests for your big dinner. It sounds like the social event of the season, and I am thrilled to be a part of it. Your friendship means the world to me.

Tammi

Just because you have already accepted the invitation does not mean that you can't offer a quick, casual note of thanks—or of added thanks. Notes like this are truly life's grace notes. They enhance the experience of friendship.

25 Words to Use

achieve	grateful	sacrifice
accomplish	gratitude	selfless
acknowledge	heartfelt	sincere
appreciate	invaluable	succeed
commitment	opportunity	thanks
contribution	pleasure	thoughtful
dedication	priceless	tremendous
generous	privilege	
goal	profound	

15 Words and Phrases to Avoid

blame	made the effort	thanks a million
debt	must	tried your best
eternally indebted	old college try	
greatest in the world	shocked	
have to	sorry I had to ask	
how can I ever repay you?	surprised	
	thanks a bunch	

Cheers and Encouragement

$\mathcal{S}$orrow, misfortune, and tragedy can create powerful emotional bonds among people, especially if accompanied by effective communication. This is an area addressed in Chapter 12. It is also true that occasions of positive enterprise and great expectation call for communicating from the heart, both before and during the event. This is what we'll cover in this chapter. After the successful completion of a project, it is time to convey heartfelt congratulations, which reinforce and celebrate the achievement. This is the subject of Chapter 9.

Finding the Heartline

Actions, begins a well-worn cliché, speak louder than words. Yet think of some of the most momentous actions the world has known. Take, for example, the American Revolution. Is it possible to think of this event without the words of the *Declaration of Independence?* Or the Civil War: Lincoln's *Gettysburg Address* comes to mind. World War II? Perhaps it is President Roosevelt's stirring request to Congress for a declaration of war following the attack on Pearl Harbor, a "date that will live in infamy," or Winston Churchill's promise to offer the British people nothing but blood, tears, and sweat.

The fact is that actions without words are often events without meaning or, at least, with compromised and diminished meaning. Words—the right words—shape, ennoble, intensify, guide, and elevate action. Often, they make the difference between the success and failure of an enterprise.

Finding the heartline in the midst of such an enterprise depends on using words that build, reinforce, and affirm the self-confidence of everyone involved. How is this done?

- By demonstrating knowledge, awareness, and appreciation of the realities involved in the enterprise.

- By drawing on experiences that demonstrate past success in similar situations.

- By showing that the experience and skills of those involved in the enterprise are adequate to achieving success.

- By reminding all involved of the objectives and goals of the enterprise.

- By ensuring that all involved in the enterprise understand the benefits of achieving the objectives and goals.

Sidestepping the Pitfalls

The most common error made by those who would cheer and encourage is a failure to demonstrate a grasp of the realities of the situation in question. People readily see through fantasy and empty rhetoric. Instead of finding encouragement in hollow words, they find reason to doubt the feasibility and outcome of the enterprise.

- Avoid empty rhetoric, including such meaningless expressions as "You can do it," "We can do anything," and the like.

- Avoid hollow predictions of success that are not based on facts, experience, or reasonable expectations.

Just as it is important to avoid empty, groundless, inflated enthusiasm, it is even more critical to avoid projecting negativity or pessimism. In planning a project, it is essential that you express any doubts and reservations you may have. The planning stage is no time for thoughtless optimism. Once you and your group are committed to a course of action, however, you should keep all doubts to yourself—unless you are thoroughly persuaded that a radical change of course is required. That is, if you are burdened by doubt, be prepared to propose a change of plan. If, on the other hand, you are committed to the plan, do not share your doubts and fears. Keep the tone and climate thoroughly positive.

Negativity to be avoided includes the following:

- Expressions of doubt.

- Predictions of disaster and doom.

- Complaints about objectives, goals, and the people involved in the project or enterprise.

Perhaps the greatest mistake people make in situations where morale-lifting encouragement is called for is a failure to know and to marshal the facts of the enterprise.

- Know what you and your group are about.

- Know the objectives and the goals of the project.

- Know the dangers.

- Know the benefits.

- Know the risks and the rewards.

- Know what means are necessary to achieve the ends that the group agreed on.

Those you work with have an uncanny ability to penetrate even the thickest layers of baloney. Know the facts—and use them.

Saying It: To Family

ENTERING COLLEGE—WORDS TO A SON OR DAUGHTER

I'm very proud of you, and I'm very excited for you. College was one of the very greatest experiences of my life, and I bet you'll find it the same for you. What you've done in high school—the study skills you've learned and already demonstrated—will really get a workout in college. It feels good to stretch. That's what college did for me. It gave me a chance to realize just how much I could achieve, and, let me tell you, you find out that you can do a lot more than you think. That's really what it's all about: Finding out what you can do and always pushing the envelope. But that's a way of working and living you're already very familiar with. I think you'll do great in college. You'll find it challenging and different from anything that came before—but you'll also find it, well, comfortable. What can I say? Have fun!

Although it may not always seem to be the case, children at the threshold of adulthood want their parents to share experience with them—and not just experience, but the feelings associated with experience. This need is especially acute as the young man or woman is about to embark on a milestone event such as entry into college. Here the speaker combines two approaches to encouragement:

1. He shares his assessment of the positive feelings associated with the experience.

2. He creates a context for success by reminding the young person of her record of high school achievement.

Both of these steps create continuity with past experience while simultaneously acknowledging the newness of the impending adventure. Yes, this is a new, challenging, exciting, even somewhat frightening episode of life, but I have been through it—with great feelings and positive results—and you have already demonstrated many of the skills you'll need to get you through the experience successfully.

A NEW BUSINESS VENTURE—PHONE CALL TO A SISTER

Hi, sis. I heard the exciting news about the franchise you and Dave just bought. From what I've heard, it sounds great. I've seen these businesses blossom here in Cleveland, and I would think the demand would be even greater in a place like Pine Bluff. People need a one-stop-shopping center for the kind of service you'll be offering. Seems to me you'll have plenty of opportunity for growth down the line.

So, when do you close on the deal, and when do you open your doors?

Notice the absence of *empty* enthusiasm here. There are no exclamations of "Congratulations!" or "I know you can do it!" Instead, the speaker conveys her sense of excitement for her sister, and she offers the genuinely encouraging example of similar enterprises with which she is familiar. That is, the speaker is careful to base her prediction of success on a precedent, not on mere wishful thinking.

Two additional features of this little speech are worth noting:

1. The comments do not remain focused on the past or the present, but turn toward the future. Encouragement is about what one has done and is doing, to be sure, but, most of all, it is about the great things yet to come. This speaker talks about the potential for future growth.

2. The speaker ends by inviting her sister's comments and conversation. She shifts the focus to her sister. Nothing is more encouraging than showing genuine interest in the other person's enterprise. The way to show this interest is to invite the other person to talk about what she is doing.

MATURE CAREER CHANGE—PHONE CALL TO A PARENT

So, Dad, Mom tells me you've finally decided to pursue your dream. I'd like to tell you that I admire your guts, leaving the firm to go off on your own. But, in your case, I don't think the move takes a great deal of courage. You've got everything it takes to make a huge splash with your own agency. If ever there was betting on a sure thing, this is it. Growing up, I saw how you carried promotional operations for the firm, and, sometimes, I also saw how frustrated you were by the dumb decisions of others. Well, it's about time you were in a position to call the shots. I'm really excited by this move. The industry is going to sit up and take notice.

The speaker immediately identifies with his father's motivation: pursuing his dream, following his own direction. This is a very effective strategy for communicating encouragement—provided that you know the other person well enough to understand his motivation. Don't guess. Don't put yourself in the position of trying to tell another person what he is thinking or feeling. This does not create encouragement, but, rather, frustration and, perhaps, a degree of anxiety, since the other person feels misunderstood.

It is often difficult to avoid falling back on hollow words of encouragement. Here, the speaker stays away from this by recalling the perception he has had of his father. Basing encouragement on shared experience is highly effective. Nothing is more heartening than the evocation of a positive track record, a continuity with a successful past combined with the prospect of improving on that past.

Saying It: To Friends

ON A BUSINESS VENTURE—PHONE CALL

> Gene, I just received your mailer announcing your new business. What a great idea!
>
> It's going to be exciting watching you grow. And based on my work with you when you were with Acme, Inc., I know that you *will* grow. You have the brains, you have the experience, and you have the contacts. You can count me among your customers from day one.

News from a friend concerning a new venture is your cue to make a phone call, write a note, or send an e-mail to express your best wishes and to provide encouragement and a vote of confidence. The most powerful expression of confidence you can make is based on your experience with your friend. Invoke your past together. Use this as the foundation for voicing your excitement and enthusiasm.

CAREER CHANGE—CONVERSATION

> No, Bob, I don't think you're crazy to leave Benson & Goulding for an entry-level position in something you really love. You owe it to yourself to be the best—and I'm inclined to agree with you: You can't be your best at Benson & Goulding, doing what you're doing now.
>
> You know, Bob, you're not alone in making a move like this. I read somewhere that, according to the Bureau of Labor Statistics, the average worker changes employers seven times in his working life—and changes *careers* at least three times!
>
> So, I know it's scary. But you've made the decision, and I'm confident you will make a go of it. Just to hear the way you talk about the new field convinces me that you'll do great things.

A large part of encouragement is providing reinforcement for decisions that have already been made. Base that reinforcement on whatever facts you can muster. Remember, facts—not fancy words—are the most powerful instruments of persuasion.

TO A DISCOURAGED STUDENT

> John, I really am sorry that the scholarship didn't come through for you. It's bad enough that you won't be getting the money, now don't beat yourself up over what you think this disappointment says about you. You know your

record, and so do I. You are at the very top of you class, and nothing can change that. No one's denying that the scholarship would have made this coming year easier for you. But you can get along without it very nicely, too. Keep your eye on the prize. Don't let this distract you.

I don't mean to sound preachy, but you know that a big part of study is independence from outside reward and pats on the back. You need to just keep doing what you've been doing: achieving excellence for the sake of excellence—and to satisfy yourself. And if you do need some outside approval, well, just to turn to me.

Providing encouragement when the chips are down is a vital service, but it is not easy. "Feel good" speeches are not always appreciated by someone who has just suffered a disappointment. Your words of encouragement should, first and foremost, put the setback into perspective. This is a crucial first step toward refloating a sinking morale. Part of this process of maintaining perspective is to offer a mirror to your friend. Let his achievements be reflected in you. Remind him of what he has done and what he is capable of doing. Provide him with the means of seeing past a temporary problem. Finally, it is *always* a good idea to end on a note that reaffirms your friendship and the esteem with which you regard your friend. Don't let him feel diminished, let alone abandoned, by you.

Writing It: To Family

BUSINESS VENTURE—LETTER TO SON OR DAUGHTER

Dear Pat,

I'm writing because I am so thrilled about your plans for the store. You have done a magnificent job lining up the financing, and your knowledge of the industry and the retail picture is so thorough that I see nothing but success in your future. I am very excited about the location you have chosen, which, I agree, is both a high-demand area and one with remarkably little competition.

You know better than I do the nature of the challenges you will be facing, but I know—maybe even better than you do—how well equipped you are to handle those challenges and to turn them into opportunities.

Pat, dear, I can hardly wait to see the grand opening next month. This is going to be big for you, and it makes me very proud.

Love,

Dad

For something as momentous as a new business venture, a letter from father to child is highly appropriate and most welcome. In this age of rapid, casual communication, there is something ennobling and even ceremonial about a written, mailed letter. The document does not have to be profound, but if it is written in sincerity, it will be meaningful the moment it is read, and it will be preserved and treasured over the years.

In this letter, the father avoids preaching or dishing out advice. He gives a realistic, encouraging assessment of the child's skills and knowledge—the complete competence that will virtually ensure success. He does not deny that challenges lie ahead, but, again, he expresses confidence in the ability of his son or daughter not only to meet the challenges, but to capitalize on them.

While keeping the focus on the recipient of the letter, the writer also expresses his own love and enthusiasm.

CAREER DECISION—LETTER TO A DAUGHTER

Dear Meg,

I'm so happy we spoke yesterday about your decision to enroll in graduate school to continue your studies in anthropology. It is something you love, and so few people have the courage and determination to pursue what they love. I am very proud of you for having that courage.

The course work you've described to me does sound challenging, but also deeply fascinating. I believe it will expand and enrich your life, and I am also convinced that whatever the field of anthropology gives you, you will return to it a hundred-fold in terms of advancing knowledge and understanding.

I am eager to follow your adventure for the next few years.

Love,

Mom

This is a letter to a young adult daughter, and it recognizes and respects the woman's maturity. There is no debating or second guessing the young woman's choice. There is no discussion of possible financial hardships that a career in anthropology may present. Instead, the writer focuses exclusively on the positive aspects of the decision: The daughter is embarking on a career in a field she obviously feels passionately about.

REMARRIAGE PLANS—FATHER

Dear Dad,

It was great seeing you this weekend! I was thrilled by the news about Mary. You've been alone so long since Mom died that I was beginning to think you had given up on looking for someone. And Mary isn't just someone. She really seems to be *the* one. She is a lovely, funny, sweet lady. I liked her instantly.

Dad, I know the two of you will be very happy together. The chemistry is very apparent and very positive. I loved seeing the two of you together, and I absolutely believe you will be great for each other.

Love,

Sarah Ann

This letter not only provides important affirmation of the father's choice in remarriage, but also signals to him in unequivocal terms that the choice creates no conflicts. The single most encouraging thing the daughter can do in this case is to let her father know that she supports his plans and that she is happy for him. Why convey this in a letter instead of a conversation? In truth, it is best to do both; the letter should reinforce the conversation.

Writing It: To Friends

NEW BUSINESS VENTURE

Dear Max,

I greatly enjoyed talking with you about the new Internet business you are starting up. We both know how competitive the field is, but the more I've thought about your approach, as you explained it to me, the more I am convinced that you've really taken hold of something sensationally promising. If anything, I think that your projections are conservative. I'm just speaking from my own perceptions and business needs, of course, but if my case is at all representative, you should do very well indeed.

My confidence and enthusiasm are based on even more than my perception of the field. They are also founded on my experience with you, both as a friend and as a business associate. You have a way of making things work—and work very well.

All the best,

Sam

CAREER CHANGE

Dear Jane,

I was surprised by your announcement the other day about your radical shift in career direction. But, of course, I should not have been surprised at all. You have always been both adventurous and imaginative. In this context, your upcoming career move seems perfectly logical.

Naturally, I cannot tell you whether or not I think you are making the "right" move. I do believe, however, that it is a bad idea to fail to follow your dream, and I support your decision to set off in a new direction. I think this is important for you. And if anyone can pull off this kind of career move, I know that you can.

Best of luck,

Bill

Providing encouragement does not require you to generate false confidence in a positive outcome. Just don't dwell on your doubts. Instead, identify the most positive approach to the subject and pursue that course. Hollow encouragement or fabricated optimism is highly transparent and instantly discovered. The result is a loss rather than a building of confidence.

RETIREMENT PLANS

Dear Pat,

I envy you. The ideas you have for your upcoming retirement are simply remarkable. It's as if you've decided to "retire" into a whole new career. I certainly enjoyed discussing your plans, which are very inventive and highly worthwhile. You've managed to turn retirement into a whole new beginning.

The very best to you,

Ben

This brief letter is effective because it focuses on the most valuable and important aspect of the recipient's retirement plans—a retirement that really amounts to a second career. The most effective encouragement identifies special strengths or unique features of a plan, enterprise, or course of action and acknowledges as well as praises these.

E-Mailing It: To Family

CHANGE OF COLLEGE MAJOR—E-MAIL TO A SISTER

Joan:

I'm excited by your decision to change from pre-med to pre-law. I've always pictured you in a public-speaking role more than as a scientist, so I really do think that you are finding your groove by making the switch. I have known you to achieve nothing short of excellence, and I have every reason to believe that you will continue to do so in your new field.

Love—and have fun!

Pete

Be cautious when you offer an opinion on the wisdom of a course of action. However, if you really do approve of the choices that have been made, say so—and give your reasons. This is the most effective vote of confidence you can give. Does it assure the other person that she has made the right decision? Of course not; but it does let her know that you, at least, agree with the decision—and that, furthermore, your agreement is based on sound, well-thought-out reasons.

VACATION PLANS—E-MAIL TO PARENTS

Dear Mom and Dad:

So you're finally taking that world cruise you've been talking about since I was old enough to understand what you were talking about! I think it's a great idea. You deserve it—nobody deserves it more than you do. And, even more important, nobody will get more from it or appreciate it more than the two of you. Every trip, every vacation we ever took as a family you made special by your appreciation and understanding of each new site. I learned a great deal, and I had a wonderful experience. Now it is about time to do the same for yourselves. Bon voyage! I'm eager to see your pictures and hear your stories.

Love, Ned

The core of the encouragement here is assurance to the parents that this "extravagance"—a world cruise—is fully justified. They deserve to indulge themselves. This approval and affirmation, coming from a son or daughter, is bound to enhance the parents' experience of the cruise. Notice that the writer focuses exclusively on the positive:

The parents deserve the trip. He does not bring up any counter-position, such as "I know some people might think a cruise like this is extravagant and a waste of money, but . . ." When you provide encouragement, the cons are usually present by implication. Most of the time, it is better to avoid trotting them out explicitly. Instead, focus exclusively on the pros. This, of course, does not apply if you are actively helping another person to make a decision. In that case, it is essential to enumerate and to weigh the pros as well as the cons. But the essence of encouragement is reinforcement of a decision already made, not an occasion to raise doubts.

FACING SURGERY

> Dear Mom—
>
> Just a quick note to tell you what you already know, that we love you, and we are sending you all good thoughts. I am very impressed with Dr. Goodson and would have no qualms about putting myself in his very skilled hands. As for you, having been raised by you and loved by you, I know how very strong you are. That strength will get you through this, as it got Cindy and me through so much.
>
> Mom, I'll see you after you come out of the recovery room tomorrow. You know that we'll be there to help you in every way.
>
> Love,
>
> Matt

If you know that your correspondent regularly reads his or her e-mail, this form of communication is ideal for quick, informal, even intimate messages. No occasion cries out more loudly for encouraging words than when your correspondent is facing a challenging, frightening ordeal such as surgery. Try to base your encouraging words as firmly on reality as possible. Usually, it is not necessary or advisable to discuss the details of diagnosis, prognosis, or procedure. These are matters between the doctor and her patient. However, if you are familiar with the reputation of the physician or the hospital, state your high opinion of these. Also draw on your experience of the patient. In this case, the writer assures his mother that he has experienced her strength and that this proven strength will carry her through.

At moments like this, it may be difficult to avoid expressing your own anxiety. Difficult though it is, do avoid it. Keep the focus on the correspondent, the patient. Address her situation and feelings, rather than your own. As you focus on the other person, maintain a thoroughly positive tone.

E-Mailing It: To Friends

NEW PROJECT IDEA

Danny:

I'm glad we talked this morning about the new software. I like the idea. I like it a lot. Based on my own experience with off-the-shelf accounting software, I'm convinced that your "custom modular" approach will be greeted with high enthusiasm.

I hope that you will contact Jim and Karen about venture capital. They love ideas like this.

Keep the faith and stick with it. This seems to me a real winner.

Cynthia

You don't have to be an expert to base your enthusiasm on facts. Just point out that you are drawing on your own experience. Do this, and your words of encouragement will not ring hollow. Note also here that the writer uses the terminology her correspondent has given her: "custom modular." This suggests that there is depth of comprehension, not just wishful thinking, involved in the assessment of the idea and the prediction of its success. Finally, the writer reiterates the item of practical aid she has offered—the names of potential investors. Repeating this information adds substance to the good wishes offered.

COPING WITH AN ILLNESS

Dear Penny,

Mike told me about your diagnosis. I was shocked, of course, and frightened, as I know you must have been. But, almost immediately, I remembered how strong you are, how resourceful, and how wise. When Mike told me about the medical team you had assembled, I realized that you were not about to let this thing get the best of you. You were fighting, and you were fighting intelligently.

And, of course, you're not in this alone. Your family, like you, is strong and loving and supportive. I know you have a horde of friends who are behind you, rooting and praying. I am one of them. Penny, if there is anything I can do to help you during this time, please, please, please don't hesitate to call.

I am thinking of you.

Love,

Marcia

Responding to a friend's illness generally calls for three things:

1. An expression of sympathy and fellow feeling

2. Encouragement and hope

3. A realistic offer of help

In expressing sympathy, take care. Do not tell the other person how horrible the situation is. Do not intensify a sense of calamity. Do not convey hopelessness. Do not paint a dark picture. Just let her know that you understand the situation is painful, difficult, and frightening. Make it clear that you do not take it lightly.

Base your offer of encouragement on what you know about the person—her strength, her supportive family, the level of medical care she is receiving. Do not offer false hope. Do not simply say, "I'm sure it's nothing" or "You'll come through this just fine." Do not offer medical opinions—unless you are a physician. Offer realistic encouragement only, but *do* offer it. Focus on the positive.

Finally, to the extent that you are able to do so, offer realistic help. Be prepared to act on this offer.

25 Words and Phrases to Use

ability	knowledge	thoughtful
adventure	optimistic	timely
calculated	planned	understanding
confident	prospects	venture
enterprise	right time	well-equipped
enthusiastic	skills	wisdom
exciting	smart	wise
experience	strength	
future	support	

25 Words and Phrases to Avoid

a breeze	luck	terrible
cinch	mistake	tough
crap shoot	no problem	tragic
dangerous	no sweat	trouble
don't worry	piece of cake	what will be will be
easy	risky	you'll be fine
failure	simple	you'll do fine
hopeless	sudden	
impossible	sure thing	

9

Celebration and Congratulation

$\mathcal{C}$ommunicating celebration and congratulation is, if anything, easier than conveying encouragement (Chapter 8). The reason is that the success of the enterprise or project has already been achieved, so there is less risk of saying the wrong thing—of instilling doubt or worry instead of confidence, or of providing false confidence when this is not warranted. Nevertheless, inept or ineffective congratulations can create hard feelings, ill will, or disappointment. The same is true in the absence of any congratulation or celebration at all. In contrast, effective, heartfelt congratulation and celebration is a reward that makes everyone involved in the enterprise feel great. Even more, an effective congratulation contributes to the climate and conditions that may promote future success.

Finding the Heartline

The secret of effective expression of congratulation and celebration is to develop a dual perspective. Look backward, at what has been accomplished and achieved, but also look forward, to what the achievement predicts about the future. Too many congratulations are one sided, looking to the past only. This neglects the opportunity to make the achievement enduring and dynamic by applying it to the future. Congratulations are not just about history. They are also about the future.

As with so many other acts of communication at momentous times, it is important to begin by identifying the facts of the event and focusing on them.

- Focus on the facts; recount them.
- Identify the significance of the facts. What does the accomplishment mean? What effects does it have?

After dealing with the facts, celebrate those who achieved them.

- Name names. Who did what?
- If appropriate, celebrate the teamwork involved.
- Finally, express your feelings and your appreciation.

Sidestepping the Pitfalls

The biggest mistake that is made where congratulations are called for is simply to fail to offer them. Any acknowledgment is better than none at all. Beyond this, avoid the following:

- *Empty, inflated praise.* When your friend makes employee of the month, don't tell him that it is "without a doubt" the greatest accomplishment in human history.

- *Faint praise.* Unless you can deliver heartfelt, unqualified congratulations, don't bother. Do not qualify your praise: "This is a great accomplishment for someone like you."

- *Uncomprehending congratulations.* Be certain that you understand what you are praising or celebrating. If your son graduated summa cum laude, don't congratulate him on graduating magna cum laude.

- *Pinning the person to the past.* Too often, well-meaning offers of congratulations are delivered as epitaphs. They imply that the achievement is over and done and that the achiever will never do better: "This is your masterpiece!" A statement like this is counterproductive. An effective congratulation celebrates achievement, but it also inspires new achievement. Look to the future as well as the past.

Saying It: To Family

WEDDING ANNIVERSARY—TO PARENTS

Are you both on the phone? Mom, Dad, I just wanted to congratulate you on loving—and deserving—one another for thirty years. In lesser people, this would be a remarkable achievement, but for a couple like you, loving and loyal, it must have come naturally. Your marriage is a lesson I have learned much from, and will always look to in my own life.

Too often, anniversary congratulations put such emphasis on the longevity of the relationship that the union comes off sounding like an epic ordeal or even a prison sentence. This phone call seeks both to recognize the achievement, but also to lighten the tone and ensure that the message is entirely celebratory. Note also the self reference—the "lesson" the son or daughter has learned. This both personalizes the congratulation and orients it toward the future.

HIGH SCHOOL GRADUATION—WORDS TO A SON OR DAUGHTER

Pat, this is a great day for you—and for your mother and me. What you have achieved no one can take away from you, and you are now ready to take the next step—into college—with real, solid, fullydeserved confidence. We are very proud, and you should be, too.

Let the achiever know that what she has accomplished not only enriches her life, but the lives of those close to her. There is nothing selfish about sharing in the achievement of another.

Note that these comments "define" the achievement of graduating from high school. That is, the speaker tells his daughter that she can legitimately derive confidence from the achievement. Congratulations should build confidence, and defining the achievement in this way does just that. Be careful, however, to avoid telling the achiever what to think and what to feel. Don't let your words pigeonhole the achievement by defining it too narrowly.

ON A SUCCESSFUL BUSINESS VENTURE—PHONE CALL TO A BROTHER

Max, it's Tom. Dad just told me that you closed the Anderson deal. I know how hard you've worked for it, and I'm just so happy that Anderson saw the light and chose you. That firm will be glad it did, and I'm thrilled that your hard work paid off. This should mean a great deal for your business and will open up a whole new market for you. It is very exciting.

Effective congratulations recognize that good things don't just happen. They're *earned* and *achieved* through hard work. By acknowledging this, you ensure that your words will not inadvertently diminish an achievement.

Saying It: To Friends

PURCHASE OF A NEW HOUSE

> Hey, Buddy. Sally just told me the great news. You've closed on the house! This is wonderful. That house sounds like a dream, and I know the neighborhood well. It is a wonderful place to live. I know how tense a closing can be, but you guys handled it beautifully. I can hardly wait for you to get moved in so that Betty and I can visit!

Closing on a new house is an important achievement that deserves congratulations. This is an occasion for 100 percent celebration. Do not debate the pros and cons of the house or the location. Be fully positive. To the extent that you can, draw on your personal experience and knowledge.

AWARD RECEIVED

> Jane, I can't say I'm surprised, but I sure am thrilled for you! If any project ever deserved the Smith Prize, yours certainly did. I think that was apparent to everyone. Your approach is so innovative and exciting that the jury really had no choice. Add to that the quality of the execution of the project, and it was a no brainer.
>
> Jane, I have some idea of just how prestigious the award is, but what, exactly, will it mean for you?

You don't need to know everything to deliver heartfelt and persuasive congratulations. The speaker here provides several good reasons why the recipient deserved the award, and he acknowledges its importance; however, he also asks the recipient to tell him more. There is nothing at all wrong with this approach. Just make certain that your remarks in no way diminish the importance of the achievement.

BUSINESS DEAL

> Well, Joe, you've bagged the whale! The Young account is quite a prize, and no one has worked harder or more intelligently than you to get it. The campaign you mounted was brilliant. I have to confess that it taught me a thing or two. Best of all, the people at Young will not be disappointed. Brilliant as the campaign was, the fact is that you can also deliver on what you promise. Congratulations!

Take care to avoid implying that an achievement was the product of good fortune, accident, hype, or that in any other way it was undeserved. Here, for example, the speaker praises the campaign that earned her friend the business he sought, but then is careful to point out that the campaign was based on solid achievement and ability.

Writing It: To Family

WEDDING ANNIVERSARY

Dear Mom and Dad,

A note for you on a very special day—your fortieth anniversary! I want you to know that, all my life, you have been for me an example of love, strength, and understanding. My family has benefited from your achievement in ways that make us all very, very grateful.

The very best to you today!

Love, Ted

BUSINESS ANNIVERSARY—NOTE TO AN IN-LAW

Dear Karen,

Your first year, come and gone already! And what a splash you've made! I don't personally know of any shop that has done so much in so short a time. In this past year, you've built a reputation that should propel you to ever greater heights. Press coverage has been tremendous, and word of mouth— well, let's just say that I hear an awful lot about you.

All of this is richly deserved, Karen. Your shop is a delight and a pleasure. I look forward to the next year and the next and the next . . .

All the best,

Stan

Anniversaries are such natural times for celebration and congratulations that it can be difficult to sound enthusiastic, let alone original. Don't strain yourself. Just identify the facts and address them. In this case, the writer begins with the fact that a year has passed and then continues with some details of the excellent reception the enterprise has received. The writer ends on a personal note, with the opinion that the shop is a delight.

COMPLETION OF MEDICAL DEGREE—TO A SISTER

Dear Doctor Sis,

I am so very, very proud of you. Of course, I knew you'd do it. All of our lives, you would set your mind to do something, figure out how to do it, plan how to do it, then you did it. This was no different—just longer and harder.

I realize you've got a lot of hard work ahead of you, a long, demanding, and very exciting residency. But you'll come out of it what you are destined to be: a great physician. It will be a terrific life for you, and you will, I believe, give a great, great deal to so many others.

Congratulations and love,

Ben

A truly significant achievement deserves a thoughtful letter written from the heart. People love to share good feelings, especially on occasions of achievement. Be generous with your feelings on such occasions. Here the writer recalls the childhood experience the two shared. Personalize your communications with facts, events, memories rather than mere words or prefabricated emotion.

Writing It: To Friends

ENGAGEMENT—TWO FRIENDS

Dear Sally and Gary,

It's about time! Mary and I have been biting our nails in suspense for almost a year now, wondering when the two of you would realize what all of us could see from the first time you guys met. You are made for each other. You—as a pair—are meant to be. I can't tell you how relieved we are now that you've finally recognized your destiny.

We know the two of you so well. We know what wonderful people you are. You deserve each other and will have a life of love together that will, I predict, be the stuff of legend.

Congratulations, best wishes, and love,

Frank and Mary

When you write to a good friend, visualize him or her. Hold a conversation. Writing to friends does not have to be very different from talking to them. Good-natured kidding is appropriate and welcome. Just make certain that it is good-natured and not belittling. Share good feelings good naturedly.

CAREER PROMOTION

Dear John:

Great news yesterday! Your firm is getting a great associate director. You will take your department to record heights. The fact that the firm realized who you are and what you can do speaks volumes for its wisdom. It knows it's lucky to have you on the team.

John, congratulations!

Carrie

Try a new approach to congratulations on a career-building promotion. Instead of patting the promotee on the back, reverse the situation by congratulating the company that did the promoting. The lucky one here is not your friend, but the firm that has hired and promoted him. There can be no higher or more genuine praise than this.

AWARD

Dear Janet,

Let me add my voice to the swelling chorus of congratulations on the recognition and honor you've received. Your moving and generous acceptance speech told the truth: The competition was extraordinary and extraordinarily worthy. But you were also too modest. I think it was clear to the membership from the moment the first reports on your project came in: You had achieved something memorable and remarkable, something well beyond any competitor.

I am thrilled for you, and I'm honored to be your friend.

Congratulations,

Sarah

An award is public recognition for an achievement. Even when communicating congratulations to a close friend, acknowledge the public nature of the award. Here the writer "adds" her voice to the "swelling chorus of congratulations"; she recognizes that hers is not the only congratulatory message that will be received, and, indeed, she celebrates that fact.

E-Mailing It: To Family

BIRTH—CONGRATULATIONS TO SISTER AND BROTHER-IN-LAW

Em and Ted,

If you're anything like Bill and me, you're thrilled, tired, and a little scared just now. Let me tell you, the thrill never really ends, and you will be tired more than a few times, and, more than a few times, you will be a little scared, but, all in all, you really have just begun the most rewarding years of your lives together. And you'll have a lot of fun, too!

Congratulations, you two—or, rather, you three. Kiss little Jenny for me.

Love,

Marcia

A birth is such a momentous event that many of us feel inadequate to find suitable words, words that are profound enough for the occasion. The best approach is not to try to make a great oration or launch into a flight of poetry. This is a time to summon up your own experience and to share it. Birth is the beginning of a voyage, and the novice voyagers will greatly appreciate any wisdom and knowing emotion you can share with them. Do, however, avoid reeling off a list of advice items, and do not tell the couple how they *should* feel.

BIRTHDAY GREETING—TO A BROTHER

Ken,

Welcome to the ranks of the "real" adults—those of us who have reached 30!

I know it's a shock, but, believe me, life goes on and, as I have discovered, continues to be a lot of fun.

Speaking of fun, I'm sorry I can't be at your party today, but I wish you much happiness as you celebrate today.

Love, Sandi

Too often we forget that birthdays are occasions of celebration and congratulations. Consider a quick, personal e-mail as an alternative to a store-bought card—especially when the birthday involved is a milestone, such as turning thirty. Emphasize celebration and the future rather than the inevitable passage of time.

PROMOTION—TO A DAUGHTER

Cindy, Dear—

Your dad just told me the great news about your promotion. I can't say I'm sur-prised, but I am thrilled for you—and very proud. You were wise to choose to work for a company that obviously recognizes your talent and is willing to reward it. I know that you will continue to excel, and I hope that, through all the challenges you will face, you will find increased fulfillment and satisfaction.

Congratulations and love, Mom

In offering congratulations on a career promotion, take care to avoid implying that the promotion is in any way overdue: "Well, they've *finally* given you what you deserve." Your tone should be 100 percent positive. Here, the writer ensures that her daughter will not only feel good about herself and her achievement, but will also have good feel-ings about the company that has recognized her talent and ability.

PUBLICATION OF A MAGAZINE ARTICLE

Uncle Ed,

I just read your article in *Fishing Life* magazine. What a stunner! I particular-ly enjoyed the careful explanation of your spin-casting technique, something I've always admired. Now I feel as if I can emulate it, if not duplicate it. I'm so happy that *Fishing Life* published the piece, and I hope it will be the first of many more. It was an informative pleasure to read.

The one thing you can be sure a writer appreciates is being read. When you convey congratulations on a publication, show your genuine interest by saying something meaningful about the piece. If possible, don't just tell the author that you enjoyed what he wrote; tell him what you especially liked about the work. Flowery language, hyperbole, or lav-ish praise are not required. Solid, fact-based praise is far more welcome.

E-Mailing It: To Friends

CONTRIBUTION TO THE COMMUNITY

Gary:

A word of congratulation on your fine presentation to the Neighborhood Board meeting last night. Your report on crime prevention in the community was extraordinarily detailed and insightful. Most important, it was filled with ideas that are perfectly feasible and well within our capability as a community organization. We all appreciate your hard work, and I am delighted that you are on our team.

Best,

Hannah Cohen

An achievement does not have to be epoch-making to deserve congratulations. The ready availability of e-mail communication makes it easy and convenient to acknowledge contributions of all kinds. Timeliness is of the essence in such informal communications. Compose and transmit them as soon as possible after the occasion in question.

BIRTHDAY

Terri,

As always, today is starred on my calendar: Your birthday! I'm sorry I'm not in town to celebrate it with you, but I trust your many (other) friends will make it a happy occasion.

Here's to a great year!

Tom

Never let a birthday greeting come across as an obligation. Note the detail the writer includes here: "today is starred on my calendar." A deft touch like this is bound to make the recipient feel special—and that is what birthday congratulations are all about.

AWARD

Dear Fred,

I just read in *Marketing News* that the Grainger Prize was awarded to—who?—*you!* If it had been given to me, I'd have been on the phone to you in a New York minute. But you, you're so modest that you didn't even mention it when we spoke the other day.

Winning the Grainger is a great achievement, and you richly deserve it. As you know, you join a very distinguished roster of recipients. I've always been honored to call you my friend, now I'm even more proud to do so.

All the best,

Ray

If you hear of your friends' achievements indirectly, through a third party or in the media, dash off a timely congratulations. Let your friends and associates know that you are thinking of them and that you are always interested in what they are doing.

25 Words and Phrases to Use

accomplishment	fulfilling	skilled
achievement	hard work	success
award	news	successful
congratulations	pleased	thought
contribution	praise	triumph
delighted	proud	value
deserve	recognition	wise
distinguished	rewarding	
enduring	satisfying	

6 Words and Phrases to Avoid

it's about time	luck of the draw	surprising
luck	lucked out	unexpected

10

Asking Favors

$\mathcal{N}$obody likes asking for a favor, right? After all, from childhood, most of us are trained "not to impose" and not to expect "something for nothing." Well, it's true: Imposing on others and angling to get something for nothing are not attractive options. Fortunately, there is another option. Rethink the definition of *favor*.

Instead of thinking of your request as a bid to get something for nothing, look at it as *giving* someone an opportunity to help you. The key word here is *opportunity*. Why? Because the fact is that most people actually enjoy helping others.

* Being asked to help empowers the helper.
* Being asked to help is a compliment and a vote of confidence.
* Being asked to help provides an opportunity to feel good about oneself.

Most of the world's religions include a tenet of faith that is similar to the concept of karma found in Hinduism and Buddhism. Karma is the total effect of a person's actions in the world. As popularly and informally conceived, karma is the notion that what goes around comes around. That is, doing someone a favor creates goodwill that will ultimately benefit the doer of the good deed as much as it does the recipient of the favor.

The bottom line? The world is actually ready and willing to help you out.

Finding the Heartline

To find the heartline when you request a favor, transform your request into an opportunity to help.

Begin by providing a basis for the request. This will get you past what most people find most difficult about asking for a favor: simply broaching the subject. Try some of these approaches:

- "We've been friends so long that I feel comfortable asking you for a favor."

- "You know so much about computers that I'd like to ask you for some help."

- "Dad, I need your help."

After establishing the basis for asking for help, describe what you want. Be clear and specific. Be realistic in your request. Tell the truth—but don't stop there. Continue by explaining how the favor will benefit you. This is important, because it will give the other person a way to gauge just how much he or she can help.

Sidestepping the Pitfalls

In a letter or e-mail, conclude with an expression of appreciation, but do not make the mistake of using such phrases as "thanking you in advance." This implies that you take your correspondent's compliance for granted. It is offensive, and it may be embarrassing for both of you. In a direct conversation, be certain to express your thanks only *after* you have secured the favor. Never take compliance for granted.

Here are other all-too-common pitfalls to avoid:

- Telling the other person how much you "hate to ask" for a favor. This sends a number of negative messages. It suggests that the favor will be unpleasant or difficult to perform. It also suggests that you doubt the other person's generosity.

- Telling the other person how to feel. "I know that you must hate being asked for favors, but . . ." Why plant a negative response?

- Minimizing the extent of the favor requested. If, for example, you know that performing the favor will require an hour of time, don't tell the other person that you only need a "minute or two."

- Making promises you cannot keep. "If you help me, I'll use my influence to get you such-and-such." Such quid pro quo promises are, in fact, not requests for favors at all, but, rather, business propositions. Made honestly, there is nothing wrong with such a deal. Just be aware that it is not a request for a favor, which requires no explicit quid pro quo.

Saying It: To Family

REQUEST TO BOARD A PET

> Mom, I have a favor to ask you. Jenny and I are going out of town next month. We'll be gone for a week. I hate to board Fido in a kennel for that time. He loves you, loves Dad, and he loves your backyard. It would be great for all of us if you could take him for six days, from July 2 through the 7th.

The request is forthright and factual, with the focus on what the dog needs and loves, rather than on what the requester wants. The basis for the favor is how the dog "feels" about Mom, Dad, and their backyard. Who could resist such a request?

FINANCIAL HELP

> Hi, Dad. My old beater finally gave up the ghost—blew a head gasket—and I need a new car. As you know, the car's the only way I can get from school to my job. Dad, I found a good used (MAKE, MODEL, YEAR) for just under $10,000. I can get financing, but I need help with the down payment. Can you loan me $1,000? It would really help me out. I didn't expect to have to buy a car at this time.

Don't prey on your relatives. Don't plead. Don't whine. Don't try to make them feel guilty. State your need and all the relevant facts. Give the other person the data he needs to make the decision you want. Don't try to make the decision for him. Here, the speaker clearly states the need: A new car, because the old one is beyond repair. He goes on to detail the urgency of the need: A car is essential transportation between school and work. The speaker does not ask for a vague sum to cover a vague expense, but gives the particulars—make, model, year, and price. He then asks for exactly what he needs, then closes by telling his father that the loan will *help* him. Remember, most people derive satisfaction from helping. To help another person is an empowering and, therefore, fulfilling and satisfying experience.

ADVICE

> Mom, you and Dad have bought three houses, which, as far as I'm concerned, makes you real estate experts. As you know, we've just started looking at houses, and, before we get too far into the process, I'd like to come by with Ed to get some advice from the two of you. Any evening this week would be great for us.

Many people enjoy giving advice, but, make no mistake, to ask for advice is still to ask for a favor. Don't take advice for granted. Ask for it in a way that shows how much you value the advice and how much you appreciate the effort that will be made in giving it.

Saying It: To Friends

RESCHEDULE A PLANNED DINNER

> Harry, I'm beginning to think that everything our parents told us is wrong. For example: "Plan ahead." We planned our dinner Tuesday a month back. My schedule was clear, and so was yours. Now, suddenly, my boss needs me to go out of town to troubleshoot a major crisis with one of our top accounts. I know this is awfully short notice, but can we reschedule? I know how hard it is to rejuggle your schedule, but Dan and I really want to get together with the two of you, and I just cannot get out of this trip.

Changing carefully made plans can be very upsetting. This speaker prepares for it with mild humor followed by a clear explanation of the scheduling problem she faces. Although you should never tell the other person how to feel or discourage him by implying that the favor requested is difficult or troublesome, in a case like this, it is necessary to acknowledge that what is being requested requires effort and does cause inconvenience. Don't add to the other person's feeling of burden, but do acknowledge the effort required.

BUSINESS REFERRAL—TELEPHONE CALL

Hi, Pete. It's Sarah. I ran into a friend of yours yesterday, Eunice Williams, who, it turns out, is in the market for a new widget. I'd sure like to sell her one. Of course, I gave her our literature and discussed some of the options with her, but nothing would be more valuable or helpful than a good word from you. Would you be able to give her a call today to say one or two kind things about me? What she's particularly concerned about is after-sale customer service, so if you could speak up about our "never-on-hold" policy, I think she'll do business with us. She's a nice lady, and I would enjoy doing business with her.

Here is a good example of the straightforward approach. There is no dramatic buildup to the favor. The other person is not kept in suspense. Instead, the facts are presented:

1. I met a friend of yours.
2. I want to sell her something.
3. Your help would be valuable.

Notice that the caller is careful to indicate that Eunice Williams is genuinely interested in buying the widget. It is important for the other person to know that, in calling Eunice, he will not only be helping the person requesting the favor, but will also help his other friend, Eunice Williams. That is, he is being of assistance to the seller as well as the customer.

The caller in this case is also careful to follow an important rule when asking for a recommendation or referral: Give the other person something to say. Don't just ask for a referral or recommendation; supply an item or two to be discussed—in this instance, a mention of the "never-on-hold" customer service policy.

Finally, note how the caller shows regard for Eunice Williams, who is, after all, a friend of the person from whom she is requesting a favor. She is not just a customer, but a "nice lady" with whom it would be a pleasure to do business. Take every opportunity to present yourself as unselfish. Focus on the needs and feelings of others—especially when you are asking for a favor for yourself.

MOVING HELP

Ben, you are a good friend and a strong man, which are the two reasons for my call. I've just bought a sofa from the elderly woman who lives down the block. She's pushing 80, weighs maybe 90 pounds, and I think you'll appreciate my reluctance to ask her to help me heft the sofa out of her apartment. So, would *you* be able to give me a hand? I've got the loan of a pickup truck for tomorrow afternoon, if you could get away . . .

This caller begins, half humorously, with the basis for his favor. His friend is both a friend and a "strong man." This good-natured touch of flattery paves the way for the request. The caller builds on the humor by explaining why the little old lady can't give him a hand. Again, this serves to keep the tone of the request light, but it also signals that no one else is available, so underscores the need for the help of a friend. Finally, the caller makes it clear that he has already attended to a key transportation issue, which not only allays any anxiety the friend may have about being called on to provide transportation, but gives added urgency to the request: The job needs to be done tomorrow afternoon. In asking for a favor, it is important to eliminate vagueness. Make clear what you need and when you need it, but avoid making this information come across as a demand. Be certain to supply a reason for any deadlines.

Writing It: To Family

FINANCIAL HELP—LETTER TO SISTER

Dear Marge,

The good news is that I'm starting a new job next week, at the Acme plant, and at 15 percent more than I was making at the old job. The bad news is that the credit card people are breathing down my neck, and I won't have my first paycheck for another three weeks. Could you float me a loan of $1,250 until the 30th? I can pay you in full at that time, plus $125 interest.

Marge, this isn't a matter of life or death, but the loan will keep my credit rating intact. It would be a very great help to me. You can call me at home.

Love,

Tom

Asking for a loan can be hard, and some people find it easier to write rather than call. The writer leads off with the positive news, which directly addresses his ability to repay the loan he is about to ask for. He then makes clear the short-term nature of the loan he is requesting, but also its urgency. The writer is very specific about why he needs the money, how much he needs, how long he needs it for, and when, how, and how much he will repay. Such detail is critical when requesting a loan. Finally, the writer presents his need realistically: His life won't end if his sister doesn't lend him the money, but his standing with the credit card company will be damaged. Do not apply false or misleading pressure to the person from whom you are asking a favor. Present your case fully and honestly. Neither minimize nor inflate your needs.

EXTENSION OF LOAN REPAYMENT DEADLINE— LETTER TO SISTER

Dear Marge,

This month, I have had some unexpected expenses, including the sudden need to get my car's transmission rebuilt. If it is at all possible, can you extend the due date on my loan repayment by thirty days? If it will help, I can pay half now and the balance by the 30th of next month.

I imagine you were counting on being paid in full by the end of this month, but if you can hold out for another thirty days, it would be a very great help to me.

You can reach me at the home number or at the office, 555-555-5555.

Love,

Tom

If asking for a loan is difficult, asking for an extension of a repayment deadline can be even harder. Don't dwell on your embarrassment or guilty feelings. Doing so will only make the other person feel bad or, even worse, resentful of being emotionally pressured. The best approach is to express yourself in more emotionally neutral terms. Provide the facts, including the problem or problems that prevent you from meeting the original deadline and a proposed alternative to the original deadline. Providing alternative options to nonpayment or late payment allows the other person to avoid feeling as if she has been deceived or cornered.

SPEAK AT A MEETING

Dear Aunt Ida,

You are a natural storyteller. You know it, I know it, and our whole family knows it. I'd like to ask you to share your gift with a little wider audience— the members of my Travel Club.

We are a group of about fifty men and women—mostly women—who get together once a month to swap travel recommendations and stories. It suddenly occurred to me that *you* have some of the best travel stories of anybody I've ever heard or, for that matter, *read*.

Would you be willing to talk to us for about forty minutes? It would be fun for you, I think, and I know it would be a hoot for our club members. The meeting after next—that's on November 8—is wide open just now. Please give me a call and say you'll come and talk to us.

Love,

Betty

Flattery, when it is sincerely delivered and genuinely deserved, is a great persuader. The writer has good reasons for inviting her aunt to talk to her club, and expressing these reasons involves sincere tribute to the woman's talent as a teller of tales. The writer does not plead and does not beg, but wisely lets her reasons do the persuading for her. She merely asks her aunt to do what she is good at doing.

Writing It: To Friends

JOB FOR A RELATIVE

Dear Mary,

I swore I would never do what I am about to do: Ask a friend to interview a member of my family for a job. Well, we can both stop groaning, because the pleasant surprise is that my nephew, Gary Unger, is a bright, eager, thoroughly delightful young man who is about to graduate from State with a major in accounting and a 3.8 GPA. He interned for two summers at Acme, Inc., whose general manager, Clara Weeks, will furnish any references you require.

In all, Mary, I guess I don't feel too guilty about breaking my pledge. If you are at all inclined to interview Gary, you can call him directly at 555-555-5555 or, if you prefer, give me a call first at 555-555-4444. We both appreciate your consideration.

All the best,

Mike

Asking a friend to consider a relative for a job is a major request. It should be presented in a friendly but businesslike manner, with the emphasis on what the job candidate has to offer. Underscore the value of the referral rather than the fact of friendship.

Note that this writer recognizes that prevailing on a friend to interview a relative may put the friend on the defensive. After all, the referral does not come from an unbiased source. For this reason, the writer begins by light-heartedly addressing the issue of people who recommend relatives for jobs. Sometimes, it is best to begin a request for a favor by clearing the air.

RECOMMENDATION

Dear Carla,

Can you help me?

I interviewed at Smith and Son for the position of assistant manager in one of their best branch stores. Understandably, they're looking for a 100 percent dependable person with good people skills. I have a slew of business references, but I thought it would also be great to let these folks talk to one of my closest friends.

Could you give Jane Clark—she's director of Human Resources—a call at 555-5555? You might fill her in on our friendship and, in particular, on the work we've done together for the Community Chest. Your good words would mean a lot to me.

With thanks,

Amos

Business recommendations from friends are often useful supplements to recommendations from colleagues and professional associates. Be sure to provide all the necessary contact information. Don't try to dictate what the person should say, but do feel free to make some recommendations or outline a subject or two.

PLACE TO STAY

Dear Fran and Dan,

I will be coming through Detroit at the end of the month for the widget convention and would love to mix business with pleasure by staying with you instead of at a hotel. Can you put me up—and put up with me—for three days, from the 29th through the 31st? My days will be occupied with the convention, but I'll have the evenings free, and it would be great to get together with the two of you.

Please give me a call at 555-555-5555. Don't worry if you can't accommodate me, but it *would* be great to spend some time together, and I really want to see your new house.

Best to you both,

Paul

This writer makes it clear that he very much wants to stay with his friends, but he is also careful to avoid applying undue pressure. He closes by letting his friends know that, if they cannot accommodate him, it will not create any great problem. It is always most desirable to frame requests for favors as positively as possible.

E-Mailing It: To Family

MAKE A PURCHASE

Janey—

One of the few things I don't like about living in Smallville is the absence of anything even remotely resembling a fine food store. I need a really nice Gouda cheese, and you, dear sister, are the only person I can trust to buy some for me. You know what's good, and you know what I like.

Please buy a half-pound of the best. Have the store send it directly to me, and have them bill me directly, too. There's no big rush, but I need the cheese for a party on the 25th. People out here have never tasted great cheese, so your mission of mercy is bound to change some lives.

Madeleine

Sometimes it is fun to couch routine, even mundane requests in colorful language. Let your sense of fun convey your affection for your correspondent.

LOCATE A FORGOTTEN ITEM

> Mom,
>
> Yesterday, I was looking for my high school yearbook. I looked for a good hour or so before I realized that I never took it with me and that it is at the house, somewhere up in the attic. I'm trying to get in touch with some old friends, and I'd really like to get at the yearbook. Could I trouble you to rummage in the attic for it before I come out to visit on Sunday? You know that attic a lot better than I do.
>
> Love,
>
> Glenn

A quick e-mail is a convenient means of communicating a request for a simple favor to be performed in a timely manner. Because you don't want a request to come across as a command or a demand, consider framing it as a question: "Could I trouble you to rummage in the attic for it before I come out to visit on Sunday?" This naturally softens the tone.

BORROW AN ITEM

> Patty,
>
> I am so happy that you will be coming to the party Friday night. Could I borrow your big, beautiful punch bowl for the event? I know how much you value it, but I promise that I will guard it with my life. I could pick it up Thursday afternoon or evening.
>
> Doris

The writer paves the way for her simple request by bringing up the impending party and reminding Patty that she will be a part of the festivities. Note that the writer signals her appreciation of the value of the item she asks to borrow. A prospective lender likes to know that her treasure will be safeguarded and treated with care.

E-Mailing It: To Friends

HOUSE SIT

> Dear Ed,
>
> Maggie and I are planning a three-week vacation this summer during August, and it occurred to us both that we would be much more comfortable leaving if we knew our house was being watched by a trusted friend.

Can you house sit for us, Ed, during August? We know that there's no place like home, but it's also good to get a change of scene once in a while, and you'd be welcome to use our membership in the neighborhood swimming pool while we're gone. As far as guests go, invite whomever you want. Our house will be yours. We want you to be comfortable—because we want you to say *yes.* How about it?

Yours, Nat

A lightly bantering tone is appropriate between good friends. Here the writer applies a little good-natured pressure at the end: "we want you to say *yes.*" With your very close friends, you should feel free to express forthrightly what you want.

ADVICE

Jack,

I need the advice of someone with taste and expertise in home decorating. Since your house is the most beautiful of any I have ever been in, you're my nominee. Would you be able to accompany me to Home Showcase on Friday or Saturday to help me choose some wallpaper? I really just cannot make a decision about such things, and I need all the intelligent advice I can get. I'll take you out to lunch afterward. Is it a date?

Yvonne

Honor the person from whom you seek advice. Prove how much you value his opinion.

Generally, it is best to keep a request for a favor distinct from a quid pro quo business proposal ("You do this for me, and I'll do this for you."); however, there is nothing wrong with incorporating a modest token of gratitude into the request you make. Here, for example, the writer includes an invitation to lunch, thereby transforming the request for a favor into something of a social event ("Is it a date?").

25 Words and Phrases to Use

accommodate	caring	counsel
advice	considerate	friend
appreciate	consideration	grateful
assistance	could you	great

help	need	thought
important	permission	valuable time
judgment	please	valuable
make a big difference	request	wisdom
	thanks	

18 Words and Phrases to Avoid

a drag

chance of a lifetime

deadline

demand

don't say no

I hate to ask

I'll never bother you again

I'll scratch your back if you scratch mine

insist

must

pain in the neck

require

rush

this will be easy

you can't refuse

you can't turn me down

you must

you won't want to do this, but

11

Invitation and Welcome

$\mathcal{I}$nvitations simultaneously ask a favor and bestow a compliment. They request the presence of someone's company, even as they extend the great compliment of offering to share your valuable time with another. If you approach invitations from this dual perspective, you will make them effective and heartfelt.

Closely associated with an invitation is the act of welcoming. Welcoming is, in fact, a broad invitation to a newcomer to join your team, your community, your circle of friends. Approach welcoming from the same dual perspective that governs invitations. To welcome someone is a profound act of generosity, the extension of your hand toward a newcomer, but it is also a request for the favor of that person's acceptance of you and what you and your circle have to offer.

Finding the Heartline

Invitations are a balancing act. Not only do you need to combine a message of compliment with a request for the favor of the correspondent's company, you must also convey a sincere, warm tone without neglecting the nitty-gritty of the invitation as a communication of clear and specific information. Remember the journalist's all-important five questions: *Who? What? When? Where? Why?* Each of these five questions must be answered in an effective invitation. Miss any one of these, and the invitation, no matter how warm and sincere, will be a failure. Let's take a closer look:

126

- The *who* is the person or persons you are inviting. Be clear about this. Is the spouse or significant other welcome? What about children?

- The *what* is, first and foremost, the occasion. Be clear about the purpose of the event—a birthday party, a dinner party, a holiday celebration, whatever. Your invitation should also specify *what* type of response you want. If you want the invitee to call and tell you whether or not he can attend, be sure to ask for a reply. If the invitation is at all formal, you can write R.S.V.P. (*Répondez s'il vous plaît*) or the phrase "Please Respond" somewhere on the invitation, followed by your phone number and, if necessary, a date by which you need the reply. An alternative to the request for a response is your promise that you will call to confirm. If you make such a promise, be sure that you do, indeed, call. If you are inviting a large number of people to an event, consider substituting the phrase "regrets only" for R.S.V.P. This way, only those who cannot attend need call you.

Before we leave the *What?* question, be sure to include in the invitation any other special "whats." For example, you might specify what to wear—"black tie optional," "come as you are," "bring your swimsuit," whatever is appropriate. You might ask invitees to contribute their favorite food or drink.

- The *when* should specify the date and time of the event. Be specific.

- The *where* is the place. Again, be specific and avoid confusion. Supply an accurate address. If the event is to take place in a restaurant, get the name right and include an address. This is especially important if the restaurant is part of a chain with multiple locations. Be certain to furnish clear and accurate directions to the location.

- The *why* is the purpose of the occasion. This does not mean that all parties have to focus on a specific occasion—a birthday, an anniversary, and such. But you can make even a nonspecific event special: "Please come to my 'It's-Been-Ages-Since-We've-Seen-Each-Other' party." Specify such details as a cocktail party, a pool party, a Super Bowl party (a get-together to watch the big game on TV), a dinner party.

Remember, communicating a message of welcome is similar to an invitation in that it is an extension of your hospitality and generosity even as it is simultaneously a request that the newcomer accept your offer of friendliness. Effective gestures of welcome also recognize that the recipient of the message, as a newcomer, is in the midst of change. Most of us find some aspects of change refreshing and exciting, but also unnerving and anxiety-provoking, perhaps even traumatic. The warmth of your welcome can go a long way toward heightening the excitement of change while reducing the anxiety associated with it. Extending a message of welcome is more than a polite act; it is an opportunity to make another person feel good—about himself, about the group or community he is about to join, and about you.

Sidestepping the Pitfalls

The most common and most serious problem with many invitations is a failure to answer fully, adequately, and clearly the five questions, *Who? What? When? Where? Why?* Invitations should bring pleasure and pleasure only. Failure to present all the relevant information and to present it clearly creates not pleasure, but frustration, irritation, and even anxiety.

Another invitation pitfall is neglecting to take full advantage of an excellent opportunity for communication. While all invitations must include answers to the five *W* questions, an invitation truly conveyed from the heart should include even more. Take the opportunity to convey something of your feelings about the person you are inviting.

Gestures of welcome, fortunately, present few pitfalls. Just about any expression of welcome will be accepted with gratitude. Nevertheless, do avoid the following:

- *Pushing or forcing yourself on the newcomer.* It may take weeks or months or even longer for a newcomer to feel fully comfortable in new surroundings. This is natural. Don't force the process by claims that you want to be the person's "best friend" or that you intend to introduce her to "absolutely everybody."

- *Making the newcomer feel anxious about fitting in.* Don't imply that the new situation is fraught with dangers. That is, avoid such statements as "You need someone to show you the ropes.

Things can be very complicated here," or "Let me guide you through this minefield." Always accent the positive. It may be true that the newcomer needs guidance, but the negative aspects of this message should be avoided in an initial communication of welcome.

Saying It: To Family

LUNCH—PHONE CALL TO MOTHER

Hi, Mom. Can I take you to lunch Wednesday? I was thinking of Fabio's at, say, one. You know where Fabio's is, on the corner of Main and Fifth. It's been so long since we just went out together, relaxed, and talked. I really miss talking with you—and, with my new job, I have a lot to talk with you about.

This brief phone call says it all. In a few words, it includes all of the information an effective invitation should have. In addition, it conveys genuine warmth, the unmistakable message of love.

SURPRISE PARTY FOR SPOUSE—PHONE CALL TO SISTER

Cheryl, I'm planning a surprise birthday party for Sam on the 23rd. I'm taking him to dinner at Jason's Place. Do you know where that is? Good. And you and Ben can make it? Great!

You should get there by 6:30—no later. Go to the back room. About a dozen people have been invited. I'll be by with Sam at 7. You know the drill: Everyone yells *Surprise!*

Dinner will be catered, and the drinks are on me. Sam will be thrilled that you're there, and I'm so glad that you can make it! And, *please*, let's keep this a surprise. Be sure to tell Ben not to let the cat out of the bag.

This informal invitation covers all the informational bases, with emphasis on the surprise aspect of the party. Always be sure to include any special instructions that may be necessary; in this case, a reminder to be careful to avoid spoiling the surprise.

WELCOME TO A NEW TOWN—PHONE CALL TO A COUSIN

Hi, Cousin! Welcome to Plainville. You have no idea how thrilled I am to have you in town. It will be like old times, when we used to visit each other's houses. Like being kids again.

> Listen, let me give you a day or two to get settled, then I'd like to drive you around downtown to show you my favorite places to shop and eat. There are a lot of very nice shops and restaurants in town. I think you'll be very pleasantly surprised. I'll call you on Wednesday. In the meantime, if there is anything I can do to help you find your way or settle in, just give me a call.

The caller clearly understands that a message of welcome should help allay the anxiety of change. She immediately summons up the past, remarking that her cousin's "new" experience will be like "old times." The caller goes on to offer guidance and to make the new town sound inviting; however, she is also careful not to intrude herself on the newcomer. She recognizes the need for a day or two to "settle in." Finally, the caller sets a specific day for the next contact. A message of emotional warmth need not be fuzzy and vague. Clear information and specific plans are by no means incompatible with friendly, informal, heartfelt communication.

Saying It: To Friends

DINNER INVITATION

> Larry, I'm so happy I ran into you. I was about to call you this evening to invite you and Pat to dinner at our house. Sarah and I were just talking about how much we enjoyed getting together with you last month—we have so much in common—and we thought it would be a great idea to have the two of you over. We were thinking about a week from Friday—that's the 5th—say, 7 o'clock. We could start with drinks.
>
> Why don't you talk it over with Pat, and I'll call you this evening, around nine. We would love to get together with the two of you.

Don't expect an off-the-cuff and on-the-spot invitation to elicit a final, definitive response. Here the speaker conveys his enthusiasm for the couple he is inviting, but he also recognizes that a response to the invitation will require Larry's consulting with Pat. Instead of putting the burden of the response on the invitee, the speaker makes a clear arrangement for a follow-up call. This is a good strategy, but it requires the host to ensure that he does indeed make the follow-up call as promised and when promised.

WELCOME TO MEMBERSHIP IN A SOCIAL ORGANIZATION—PHONE CALL

> Marty, your first meeting is tomorrow evening! This is exciting for all of us. I can't wait to introduce you around. We have a great organization, with interesting and very friendly members. I'm so happy you joined us, and I know you'll be pleased, too. The organization is a great way to make business as well as social contacts, but it's also just plain fun being with a group of people who enjoy getting together with each other.
>
> Do you have all the information you need? Time and place? Do you need directions to the restaurant?

The caller takes care to reinforce his friend's decision to join the organization, assuring him that membership offers valuable business and social benefits and is "just plain fun" as well. The caller's purpose is to ensure that his friend feels good about what he is doing. Notice that he emphasizes the excitement he and the other members feel about the new member. He is careful to avoid implications of exclusivity or that the new member will be judged or evaluated in any way. Nor does he imply that his friend is lucky to have been chosen. Instead, the focus is put on making him feel welcome.

Writing It: To Family

INVITATION TO A WEDDING—NOTE TO BROTHER

> Dear Hank,
>
> Tyrone and I are getting married on Saturday, June 23. The ceremony will be held at 2 P.M. at First Christian, 1234 Young Street, here in Thornton. The reception will begin at 5, at Davidson's, 5678 Brewster Lane.
>
> Hank, as you can imagine, I am very excited, and I would be even more thrilled if you could be here. Please try. I especially want you to meet Ty, and having you share the day will make it absolutely perfect for me. Please call me at 555-555-5555 to let me know if you can make it. And, please, bring a friend!

Not all wedding invitations have to be store bought and formally engraved. For special people or in special circumstances, consider sending a personal note, in which you can express yourself fully. Just remember to include all the basic and essential information, along with your personal message.

This is an example of a strongly worded invitation. The writer wants to make clear how much she wants her brother to attend the wedding; note, however, that she stops well short of pleading. The intention here is unmistakable, but the tone is thoroughly positive and upbeat.

INVITATION TO A FAMILY REUNION

Dear Carlson Family Member:

For the first time ever, we are trying to assemble as many Carlsons as we can find for a mammoth Family Reunion.

The place is Grinder Park, Picnic Ground C, in Mason City, Utah. Please see the attached map for detailed directions.

The date is June 14.

The hour is 10 A.M. until well after dark.

The goal is fun, fellowship, and a great time. We will settle for nothing less.

Please, move heaven and earth to attend. I'd appreciate a call at 555-555-5555 to let us know if we can look forward to your being there. I've also attached a list of the Carlsons I've invited. If any of you know of anyone who is not on the list, please call me with the information. We want to reach everyone!

Love to all,

Edna Carlson
1234 Gary Street
Penn, UT 12345

When inviting a large group of people, a generic invitation can be useful. Not only does it save time and effort, it can actually create a sense of community and togetherness. This invitation spells out all of the necessary information and introduces a lighthearted tone in its statement of the "goal" of the reunion. It also focuses on inclusiveness. Where family reunions are concerned, the more truly is the merrier, so the writer leaves no doubt as to her intention to reach as many Carlsons as possible. Thus the invitation becomes something more than personal and individual. It is an invitation to participate in a group effort, a collective, a collaboration.

Writing It: To Friends

INVITATION TO JOIN A CLUB

Dear Joan,

I know that you've heard me talk about our Saturday Evening Book Club and how much I enjoy it. We're a small group—we like it that way—and so the opportunity to invite a new member does not come up often. I'm happy to tell you that we have room for a new member, and I cannot think of anyone I would rather have join us than you. Nor can I think of anyone who would enjoy membership more than you, an avid reader, a great conversationalist, and someone who enjoys the company of kind and interesting people. So, you and the Book Club seem to me, beyond question, a natural fit.

Joan, please consider this letter a formal invitation to our next meeting, Saturday evening, the 15th, at 8:30. We meet at one another's homes, on a rotating basis. This Saturday, the meeting is at Chris Jenson's house, 568 West Adams. If you like, you can come over to my house first, about 7:30, and we can go to Chris's together. The book we're discussing is *How Deep Is My Ocean* by Eunice Carver—but you don't have to read it prior to the meeting. The idea is just to sit in and see how you like the group.

Please give me a call by Friday evening, Joan, to let me know if you would like to attend—or if you have any questions. It would be wonderful to have you as a member.

Yours,

Paula

When inviting a friend to join a club, remember that such an invitation is a two-way street. The effective invitation conveys that the club is right for your friend and your friend is right for the club. You might want to think of yourself as a kind of matchmaker, someone who represents the interests both of the organization and of the prospective new member.

Note that the writer here is careful to provide all necessary information, and she thoughtfully suggests that the newcomer accompany her to the first meeting, something that might make her friend more comfortable.

WELCOME TO THE COMPANY

Pete—

Thanks for the great news! You've taken the job here at Perkins. I'm thrilled for you, and I'm excited for our firm. Most of all, I look forward to working with such a good friend.

Pete, I firmly predict that you will love working here. You are joining a great group of people, who will welcome and reward your contributions. I've arranged with Bill Williams and Clara Foley, the heads of advertising and marketing, to have lunch with you and me on your first day. They're people you should meet right away, and I want them to get to know you. I'll pick you up at your office just before noon on the 15th.

Welcome aboard!

Ann

This letter is designed to make a friend feel at home in a new job. It is 100 percent positive, and it creates the impression that the writer is determined to help her friend hit the ground running. The writer also understands that the essence of communicating welcome is to convey the *mutual* benefits of the new situation. In this case, the company is right for the new recruit, and the recruit is just right for the new company.

E-Mailing It: To Family

INVITATION TO A CHRISTMAS PARTY—MULTIPLE E-MAIL

Dear Children,

Dad and I are giving our annual Christmas Party on the 23rd, here at the house. This year, we've decided to start an hour earlier, at 7 p.m. instead of 8, for one reason and one reason only: to start having a good time an hour sooner.

There will be the usual drinks and food, and everyone gets a Christmas stocking. The sing-along, as always, is mandatory. No excuses.

Please reply to this message only if you *can't* attend.

Love to all,

Mom

E-mail is a great way to communicate to a set group of recipients quickly and with a minimum of effort. This invitation to an annual event requires little in the way of information, except to announce the new starting hour. The invitation hits the highlights—presumably treasured family traditions—and pokes fun at one tradition in particular, the sing-along. Used wisely, humor reinforces bonds among a group. Just be careful to avoid using it to belittle or diminish any aspect of the upcoming event.

INVITATION TO LUNCH

Cal,

What about lunch? Tomorrow, 12:30, at Luigi's. Dutch treat. Hit the reply button.

Hal

The closer you are to your brother, the fewer words you require. Indeed, communicating this way expresses the intimacy of family members who feel they can almost read one another's minds. An invitation can be as economical as this one, especially if it is sent via e-mail.

WELCOME HOME

Benny,

Mom just told me you're coming home for a visit. Welcome, stranger! It's been almost a year!

Benny, I can hardly wait to see you. I want to take you to the new CD store that's opened on Warren Street. This place is great and definitely raises the culture quotient of our little town. We'll have a blast.

See you soon,

Demi

A timely communication can serve as a welcome to a familiar place as well as a new place. Here a sister expresses her affection for her brother by choosing to focus on a new favorite place she wants to share. Emotions may be expressed in words, but they do lose something in the translation. It can be more effective to convey your feelings with real things, by sharing events, places, and other favorite things. Such an act of sharing is a warm welcome, which goes far beyond merely telling the family member how eager you are to see him. Reality—real places, real events—almost always speaks more clearly and tenderly than abstract words.

E-Mailing It: To Friends

TO A CONCERT—DUTCH TREAT

Terri,

I have an opportunity to buy a pair of tickets for the Big Tomato concert, which, as you know, has been sold out for months. It would be great if we could go together. The ticket is $35, and the concert starts at 8 on April 4, at the Paradise Dome.

This is *the* event of the year, Terri. I hope you can go with me. Please let me know right away.

Sonny

Some people are made uncomfortable by the prospect of sending out a "Dutch treat" invitation, an invitation to an event in which each person pays his own way. There is no need to feel any embarrassment, provided that the invitation is to an event you believe of genuine value and interest to the other person. Two rules to observe:

1. Do not apologize for requiring that the invitee pay his own way. Present this as a fact, period. Do not say such things as "I wish I could pay for you" or "I wish I could get you in for free." Payment is a condition of the invitation, and that is all there is to it.

2. State the amount of the payment as clearly as possible. If you know what a ticket costs, specify the price. If the event has a range of costs, nail down this range. The invitee needs to know what he is committing to.

GROUP ACTIVITY

Daryl,

John, Ken, Rich, Mark, and I are going to see *Curl Up and Die* at the Cineplexis tomorrow afternoon. We're going to meet at the Burger Palace around 3, then catch the 3:45 show. Come on and join us!

Danny

E-mail is ideal for short-notice, informal invitations. When you invite someone along on a group activity, be sure to mention who the other participants will be. Avoid phrases that make it sound as if the invitation is an afterthought or in any way halfhearted: "Do you want to tag along?" or "We don't want to leave you out." Close with a simple, enthusiastic phrase of invitation, as here. Since this is an e-mail, the writer reasonably assumes that the recipient will reply one way or another.

WELCOME TO MY HOME

Dear Janice,

Ron and I are eagerly looking forward to your arrival Wednesday. Ron will pick you up at the airport, Terminal Y, Gate N, when your flight gets in at noon. We have the guest room ready for you, and I've laid in a supply of your favorite breakfast food, Pop Tarts in assorted flavors. There is also a small army of your old friends standing in line to see you. We will make sure that you feel at home.

Denise

There are many ways to tell a guest that she is welcome in your home. The most effective way of making a guest welcome, however, is not to *tell* her, but to *do* things that make her feel welcome. In this case, the writer reminds the guest that she will be picked up at the airport, that she will have a comfortable room, and that her desires (Pop Tarts and friends) will be catered to.

25 Words and Phrases to Use

comfortable	include you	pleasure of your company
delighted	interesting	R.S.V.P.
eager	join	Regrets Only
excited	let us know	see you again
fascinating	like old times	thrilled
friendly	miss you	welcome
fun	opportunity	your company
get together	please reply	
honored	pleasure	

10 Words and Phrases to Avoid

come if you want   must
don't be left out   must attend
don't fail   snooty
exclusive   sorry to have to ask you to pay
lucky to be invited   tag along

12

Sympathy and Condolence

Occasions calling for sympathy and condolence are, universally, occasions of loss: loss of a loved one, loss of health, loss of property, loss of a job. And when it falls to us to communicate in such situations, we, too, often find that we have suffered a loss, a loss of words. It is not just that we do not know what to say—and are afraid of saying the wrong thing—but that, in times of grief, words seem hollow, inadequate, even profane or offensive. The most intelligent and articulate among us sometimes find it hard to say the right things on occasions of death, serious illness, or other loss. Yet it is precisely at such moments that saying it from the heart is vitally important, not just because it is the polite and caring thing to do, but because it is the *healing* thing to do. Make no mistake, your words will not work magic, but they will *work*. Even if you feel that anything you have to say will be inadequate, anything you *do* say will be more adequate than saying nothing. At the very least, loss demands acknowledgment. Without it, the loss is compounded, magnified, and made more miserable.

Finding the Heartline

Knowing the right things to say in a sad or traumatic situation requires, first and foremost, a leap of imagination. Put yourself in your correspondent's position. Under these circumstances, what would *you* like to hear? What would help *you* most? The most direct way to make this leap is to look into yourself in order to express your own grief.

Your neighbor's husband dies suddenly of a heart attack. You liked the man. You spoke with him almost daily. You lent each other

139

garden implements and shop tools. He was not a close friend, but his passing saddens you. Of course, your grief is far less intense than that of his family, but it is still real. Begin by expressing that grief.

Once you have accepted the importance of saying something, even knowing that it will not take away all of the pain, and once you have gotten in touch with your own feelings about the loss, bear in mind the following five steps:

1. Express your own sorrow at hearing of the death or loss.

2. Sympathize by acknowledging the emotional pain of loss.

3. If the loss is a death, say something good, something positive about the deceased. If possible, share a memory.

4. It is often helpful gently to remind your correspondent of the healing power of time.

5. To the extent possible and appropriate, offer your help and support. Try to offer to do something specific that you know will be helpful. Perhaps you can offer to take the kids to school. Perhaps you can offer a visit. Identify something appropriate, then offer to do it.

All effective communicators get in sync with the person they address. Strike the emotional tone appropriate to your correspondent. You will, doubtless, communicate with a family member on a different level than you communicate with a personal friend or a business friend. Think about the nature of your relationship with your correspondent.

Sidestepping the Pitfalls

The deepest and most common pitfall is the paralysis of silence. We may feel so inadequate to speak or write on this occasion, that we fail to say anything, fail even to acknowledge the loss.

- Don't expect too much of your words. No matter what you say, you will not magically erase the grief.

- Nevertheless, expect much of your words. Whatever you say is likely to help. Inadequate as your words may be, they are far more adequate than silence. Words heal. They may not cure, but they do heal.

Although you should not worry much about making the situation worse by your words, do avoid the following:

- Adjectives and nouns that may magnify the loss, for example—"your *terrible* loss," "your *horrible tragedy*," and so on. Your correspondent does not need help feeling bad.

- Minimizing the loss. Don't tell the person that "things aren't so bad" or "you'll feel better" or "it could be worse" or "it's all for the best." Acknowledge the loss simply, and with sympathy and understanding.

Saying It: To Family

DEATH OF FATHER—TALKING WITH MOTHER

Mom, I'm so sorry. Right now, I have to tell you, it's hard to think of a world without Dad. It's hard for me, and I know it must be even harder for you. But Dad knew this was coming, and he did his best to prepare us for this. That's how much he loved us all. He loved us so much that he found the courage, sick as he was, to make his leaving easier for us. I miss Dad so much, but his generosity, selflessness, and courage are still with us, still a part of us.

Mom, I'm going to be coming out to see you every week for as long as you need me. I can help you with the grocery shopping. Dad left his affairs in such good order that there's not much to do about that, but I'll be here to help you in any way I can.

You know, Mom, we'll never "get over" this. We wouldn't want to if we could. But we will live through it. Dad has seen to that.

Never deny the loss, but do seek to emphasize whatever remains. In this case, the husband/father, suffering an illness, had taken great pains to provide for his family after his passing. The speaker, recognizing this, builds on it in his remarks to his mother. The message is that the man's presence remains strong, despite his death. Note also that the speaker concludes with offers of specific, practical help.

DEATH OF FATHER'S MOTHER

Dad, this is a shock. I thought Grandma would go on forever, and I know that whatever loss I feel is even more intense for you. I hope, Dad, that you can take some comfort in knowing that you made Grandma very proud, and what-

> ever she taught you about being a parent—well, I couldn't have been raised by a better father. Grandma's life meant a lot to all of us. She's made us all better sons and daughters and mothers and fathers.
>
> If there is anything I can do to help you and Mom over the next few days and weeks, please don't hesitate a moment about calling. I'm going to be staying in town for the next four days. I can take even more time off of work, if you need me.

The speaker expresses his own feelings, then acknowledges that the loss must be even more intense for his father. He then shifts to the living legacy of his grandmother. This is important, for part of the pain of loss is the feeling that much has been left unsaid. It may be possible for you to say some of those things. In this case, the speaker lets his father know that his mother—the speaker's grandmother—had every reason to be proud of his dad. The implication is that the grandmother/mother's spirit continues to live through the father/son as well as the son/grandson. Once again, the speaker ends with an offer of practical help.

DEATH OF SISTER'S CHILD

> Jane, I hardly know what to say. Knowing and loving Ronnie was such a blessing and a joy. We all need to take some consolation in the time we had with him, but I know it's easy to say this and very hard to accept it.
>
> I have to be selfish, Jane, and tell you that I look to you, my big sister, for strength at this time. I'll share with you what little strength I have, but I need to hold you and feel your strength. You do know that I will be here for you, to help with anything you ask.
>
> Right now, we just have to believe—together—that time will ease this pain and leave us with memories of the joy Ronnie brought to our little world.

It is all right to confess the poverty of your words, the feeling that your power to make things better is very limited. Without minimizing this terrible loss, the speaker strives to put emphasis not on what has been lost, but on the meaning, influence, and joyful effect of the young life that has been lived.

HURRICANE DAMAGE TO IN-LAW'S HOME—PHONE CALL

> Frank, I just heard about what Hurricane Maurice did to your house. I know you well enough to realize that what you're mostly feeling right now is thank-

fulness that Louise and the kids came through safely. Nobody's been hurt. But I also know how much that house meant to you, and I'm very, very sorry.

People tell you at times like this that "Things can always be replaced." Well, that's a lot easier said than done, but it's also true—hard, but true. You guys are a very strong family, and I know that, step by step, you'll not only get through this, but you'll rebuild even better than before. What I mean is that you'll all come through this even stronger and closer than ever before. I have confidence in you.

In the meantime, if you need a place to get away from it all for a while—to step back from it all—please come up here to Northville. Alice and I would love to have you, and we have plenty of room.

After the loss of physical possessions, it is common for well-meaning consolers to remark that "Things can always be replaced." This is very true, but, stated glibly, the cliché is not very helpful. The speaker expresses this common sentiment in a way that recognizes its truth as well as its inadequacy. He then shifts the focus to where it more properly belongs: to his confidence in the strength and ability of his friend and his friend's family to come through the ordeal. In a situation like this, it is necessary to acknowledge the loss, but it is most helpful to turn toward the future, toward repair and recovery. Also, remember to offer as much practical and specific assistance as you are in a position to offer.

Saying It: To Friends

DEATH OF A FRIEND'S MOTHER

Karen, we were all saddened this morning when news of your mother's heart attack came. As you know, I lost my mother suddenly two years ago, and I think I understand what you must be going through and feeling right now. It is a shock that is alternately painful and numbing and confusing. I don't know if it helps much to hear this now, but you *will* get through these feelings in time.

Your mother meant a lot to me—and not just because she was the mother of my best friend. She was always so kind and cheerful, and she took time to give me advice whenever I asked for it—and sometimes even when I *didn't* ask for it! Do you remember that long discussion we had about my first boyfriend? That was a riot! She was a great lady.

Karen, if there is anything at all I can do for you, please call. I want to do whatever I can to make this time a little easier for you.

Sympathy requires understanding the feelings of another, and a good way of getting in touch with your ability to sympathize is to look inward, into your own range of experience. This is how this speaker begins, after first registering her own shock and grief. The next step is to extend and deepen your sympathy by recalling experiences in common. Karen lost a mother, but the speaker lost a friend. True, the magnitude of these losses differs, but the losses have more in common than not. Recalling her own relationship with Karen's mother, the speaker can express herself more fully from the heart and with greater meaning.

DEATH OF A FRIEND'S DOG

> Tom, I am very sad to hear about Fido. He was such a part of the family, and I loved the way he greeted me at the door whenever I came to visit. A really sweet, gentle dog.
>
> I know how difficult a decision it was to put him to sleep, but he was very sick, and, certainly, no one could have done more for him than you did. I have to tell you that I think it took a lot of courage and character on your part to make the decision that he had suffered enough and to let go.
>
> I know that no dog can replace Fido, but I hope that you and the kids will adopt another pet soon. You're all just so good with animals. It is a delight to see.

The loss of a family pet is not to be dismissed or taken lightly. Cats, dogs, and other animals readily become part of the family, and their loss produces grief similar to the death of a human family member.

The speaker expresses his sadness and shares a memory as well as kind words about Fido. He also expresses informed sympathy about the manner of the animal's death, euthanasia, taking care to affirm the wisdom of this difficult decision. Finally, the speaker looks toward the future. He does not want to imply that a new animal can replace the old, but he does suggest that a new life will help fill the void left by the passing of the family pet.

LOSS OF A JOB

> Tom, I just heard about the shake-up at B&R. I know getting laid off, after 15 years with the firm, must have been the last thing you expected just now. It's the unexpected aspect of the whole thing that makes it such a sharp, deep blow. That's just the way it is, a Sunday punch. But I know you. You may not

feel much like one at the moment, but you are a real fighter, and you have built a record in the industry that few can match.

Tom, if you want a suggestion from me, take a few days off, just to breathe, then let's get together for lunch. I have some ideas for you. You may not think so right now, but you are in big demand in this industry. We just have to get the word out. Let me help.

The loss of a longtime job can be every bit as traumatic as a death in the family. Losing a job attacks our self-confidence and, sometimes, our entire sense of who we are. Typically, it creates immediate and direct anxiety about paying bills in the short term and earning a living in the long term. If the job loss is sudden and unexpected, confusion compounds the anxiety. The danger is that feelings of worthlessness and depression will sap the strength, will, and wit required to get a new and fulfilling position. In responding to someone who has just lost his job, don't just try to assure him that "something else will come along"; instead, after acknowledging the blow suffered, do what you can to bolster his self-confidence and his sense of self.

Jobs are lost and found all the time. Inner strength, morale, and resilience, once lost, are much more difficult to restore. Focus your remarks on maintaining and rebuilding these. If you are in a position to help—even with nothing more than a brainstorming session—offer help; however, don't add to a sense of panic by implying too much urgency. Here, the speaker advises his friend to take a few days off, to let the air clear, to settle down, to "breathe." Advising an emotional interval like this is a good idea, since it may allow the other person to see his situation from a clearer, cooler, less anxious perspective.

Writing It: To Family

SERIOUS CAR ACCIDENT—LETTER TO COUSIN

Dear Jerry,

I have hardly slept since your midnight call. I am so sorry about the loss of Kathy. How hard it is, how shocking. My heart is filled with sympathy for you.

I did not know Kathy well, but I didn't have to spend much time with her to know that she was loving, intelligent, and lovely. I can only begin to imagine what her loss means to you, and the only comfort I can offer is that, difficult as it may be to feel this now, time will ease the pain.

Jerry, you have a large number of friends, and you need to turn to them for help and support. You know that you can call on me if I can be helpful to you in any way.

Love,

Tammi

The sudden loss of a loved one through accident is an especially cruel blow because it is unexpected. Accidents, by their nature, are senseless and random, a fact that often adds bewilderment and bitterness to the bereaved's grief. If you are a religious person, you may feel moved to share the comfort of your faith with the bereaved. This is best done, however, if you also know something of this person's religious beliefs; for now is not the time to raise religious issues with a person who may not be inclined toward faith in general or toward your faith in particular.

In the absence of religion, what comfort can you offer? First and foremost, you can share your sympathy, your own grief, and your concern. Second, you can remind the bereaved of the healing power of time. These things may provide small comfort, but, modest as it is, such comfort will be welcomed.

DEATH OF FATHER—LETTER TO MOTHER

Dear Mom,

We knew this day would come, with Dad so sick for so long, but I can't say that I was ready for it. Thank God, you are stronger than I am. I saw how you cared for Dad, even in the worst of his illness. It has made you stronger and stronger, and now I look to you as an example and source of strength.

I look to Dad, too. He was a man who truly lived his faith, and now, more than ever, I see the great value of that. His example of faith I have taken to heart, and I know that he has gone to a better place.

Mom, it would help me now if I could help you. I'd like to come back home for a week or two to help you out with day-to-day things, shopping, putting Dad's things in order, and so on. Please let me know when my coming out would be best for you. My boss is very understanding, and I can easily get time off from work.

Love,

Manny

Expressing your condolences does not require that you present yourself as a tower of strength. In this case, the writer recognizes the intensity of his own grief and, while seeking to comfort his mother, also asks her for help. It is a remarkable thing that seeking help from another tends to make that other person feel stronger and more emotionally capable. Asking for help empowers the other person. This does not mean that the expression of sympathy and fellow feeling is an invitation to fall apart emotionally, but, under the circumstances, it is an opportunity to create mutual reliance, an emotionally supportive situation for both people.

Note that, in this letter, the writer acknowledges his father's religious faith. If you know that the others involved in the grieving situation possess religious conviction, it may be helpful and healing to make meaningful reference to religious belief. Let your own convictions and your knowledge of the others involved be your guide in this respect.

BUSINESS LOSS—LETTER TO BROTHER

Dear Ron,

I've been thinking about what happened with your big investor. On the phone, I called his backing out of the deal a "serious blow," but, as I think about it now, the word that comes to mind is not "blow," but "setback."

Look, there's no way around the fact that Smith's bailing out is *not* a good thing; however, I am convinced that you can recover from it. The project is such a good one that I believe you will readily find a new backer—more than one, if you need to.

I wish I could offer you a list of prospects, but I don't have the contacts. If there is anything else I can do to help, however, please don't hesitate to call.

Keep the faith, brother—in yourself and in this project. You will prevail.

Yours,

Sid

Nobody's perfect. In this case, the writer sends a follow-up letter to modify a remark he made in haste on the telephone, when his brother first reported a financial reverse. A sudden loss can provoke panic or, at least, a hasty conclusion. A letter, written in greater leisure and after some thought, can reassess the original conclusion. Here the writer modifies his response from an expression connoting near hopelessness to one that allows more latitude for positive action. The writer seeks to restore his brother's confidence, without, however, denying the seriousness of the problem. Effective letters of condolence can serve one, or perhaps two functions:

- They can provide a measure of comfort and consolation in a painful situation.

- They can look toward and encourage and even guide positive action for the future.

It is not always possible to perform both of these functions, but, at the very least, a communication of condolence should avoid intensifying the negative feelings associated with the event.

Writing It: To Friends

SERIOUS INJURY

Dear Claire,

I just heard from Sarah about your terrible accident. You are in my thoughts and prayers and hopes for as speedy a recovery as possible. I know that injuries of the kind you have suffered require a good deal of time for healing and a lot of effort from you in physical therapy. Effort, however, you have never shied away from. Achieving all that you have in the professional and business worlds does not come automatically or easily. You have faced, met, and surmounted one challenge after another, and I have no reason to believe that you'll turn away from the new challenges that now face you.

And you'll have help. You know far better than I do how thoroughly supportive your family is. As for me, if there is anything I can do to help you during the challenging days to come, please don't hesitate to lean on me.

My love to you,

Nell

Serious injury is a form of loss and, like other losses, creates sadness, depression, and feelings of despair. Communication in response to such an event should acknowledge the seriousness of the injury, but should avoid medical diagnosis or speculation. Note that the writer expresses a hope for "as speedy a recovery *as possible,*" thereby acknowledging that recovery will, indeed, take time. She also express-es her understanding that the process of physical therapy required will not be an easy one. Even so, the writer expresses this in terms of chal-lenge rather than difficulty, and she defines challenge as something with which her friend is quite familiar and in dealing with which she has been quite successful. At times like this, encouragement is most welcome, provided that it is based on some plausible interpretation of reality. In this case, that reality is the writer's knowledge of her friend's personal history.

BURGLARY LOSS

Dear Tom and Martha,

I was very shocked and sorry to hear about the break-in at your house. I know that insurance covers much of the loss, but it can't erase that feeling of hav-ing been violated. I know, because I also experienced a break-in, about two years ago. It's just a terrible feeling. So, I'm writing to sympathize, but also to assure you that you will get past this thing. You'll replace the missing stuff, you'll change the locks, you'll install a security system, and you'll get on with your lives. That spooky feeling you have now does fade in time. Just hold out and be patient. Don't let whoever robbed you get hold of your peace of mind, too.

If you want somebody to talk to about this, please don't hesitate to give me a ring.

All the best,

Pete

Sometimes something bad happens to a friend, and you have spe-cial knowledge, insight, or experience that may help. This letter deals with one such case. The writer is careful to confine his remarks to his personal experience. He does not present himself as an expert on home security, but he does have something valuable to say about what burglary victims generally feel, and he shares this insight with his friends. The object is not just to make them feel better, but to help them see beyond the immediate trauma and loss. The most effective communications of sympathy and condolence share useful experience and feelings. This makes whatever has happened more understandable and, therefore, less frightening.

E-Mailing It: To Family

CANCELLATION OF VACATION PLANS

Dear Dad,

Sorry to hear that Mom's hurt foot has torpedoed your vacation plans. I know how much the two of you were looking forward to getting away to Europe. Although it's hard to find a bright spot in this, at least you can be thankful that the accident didn't happen while you were already abroad. Let's get Mom back on her feet and then reschedule. I know it's a hassle, but I'm happy to help you make new reservations and arrangements when you're ready.

Love,

Nan

It is not terrible traumas and tragedies alone that warrant a note of consolation. Sympathy and understanding are also welcome in lesser instances of life's tribulations. Here the emphasis is put on placing the incident in a larger perspective and in the offer of assistance in the rescheduling of the postponed vacation.

LOSS IN A CONTEST OR COMPETITION—E-MAIL TO SON

Billy,

Your project looked just great at the Science Fair, and I was proud to see it there. I was also proud of the original approach you took to the experiment you presented. Science fairs often exhibit a lot of ingenuity, but are typically short on original thought.

I understand you're disappointed that you didn't get a prize this time around, but the prizes represent the judgment of a small handful of people, nothing more, nothing less. What I am so pleased with and proud of is that you took a problem, tackled it, and approached it in such an inventive, original way. Well done!

Love,

Dad

We all enjoy sending congratulations to a loved one who has won a contest, but we also need to be there when the results are more disappointing. The object of the consolation is not to dismiss the loss, as if the contest weren't important in the first place, nor is it to dispute the judges' decision, but, rather, to demonstrate the writer's undiminished love for and pride in the family member. The writer here realizes that this does *not* mean communicating a message to the effect that "You lost, but *I* still love you." Instead, he focuses on the project and points out what he most admires about it. Indeed, the writer makes only secondary reference to his son's disappointment. His primary focus is on achievement, as if to point out that the absence of a prize cannot negate what has been achieved.

E-Mailing It: To Friends

ILLNESS

Karl,

We missed you at the party. I understand that you're down with the flu—big time. Well, don't try to fight it. Just stay in bed, drink plenty of fluids, get as much sleep as you can, and try to keep from going crazy with boredom. Hard as it may be to believe at the moment, you will feel better soon.

Mary

A note to a friend absent on account of illness is a very welcome morale booster. You can buy a "get well" card in a store or, even better, dash off a few lines of your own. In the case of minor illness, it is helpful to convey the message that the misery will soon pass.

LOST LUGGAGE

Jen!

Sorry to hear that you went one way and your luggage another. Unfortunately, this is something that happens all the time. As I understand it, such mix ups are usually resolved pretty quickly. I hope the airline is being reasonably helpful. In the meantime, try to relax. You know, Jen, we're about the same size, so if there's anything you need to borrow in the meantime, please let me know. You're more than welcome.

Stay cool,

Pat

Showing your concern in a minor disaster like this helps put the problem in a perspective that should help your friend to feel better. Any practical help you can render is also greatly appreciated.

25 Words and Phrases to Use

adjust	express	share
aid	feel better	shock
assist	heal	sorry
celebrate	help	surprise
condolences	hope	sympathy
cope	joy	take time
delight	patience	time
emotion	recover	
endure	remember	

15 Words and Phrases to Avoid

bounce back	forget it	shake it off
could be worse	hopeless	snap out of it
despair	it's nothing	terrible
disastrous	miserable	tragedy
don't worry	no big deal	you'll be all right

Just to Keep
in Touch

$\mathcal{N}$o law binds us to wait for special occasions, for times of joy and celebration, or for moments of crisis and sorrow, to speak or write—from the heart—to family or friends. Sometimes we just want to keep in touch.

Now, keeping in touch means different things to different people and in different situations. Some of us want to say or write something special to a family member or friend virtually every day. In other cases, keeping in touch is what we do with family or friends who have gone their own way. Perhaps a son is off at college. Perhaps a friend has found work in Tucson, and you live in Chicago. In still other instances, it is not just miles that separate us, but years as well. We may wish to get in touch with a friend or even a family member we've not seen or communicated with for years.

Any of these situations offer ample reason to reach out.

Finding the Heartline

But what do we say? If someone graduates, gets married, has a child, or, alas, dies, we have news, a subject. But what is the subject of "keeping in touch"?

Keeping in touch. The phrase is so familiar that we hardly give it thought anymore. It's just a phrase, a figure of speech, after all. We take it for granted. But think about the phrase for a moment or two. *Touch* describes both a most vital human sense and a most intimate gesture. It is all about closeness, and "keeping in touch" is an effort to maintain closeness.

Now, what things maintain closeness between people? Each of us could readily draw up his or her own list, but here's a generic one:

- Shared thoughts
- Shared feelings
- Meaningful experiences, shared
- News of mutual friends and acquaintances

The most effective attempts at keeping in touch combine items from all four of these categories. Keep this in mind when you pick up the phone or sit down to write. And here are some other rules of thumb for keeping in touch:

- *Communicate with enjoyment.* If you set about the task of keeping in touch as if it were a chore, the result will be disappointing both for you and your correspondent. If you approach the task with pleasure, that feeling will illuminate whatever you have to say.

- *Be personal.* This does not mean confessing your innermost secrets. But it does require you to go beyond simply reeling off a list of things you have done lately. Talking about interesting things you've done or are doing is great, but animate this material by including what you've been thinking and feeling, too.

- *Zero in.* You don't have to deliver a novel-length account of the last decade or so. Instead, choose one event (or two) and tell a story about it. It is always more interesting to hear in detail about a specific event than it is to plow through a laundry list of one event after another. Good writing or speaking shares sensations, sights, sounds, and it shares emotions. When the American writer Stephen Crane wanted to write a realistic novel about the Civil War, he didn't summarize one battle after another, but, instead, focused on the experience of a small group of men in a single engagement. He explored this in detail, and while *The Red Badge of Courage* is certainly not a comprehensive history of the Civil War, it communicates far more about the nature and reality of that war—and war in general—than any number of dry-as-dust chronicles. You, too, can make your experience vivid by focusing on a small aspect of it and delivering the information in detail. After all, it is always more fun to read or hear a story than it is to read or hear a list.

- *Yield to the adventure.* A good storyteller lets her story lead her as well as her listeners. Select a subject, focus on it, and start talking or writing about it. See where the tale takes you.

Sidestepping the Pitfalls

The most common pitfall where keeping in touch is concerned is simply this: failing to keep in touch. Remember your high school physics—and the principle of inertia. The relevant part of this natural law goes something like this: If a body is at rest, it's difficult to get it moving. A similar principle applies to keeping in touch. We may think about doing it. We may say, *I really ought to write my cousin* or *I should give Bill a call*, but actually doing these things is another matter. The hardest part about keeping in touch is getting started.

Once you overcome the inertia, you face at least three more pitfalls:

1. *What do I say?* As mentioned earlier, occasions of great joy or deep tragedy automatically give you a subject. The subject is less apparent when you simply decide to get in touch with someone. Reread the pointers given in the previous section for some topic ideas.

2. *Forgetting to be human.* For most people, this is more of a problem when writing than when speaking. We tend to forget that writing or speaking from the heart is the communication of one person to another. The result is that we slip into a dull, dry, impersonal, artificial kind of speech. The most effective way to avoid this, to keep from forgetting that you are a human being communicating with another human being, is to use your imagination. When you are on the phone or—even more important—when you sit down to write, imagine your correspondent sitting in the next chair or across the table. Imagine that you are having a conversation with him or her. When we learn to read, we are taught to avoid moving our lips. When you write to a friend or a family member, it's okay to let your lips move as you write. *Talk* to the other person.

3. *Biting off too much.* Even if you've not communicated with your old buddy for a decade, two decades, or longer, you need not feel obligated to do all of your catching up in a single phone call, let-

ter, or e-mail. Be selective. The first attempt at keeping in touch can trigger a whole series of letters or calls over the years. Don't worry, you'll cover a lot of territory—by and by.

Saying It: To Family

MISS YOU, MOM

> Hi, Mom. No, nothing's wrong. I'm just calling because I miss you. This morning, I was scrambling some eggs, just the way you used to, with olive oil, and I thought about the million or so breakfasts you made me on those chilly mornings before school. I just remembered how great it all was, and then it occurred to me that I hadn't called for a while.
>
> What's new with you?

The caller zeros in on the homiest of memories to share with his mother. The act of scrambling eggs is pretty simple, but contained within that act is a wealth of feeling and memory. Keeping in touch is touching precisely such moments, such gestures, such actions, then sharing them.

One of the keys to a satisfying keep-in-touch phone call is to invite the other person to talk. Don't feel obliged to deliver a monologue.

MISS YOU, MOTHER TO DAUGHTER

> Hello, Mary. I know I dropped you off at State just two days ago, but, a minute ago, I walked into your room to put some things away, and there was your bed—neatly made! So it hit me: You are indeed away. And I missed you, so I just wanted to see how you're settling in.
>
> Is there anything I can send you? What's your new roommate like?

Sending a child off to college is an intensely emotional experience for many parents. This mother conveys her feelings not with gushy, strongly weighted emotional words, but with gentle humor. The girl's bed is neatly made, so the mother *knows* she is no longer at home.

There are some other important things the caller does *not* do in this conversation:

- She does not scold her daughter for failing to call. Too many efforts to keep in touch are spoiled by words aimed at making the other person feel guilty for letting the relationship lapse in some way.

- She is careful to avoid giving the impression that she is overprotective or prying. The questions this mother asks focus on her daughter's needs and her surroundings. They are not intrusive.

- She doesn't smother her daughter in sage advice. By all means, share your wisdom with your children, but recognize their need for independence, too.

WHY I HAVEN'T CALLED—SON TO FATHER/MOTHER

Hi, Dad (Mom). Maybe you've forgotten the sound of my voice. This is Ted, Ted Williams, your son. Before you bawl me out for not having called in so long, let me tell you my excuse: I'm a lazy bum. I was going to run down the list of what I've been doing, studying for midterms, working day and night on my chem lab project, and all the rest. But the fact is that I was just too lazy to pick up the phone.

So, let me tell you about what's been happening here. The big news is that I've gotten a research grant for next year . . .

It's a vicious cycle. For one reason or another, you put off making the call you've been meaning to make. Then, the longer you put it off, the more difficult it is to make the call. After all, how do you explain why you've stayed out of touch for so long? Pretty soon, you actively look for reasons not to call.

How do you break this cycle of inaction?

Just make the call. If you want, you can begin with the reasons for not having called. You may have very good ones. Avoid outpourings of guilt, however, because these will only make the person on the other end of line feel bad. He or she does not want to be the cause of your guilty conscience. The caller in this case uses gentle humor and frankly admits that he has no good excuse for having failed to call—although he does manage to alert his parents to the fact that he has been very busy indeed.

Once the caller has cleared the hurdle of excusing his failure to keep in touch, he goes on to some real news, focusing on his research grant rather than including it in a list of lesser, and less significant, activities and events.

Saying It: To Friends

MISS YOU

> Jane, you've been on my mind a lot lately. It's just not the same around here since you left. I miss talking to you, of course, and I miss the sound of your kids playing up and down the block. Our new neighbors are very nice people, don't get me wrong, but it's not the same as having someone you just feel so comfortable with, to sit down with and solve the world's problems.
>
> Speaking of problems, the town still has not put in a traffic light on our corner. There have been at least three wrecks since you left. Remember how we worked together on all those petitions? We put in a lot of time together on them, and I haven't given up hope that they'll ultimately have an effect.
>
> So, how are you settling in? The kids adjusting to the new school yet? And what about *your* new neighbors? What are they like?

Telling an absent friend that you think about her and that you miss her may sound like a cliché, but it is really a valuable gift from you to her. It is a moving—a most touching—sentiment, especially if you add a few specific details, former conversations, the sound of the children playing, and so on.

Note that the item of news the caller chooses to focus on is one she knows is of common interest to her and her friend. Emphasizing shared experience is a way of reestablishing the familiar connections from which the fabric of a friendship is woven.

COMING TO TOWN

> Hey, Max! The Candy Convention is coming to Chicago during the last week in August. I'm going to attend, and it sure would be great to see you while I'm in town. I'll be tied up at the convention until about noon on the 23rd, but I'm free after that. I could come by and spend the afternoon and evening, then take the late flight. It would be a lot of fun to get together, if this will work out for you.

Perhaps you feel self-conscious about inviting yourself to a distant friend's house. This is understandable, but it's best to avoid betraying any reluctance when you want to call on an old friend. Present the circumstances clearly, be specific about time, and express your enthusiasm for a reunion. Just be sure to leave your friend an out—"if this will work out for you."

PLEASE VISIT

Karen, Larry told Jane and me that you were going to be coming out to Jacksonville on business next week. I don't know what your schedule's going to be like, but it would be a lot of fun for all of us if we could get together. We could pick you up from wherever you're going to be and bring you back here. Maybe you could arrange a Sunday flight, and, that way, we could have you as a weekend guest. It would be wonderful to revisit old times together.

A spur-of-the-moment invitation to a friend who just happens to be coming through town can be most welcome. Of course, you must also be prepared for the possibility that your friend won't be able to accept, and you must never present this form of keeping in touch in any way that seems coercive. Be enthusiastic, be specific, and offer whatever you can to make it easy and convenient for the other person to accept, but also express your understanding that she may not be able to accept. This does not mean saying, "I know this might be impossible for you," which might be read as a lack of enthusiasm on your part, as if the invitation were extended half-heartedly; however, do include an acknowledgment of the possible difficulties of getting together: "I don't know what your schedule's going to be like."

Writing It: To Family

MISS YOU, LETTER FROM FATHER TO DAUGHTER

Dear Cindy,

Your mother and I were so happy to hear from you last night, and we are thrilled by the news of your success at college. We sat up much of the night talking about you, not so much about where you are now—though we're so very proud of that!—but about our old times together, how we used to sit together and read or watch TV, those great road trips we took together, the first time we went to the Grand Canyon. Cindy, believe it or not, it's not easy for old folks like us to get accustomed to not having you around every day!

Anyway, Cind, please keep calling. We love to hear from you—and often. And we are very excited for you and your success.

Love,

Dad

Psychologists have long known about positive reinforcement. If your child's action pleases you, reward it, reinforce it. If you want your daughter to stay in touch, respond positively and enthusiastically. A sweet, thoughtful letter is such a response.

Note that while the writer recalls the "old times," he does not wallow in them, and he by no means denies the value and accomplishments of his daughter in the present. Still, he communicates about shared experience, and he is able to admit that it is difficult for parents to let go. Letters have always been ideal vehicles for expressing feelings, and this is precisely what the writer does here.

WHY HAVEN'T YOU WRITTEN? LETTER TO BROTHER

Dear John,

The guy who runs the newsstand on the corner thinks I've gone wacko. You see, I've started buying up all the supermarket tabloids he has on sale—you know, the ones with the headlines about TWO-HEADED BABY BORN TO 80-YEAR-OLD GRANDMOTHER. I keep looking in them for a story about how *you* have been abducted by aliens and taken to Venus. How else to explain the fact that you've apparently left this planet?

John, you haven't written in ages! I'm starting to get concerned. And if this desperate attempt at humor doesn't get a few lines from you in return, I'm really going to start to worry.

I'd love to hear from you!

Love,

Barbara

Never scold another person into writing, but a letter asking for a response is perfectly reasonable, polite, and even welcome. It shows your concern and caring without, however, making any insistent demands. Mild humor is an effective means of ensuring that your request for correspondence doesn't sound too insistent or even indignant.

TO A HOMESICK SON

Dear Daryl,

It was good talking to you last night. Your Dad and I are so sorry that you're feeling homesick. I know it's painful—I know, because I've been through it myself. The bad news is that it makes you feel pretty low, but the good news is that it's strictly a temporary problem. It doesn't *feel* temporary now, I realize, but, trust me, you'll feel better soon. In the meantime, call us as often as you want. We love to talk to you—anytime. After all, Daryl, we miss you, too—very much!

Love,

Mom

Homesickness is a common complaint, and it hits some kids hard. Your response should be understanding and sympathetic. Don't deny or minimize your child's feelings, but do what you can to persuade him that the problem, though intense and real, is temporary. Few things are more convincing than sharing personal experience, as the writer does here. While you should avoid minimizing the problem, don't allow your response to magnify it out of proportion, either.

Conclude as positively as possible. The most positive step you can take is to offer a reasonable means of relief, namely an open and warm invitation to call home—often. Finally, note that the writer turns the tables on her son by confessing that the feelings he has are in some ways reciprocal. She and her husband miss their boy.

Writing It: To Friends

TO AN OLD FRIEND

Dear Ron,

It was great seeing you again, buddy, after much too long. Too long, yes, but it was oh so easy to get back in the groove with you. It was like old times. It was as if all those years hadn't passed by at all. The feeling, Ron, was very special, and I wouldn't like to lose it in another long silence. So let me fill you in on what's been happening since you left.

The big thing, which has us really fired up, is Jenny's success in the local band. She just got promoted to first clarinet—this after only a year marching with the band. We're thrilled, and I just love to see Jenny enjoying something so much, taking such satisfaction in a hard-won accomplishment.

As for me, I mentioned while you were here that it looked as if I'd be stepping up to assistant manager for the district, and, thank goodness, that's just what happened. It means I have to work longer hours, unfortunately, but the challenge is a welcome one—and so is the extra money.

Ron, my friend, what's been happening with you since we parted? I'd love to hear all about it.

Yours,

Ben

Friendships don't just happen. They require a certain amount of work. Call it maintenance, if you like. Neglected, a friendship fades away. Take positive action by following up on a pleasant visit with a phone call or letter. Make clear your desire and intention to stay in touch, and reinforce this message by sharing choice current personal events with your friend. Close by inviting him to share likewise.

MISS YOU

Dear Kathy,

Last night, I was cleaning out the bureau drawer and ran across a packet of snapshots from a dozen years ago. They were photos of that trip you, Dave, Martin, and I took together to Yosemite. Suddenly, the smell of the cool, crisp air, the sounds of the birds, the deep green of the forest, all of this came back to me in a flood. And so did memories of the great pleasure we had there together and all the fun we've had over the years. That, I realized, was the secret formula of our friendship: that we always enlarged and amplified the enjoyment we took in whatever we did together.

So, my dear friend, I'm writing to say how much I miss you—how happy I am for the times we had together, but how much I wish we could be together much more often. Let's plan a new trip together. We're open to vacation plans any time in August. What about it? Life's too short to spend so much of it apart.

Love,

Ella

Time and distance are formidable obstacles and undeniable facts of life, but a good letter to an absent friend can do much to overcome these barriers. Feelings of friendship, after all, live in the heart and mind, places in which time and distance can be compressed.

The writer evokes strong emotion here not through the use of flowery language, but by recalling and sharing specific moments from the past, including sights, sounds, smells, and feelings. If you can awaken the senses of your correspondent, you can be confident that your letter will come across as real, vivid, and touching. A key to communicating from the heart is to tie your language to the real world, to real events, to actual experiences, and to vivid emotions.

WHY I HAVEN'T WRITTEN

Dear Jack,

No, I have not dropped off the end of the Earth. Even more important, the fact that I haven't written in so long is no indication that I've stopped thinking about you.

My excuse?

Well, there is no adequate *excuse* for my not having made the time to write a few lines. I do have an *explanation*, however. I have been swamped, what with starting up my own business—it's what we always talked about, a specialty CD shop—and attending to my aunt, who is in the hospital again. Swamped, yes, but I could have found a few moments to drop a line or two. It's just that I never feel I can say what I want when I dash off a note.

So, please take this brief letter as my promissory note to you—an IOU on a much longer letter, which I promise to write as soon as I can. In the meantime, how about letting me know what's happening on your end?

All the best to you,

Patti

The writer hits on an important truth here. Often, we fail to make time to write to those we care about not because we have absolutely *no* time, but because we feel we have insufficient time to do full justice to what we want to say. The result? Neither a long nor a short letter, but no letter at all. If you find yourself in this bind, you owe it to yourself to do at least one of two things:

* Find time now to write the letter you want to write.

* Write a short letter now, promising more later.

Don't burden your correspondent with a long, guilt-ridden explanation of why you haven't written. Acknowledge that you have not written, offer a brief explanation, but point out that you regret having been out of touch and that you want to reach out now, to make up for lost time.

E-Mailing It: To Family

WHAT'S HAPPENING?—E-MAIL TO SISTER

Hi, Sis—

Been thinking about you. It's been weeks since we've spoken. What's been happening? In particular, how's the job search going? Anything interesting come up? Have you thought about contacting Mary Williams at Union Company? If not, she's someone you probably should talk to. She knows the market in your town pretty well. Maybe she can provide some leads.

Anyway, how about a call or e-mail to get me up to date on your life and times?

Love,

Mike

Prodding someone to call or write should never come across as a demand. Instead, express interest by asking for news. If you can be specific in your request, so much the better. Note that this message also adds an offer of help.

MISS YOU—MOTHER'S E-MAIL TO SON AT COLLEGE

Dear Matt,

I'm getting to love e-mail. I can just sit down and fire off a few lines to you whenever I miss you—which, Matt, is pretty often. I know that you'll take off like a rocket in college, but I hope that you won't accelerate so fast that we'll lose touch with you. You know, all you have to do is click on the reply button to send a message back to me. Tell me a little bit about your classes, about your professors, and about your roommate. And is the food decent?

Love,

Mom

E-mail invites reply, because technology has made it so very easy to respond to messages. Exploit this when you want a response. But don't depend on the technology to prompt a busy, lazy, or otherwise reluctant correspondent. Try *telling* him what to write about. This makes his job that much easier, and it improves the odds of your getting the reply you seek.

PARENTS TO WORRIED DAUGHTER

Dear Meg,

I have been thinking about your phone call. I'm not going to tell you to stop worrying about your grades. Look, they're important, but you and I both know that they don't always accurately reflect your performance or your ability. Don't be discouraged. You have a lot of time to pull those grades up. Take some positive steps: Organize your study time more efficiently, and *talk* to the professors. When you are studying, jot down every question you have, then take these to your professors. Remember, your success is *their* success, too. They want to feel that they are doing a good job. They want to help. Once you realize that you do not have to go this alone, I think you'll feel better—and your grades will improve.

Please, Meg, call us anytime you need to talk.

Love,

Dad

E-mail is an ideal medium for quick afterthoughts, following a conversation or phone call.

It is painful to see a loved one wracked by worry. The natural impulse is to assure her that "everything will be just fine." The impulse is natural, but it isn't necessarily helpful. In the first place, such reassurances usually come across as hollow, a denial of reality. In the second place, it is quite possible that your correspondent's worry has a legitimate basis in the real world. It is not helpful to encourage ignoring it. Instead, admit the problem, sympathize with the bad feelings it is causing, then try to offer some genuine help and advice, if at all possible. Do not say anything that either reinforces or magnifies the bad feelings that already exist, but try to advise a course of action that may improve the situation that is causing distress.

E-Mailing It: To Friends

COMING TO TOWN

Jim:

Marilyn and I will be passing through Middletown next week on our way to New York. We haven't seen you and Cynthia for over a year—and that's a year too long. Are you guys going to be home and open to a pair of wayfarers on the 6th? I expect we'll be in the neighborhood by three in the afternoon. We'd love to take you out to dinner and chew over old times.

Click on reply. Say yes, if you can.

Best from both of us,

Dan

E-mail is fast and easy, which makes it a good medium for arranging impromptu visits. Give as much specific information as you can, and communicate your enthusiasm while also allowing for the possibility that your friends may not be available.

GREAT TO SEE YOU AGAIN

Dear Ralph and Eunice,

It was so wonderful seeing you again after way too many years. Tom and I have talked about practically nothing else since. We've both remarked how the two of you have hardly changed, but how "little" Mike has grown into a fine young man. It is so inspiring—I can't think of another word—to see your family, solid, sane, fun, and loving people, all of you.

Let's make a vow to stay in touch and to try to see more of each other.

Love,

Nancy

A note acknowledging the pleasure of a visit after long absence is more than a polite gesture. It is an effort to reach out, to ensure that the visit will help reestablish a lapsed friendship. It is a gesture of reconnecting.

Don't be shy about expressing your genuine admiration for a friend. Don't be shy, but do try to be specific, as the writer is here. She makes the effort not just to express her affection and admiration, but to explain why she feels the way she does. She also makes it clear that she speaks for her husband's feelings as well.

25 Words and Phrases to Use

admire	embrace	faith
affection	encourage	friendship
delight	exciting	fun

get together   miss you   share
great time   news   too long
hear all about it   old times   too many years
hear from you   please reply   wonderful
keep in touch   pleasure
memories   reach out

10 Words and Phrases to Avoid

ashamed of yourself   must reply
don't know what to say   no time to write
everything will be fine   shame on you
get together sometime or other snap out of it
have to hear from you   why haven't you called?

Part 3

Talking with Children About . . .

*E*ffective, loving communication with our children
is the subject of this section.

14

Anger

"*I* hate my brother!"

It's an exclamation at least as old as Cain and Abel, and what parent has not heard it? Or its equivalent:

"I hate my sister!"

"I hate my teacher!"

"I hate Tommy!"

"I hate you!"

How do you respond?

Whatever else it is, anger is the verbal expression of energy. Energy is difficult to control or contain. Set off an explosion, and it affects everything in the vicinity—usually adversely. Thus you may find it difficult to respond to your child's anger with anything other than anger. As energy begets energy, so anger begets anger.

But you *are* an adult, and you have learned to exercise adult-level restraint. Instead of responding to your child's provocations with anger—which will only escalate the prevailing rage—you respond calmly: "Oh, you know you don't mean that!"

Does this restraint, admirable though it may be, resolve the problem?

Hardly.

Responding to anger with anger is as effective a means of dealing with rage as throwing gasoline on a blaze to put out the fire. However, simply denying the child's feelings is equally ineffective. It may even be more destructive.

Yet it is understandable. Looking around at present-day popular culture, at our songs and TV shows, it may be hard to believe that our society sets any value at all on courtesy. More often than not, it defines courtesy simply as avoiding—or ignoring, if necessary—unpleasant emotions and the expressions to which those give rise. Therefore, if we manage to avoid a knee-jerk response to anger—that is, expressing anger in return—our next automatic choice is to deny the anger altogether.

Denying feelings does not deal with feelings. It only cuts off communication.

What's wrong with this? Well, let's pause here to discuss the reasons why communication is so important. It is a daunting subject to which vast volumes have been devoted, books by eminent philosophers, scientists, psychologists, and even theologians. *How to Say It from the Heart* is a humble handbook aimed at helping you to write and speak more effectively. So allow me to boil down the discussion to a mere three points.

1. *Verbal expressions of anger are intimately related to physical expressions of anger.* Verbal violence and physical violence are both forms of violence. Most outbursts of physical violence begin with verbal violence. Cope effectively with verbal violence, and you will reduce the incidence of physical violence. Denying verbal violence—ignoring or rejecting the expression of anger—is not an effective way to cope with anger and, therefore, will do nothing to forestall the physical expression of anger.

2. *Effective communication, especially where strong emotions are involved, is essential to future success.* What parent does not want a bright future for his or her child? We spend hours at parent–teacher conferences, we willingly pay for tutors, we buy books, we drag the kids to museums. Yet too many of us fail to realize that the denominator common to most success is a highly developed ability to communicate. Your conversations with your kids, from a very early age and until they grow into young adulthood and leave home, are the chief vehicles by which children arrive at their communication skills. To turn away from an emotion is to forsake an opportunity for communication, and to miss such an opportunity is to fail to build your child's communication skills. This, in turn, diminishes his or her chances for future success.

3. *Communication contributes to good health.* We all know people who "bottle up" their emotions. They are flushed of face and tight

of lip. They walk through life stiff, complaining of their aching backs, their high blood pressure, their sour stomachs. The ability to express emotion verbally—including strong and painful emotion—is essential to physical well-being. To help a child develop effective ways to talk about his feelings, including (and especially!) anger, is as important to his future health as the good food you feed him.

Finding the Heartline

Find the heartline in talking to a child about anger, and you have a key to effective communication with children on virtually any subject and in any circumstance.

The first principle to bear in mind is the necessity of recognizing and maintaining the connection between feelings and words. In the case of anger, this means accepting the child's feelings and dealing with them in words. When a child says he hates his sister or he hates his teacher or he hates you, don't tell him he can't mean or doesn't mean what he has just said. Hard as it is, accept the fact that, right now, at this moment, in these circumstances, this is precisely what he means. Be prepared to use words to deal with this.

In addition to this prime directive of communication with kids, this overriding truth, consider the following when you speak to your child about any powerful emotion:

- *Theories of language aside, the only meaning a communication has in the real world is whatever the listener understands it to have.* This is true whether you, an adult, are speaking to another adult or whether you are speaking to a child. The problem is that when you speak to a child, her understanding may be quite different from your intention, because, as a child, her experience, her frame of reference, is different from yours. Try to understand the child's frame of reference before you speak.

- *Communication is developed through feedback.* Exasperated, we sometimes feel that communicating with our children is like putting a message in a bottle and sending it out to sea. The communication is one way, and there is a very little guarantee that it will reach its intended recipient. While this image may accurately reflect our frustration, especially when trying to communicate in situations of intense emotion, it is not a good model of communication. All conversation is based on the model of the feedback loop.

Let's pause a moment to look at the feedback loop. Here is a snatch of conversation:

You: I went to the store.

Him: What did you buy at the store?

You: I bought a new dress.

Him: How much did the dress cost?

It would be easy—if, perhaps, a trifle tedious—for you to continue this dialogue from this point. And you don't have to possess the imagination of a Charles Dickens or a Stephen King to do so. Why not? Because of the feedback loop. The first words "*Him*" utters are feedback to the first words of "*You*." They don't come out of thin air, but directly from "*You*'s" statement. For one thing, they share a word in common, "store." Because "*Him*" knows what one does in a store, the natural feedback to "*You*" is "*What did you* buy?" Similarly, this question prompts feedback relating immediately and directly to the content of the question. "*You*'s" response employs the past tense of the verb in the question "*Him*" asks:

Him: What did you *buy* at the store?

You: I *bought* a new dress.

Now, the fact that this conversation runs on a feedback loop does not mean that "*Him*" has no choice in his next response. He could have asked what color the dress is, what it is made out of, where the hemline falls, and so on, depending on what most interests him. In this case, the question concerns cost. It is one response out of many that are possible—but the important point here is contained in the phrase *that are possible*. The content of the statement "I bought a new dress" does not dictate what "*Him*" says next, but it does narrow the relevant possibilities. That is, "*Him*" might next have said, "Louis XIV was called the Sun King," but, then, we would no longer have a conversation. But, "*Him*" does say something that constitutes feedback, and this leads us to the next heartline principle:

- *Your child bases what he says on what you say.* If you speak accusingly or angrily or disparagingly to your child, you will be paid back in kind. This applies not only to a particular conversation, but to the context of communication you build up over the years.

Let's take time out again. Your child, playing recklessly after you told him not to play in the living room, knocks over your favorite vase, which shatters on the floor.

You: What's the matter with you? You are so clumsy!

Your child: You shouldn't have put that there if I'm so clumsy.

There's only one direction the conversation can go from here: to a place of greater and greater anger. Clearly, the child misbehaved. Clearly, it is his fault that the vase is shattered. Clearly, both of you would be best served if the kid would sincerely apologize.

Why doesn't he?

One reason is that you have not provided the right words to elicit that feedback. By verbally attacking the child, you invite defensive—not contrite—feedback. Such feedback, in turn, provokes even angrier feedback from you, and you have the makings of a vicious cycle of escalating emotion.

Let's not leave this point without exploring an alternative to verbally attacking your child. The shattered vase is a bad thing. It is no wonder that it makes you angry, especially after you told your child not to play in the living room. Don't deny your feelings about the incident, but do focus your remarks on the incident, the event, the issue, rather than on your child, his character, or his abilities.

You: Oh, Max! That was my favorite vase! I feel terrible about it!

Your child: I'm sorry . . .

And, from here, the conversation can take a more constructive turn, aimed at controlling anger without ignoring it. Another heartline principle, then:

- *Focus on issues, not personalities.* This is a principle to apply to all communication, especially those involving strong negative feelings. If the child breaks the vase, talk about your feelings concerning the loss of the vase. Do not focus on how you feel about your child at this particular moment. Do not use the event as a lever to pry open the child's character flaws. Events, like feelings, are often quickly past, over and done with; but character, self-image, self-esteem, and personality endure. Do not allow momentary feelings born of particular incidents to label enduring qualities of self. Separate events—and the feelings elicited by events—from the person that is your child and how you feel about him or her.

- *Look to language for the cause of communication problems before you blame your child.*

Let's give this principle some thought. Even people who don't care much for classical music generally agree that Beethoven's *Fifth Symphony* is a great piece of music. But what if you had never heard it played by a full symphony orchestra and instead heard a novice kazoo player struggle through it?

"Who *is* this guy Beethoven? His music is incredibly lame!"

Of course, we *have* heard the *Fifth Symphony* played by an orchestra and, hearing a kazoo rendition—a bad one at that—we understand that the fault lies not in Beethoven's music, but in this particular expression of it. Similarly, we need to recognize that many of the problems we experience in communication, including negative feelings that may result from certain exchanges, are due not to the person talking to us, but to language itself. Understand that not everyone is a great communicator with a virtuoso command of language. This is especially true of your child. As a speaker, Sir Winston Churchill possessed a philharmonic orchestra of eloquence. Your six-year-old is still learning the kazoo.

- *You don't have to be a child psychologist to talk effectively with your child.* Understand that your child probably will see most issues from a different perspective than you. Understand, too, that, depending on his age, your child's vocabulary is less extensive than yours. But, aside from this, you may speak with a child *essentially* as you speak with an adult. More precisely, you may speak with a child the way you might speak to a respected subordinate at work. This means expecting *and giving* courtesy and attention. It means not talking down to the child. It means listening to him without interruption—anymore than you would cut off or interrupt an adult partner in conversation.

Sidestepping the Pitfalls

The pitfalls in communicating with children are many, and they are yet more numerous and deeper when strong emotions, especially anger, are involved. The major pitfalls may be expressed as negative versions of the heartline advice just given. That is, parents should look out for and avoid the following:

- *Denial of feelings.* This is both the biggest and the most common pitfall in talking with kids about anger. If a child expresses anger, do not reply that he "doesn't really mean it." Accept the feeling. Engage it. Discuss it.

- *Focusing on the child instead of the issues.* Focusing the discussion on your child—his personality, his "attitude," his character, his skills (or lack of them)—almost always intensifies anger, making both you and your child feel worse. Point the conversation at the particular event in question and about the feelings you and your child have about the event.

- *Sending out angry messages.* In communication, you really do reap what you sow. If you habitually speak to your child—or other family members—in angry tones and with angry content, you will get anger in return. On a smaller scale, if you respond to your child's anger with anger, you will only intensify his anger.

- *Blaming the child instead of his language.* You have no right to expect great eloquence from your child at any time, but especially not when he's angry. Recognize that much of what he says— or fails to say—is a product of his limited command of the instrument of language.

- *Talking down to the child.* Children, of course, are not "little adults." Nevertheless, you are better off talking with them as adults who are subordinate to you than you are talking down to them. Expect and deliver the same courtesy and attention in your conversations with children as in those with adults.

Angry Scenarios

The following three scenarios call for different responses, but it is important to make two basic responses to all three—and, indeed, to any conversation with your child about feelings:

1. *Pay attention.* Stop whatever you're doing, turn to your child, pause, make eye contact.

2. *Do not avoid, evade, or otherwise ignore your child's feelings.* This does *not* mean that you have to understand exactly what your child feels. Just acknowledge the fact of the feelings with a phrase such as, "I see you're very angry" or "I see you're upset."

If your child is having difficulty putting angry feelings into words, you might try to help: "When your brother did that to you, it must have made you very angry." Or: "I bet that was embarrassing, huh?" Or: "That probably hurt your feelings."

LITTLE BROTHER SNOOPS IN BIG SISTER'S ROOM

Child: I hate Billy! He's always messing up my stuff. Next time, I'm going to go into his room and break one of his toys!

The temptation is to "correct" this threat, because the behavior it mentions is definitely out of bounds, against the rules, and unacceptable. But replying with a "You'll do no such thing, young lady" ignores feelings and will only escalate the anger. Here is an alternative:

Parent: Oh, Debbie. I'm sorry. Nobody likes their stuff getting snooped into. I can understand why you're so upset. Let's talk about what we can say to Billy.

The parent neither denies her child's feelings nor condones her proposed action. Instead, she offers justification as well as sympathy for the feelings, and she proposes an alternative course of action—communication with Billy rather than vengeance against him. Moreover, she offers her help in resolving the situation that caused the anger. This is especially important because frustration—a feeling of powerlessness—fuels anger. Children see themselves as low on the family totem pole. They often feel powerless, frustrated, and therefore, angry. Demonstrating to them that what they say to you can produce a desirable and positive effect does much to relieve the frustration. Also important is the shift in focus here from the character of Billy to the issue at hand, invasion of privacy. Issues are always easier to deal with than people.

"IT WAS BORING AND I HATED IT!"

Dad took time off work and spent more than a few dollars to take his two sons to a baseball game. John loved it, but Mike squirmed and complained through much of the game. When it was over, he screamed out: "It was boring and I hated it!"

The temptation is for Dad to say something like, "What's wrong with you? Look at John. *He* had a good time—just like everyone else!" Instead, Dad bites his lip, swallows his own disappointment, and addresses his son's feelings: "I'm sorry you were bored. That must have been very disappointing. Tell me, what was boring about the game?"

This may spark a conversation. It acknowledges Mike's feelings, and it reinforces his willingness to share those feelings with his father. Perhaps the conversation can be led to a practical question: "What would you like to do next time? Where would you like me to take you?"

"MY MATH TEACHER IS A JERK!"

Your house rule is that children must not be disrespectful to an adult. Furthermore, you want your child to respect adult authority, especially the authority of teachers. Naturally, therefore, the temptation is to jump in and "correct" the child:

> Sarah, you can't call your teacher a jerk. That is not allowed. Period. And what do you expect if you spend so little time on your math homework? In this life, you get the treatment you earn. Work hard, and you will be rewarded. Goof off, and you'll suffer the consequences.

All of the above is perfectly logical, but such reasoning won't help Sarah cope with her anger just now. Feelings are like a house afire. You could stand next to the homeowner and watch the flames, remarking to him about the consequences of smoking in bed or overloading an electrical outlet or piling up oily rags next to the kindling stored in the basement. Alternatively, you could call 911 and, in the meantime, get your garden hose going. It is always best to begin by fighting the fire.

Dad might reply to Sarah:

When Mrs. Smith criticized you, that must have made you angry. I always hated being chewed out in class, especially in front of everybody.

Or:

You used to like Mrs. Smith, didn't you? Sounds like you're pretty angry with her just now.

Or:

It does hurt to be criticized like that. I know how it feels.

From here, father and daughter can talk more about her feelings. Once the girl's anger has been acknowledged, Dad can direct the conversation toward ways in which the *cause* of the anger might be eliminated in the future:

It sounds to me as if Mrs. Smith was disappointed in your answers to the problems, because she's used to your doing better work. Can I help you with your math homework?

Note that not all anger scenarios will result in "creative" solutions or practical plans for remedying an unpleasant situation. Such is life. Resolving an underlying issue is desirable, but it is less important than addressing feelings rather than ignoring or denying them.

25 Words and Phrases to Use

angry	must have hurt
appreciate	next time
feelings	say
frustrating	sympathize with
help	tell me
How did it make you feel?	think about
I see	together
it's okay	understand
let's talk about it	use words
mad	we
made you feel bad	What can I do?
make better	What would you like to do
must have been difficult for you	about it?

25 Words and Phrases to Avoid

ashamed of yourself
bad
behave
don't say that
don't talk to me like that
get away with it
I don't want to hear that
it's wrong to feel that way
nasty
naughty
nice girls (boys) don't say that
nobody says things like that
see it logically

shut up
stop crying
stop whining
straighten up
suffer the consequences
that's not nice
that's what you get
that's the way it is
You don't mean that!
you'd better
your fault
you're wrong

15

Death and Divorce

$\mathcal{Y}$oung parents buy their first home. They want a safe neighborhood for their new little son or daughter. They want a location on a cul de sac, away from speeding traffic. They want good, safe schools nearby. They "babyproof" the home, putting special latches on drawers, plastic inserts into electrical outlets, spring-loaded gates at the top and bottom of the stairs, and moving household cleaners out from under the sink. They dote. They worry. They want to protect their precious child. It's only natural.

It's only natural to want to protect children from harm and hurt. That is why it's so difficult to talk with kids about the biggest hurt of all, death—death and that other major loss, divorce.

But death itself is natural, and, like it or not, divorce is also a fact of life, with one of every two marriages ending in legal dissolution. We cannot protect, cannot insulate our children from such losses. We have to deal with them and, even more important, help our children to deal with them.

Is this, then, the grim reality?

There's no denying, it *is* reality. But it doesn't have to be grim.

Why not? What's the alternative?

First, here's what the alternative is *not*. It's not making light of the loss. It's not telling the child that "he'll get over it" or "it's not so bad." The alternative to *grim* is not *denial*. Never minimize or deny a child's feelings.

The true, valid, productive, and positive alternative to *grim reality* is *opportunity*. Death and loss are universal. There's no escaping them. Your child sees death on television and in the movies, and she

182

sees death when the daisy in the window box droops and withers and when you swat a fly. When this reality is experienced close to home, close to the heart, the opportunity is for understanding, accepting, and moving beyond. The opportunity is for learning to deal with a most basic condition of existence. As parents, as caring adults, we wouldn't dream of denying our responsibility to equip children for life: to feed, to clothe, to educate them. In matters of death and loss, we have both the responsibility and the opportunity to help children learn and grow and gain productive, healthy understanding.

Finding the Heartline

Death and divorce create powerful emotions for adults as well as children. The drive to protect our children is natural, and so are the facts of death and other loss. It is natural also to assume that dealing with death or divorce is all about feeling. The assumption is natural, but misleading. Dealing with serious, painful loss involves feelings, to be sure, but it most directly requires work toward achieving four goals:

Goal 1: Understanding

Goal 2: Mourning

Goal 3: Remembering

Goal 4: Continuing

In talking with children about death—or about divorce—the way to the heartline is via these four goals. To shortcut any of them is to deny the child the opportunity to realize from the experience of loss something more than mere pain and emptiness—and to realize something much greater. Achieving all four goals not only helps the child to cope with the loss, but also to gather from it something positive for now and for the rest of her life.

GOAL 1: UNDERSTANDING

Too often, in dealing with a crisis or any occasion associated with strong emotions, we separate feeling from understanding, as if the two were incompatible. In truth, they are not only compatible, but inseparable and seamless. One of the elements that produces fear in a child confronting death or other loss is bewilderment. It is a cliché to say that we fear the unknown, but it is a cliché precisely because it is so true. Understanding reduces fear. Thus, the first goal in helping a child deal with death and loss is understanding. This is a priority item.

But how do you explain death to a child?

Begin by focusing on the needs of the child, not on your own need to soften the facts of death. In our culture, death is treated very nearly as an obscenity. Many of us go through our entire lives without ever seeing a dead person—other than portrayed on television or in movies. We indulge in euphemisms for *death* and *die*. Mother "passed on" or "passed away." Or: "I lost my mother years ago." Or: "My father's deceased."

Before we can speak frankly with children about death, we must reject for ourselves the attitude that approaches death as impolite or even obscene.

Grandma died. That is the fact. Do not, therefore, tell your child that "Grandma passed away" or that "Grandma is sleeping now." Tell her that "Grandma died."

For young children—preschoolers and early primary schoolchildren—it is not enough to state this fact. The child wants to know what happens physically to the person who died. Tell her the facts, not in clinical detail, but straightforwardly:

> Grandma's body stopped working. A dead person can't eat or talk or walk or breathe. A dead person doesn't feel anything or do anything.

Depending on the child's age and level of understanding, she may or may not accept your explanation of the physical facts of death. Preschoolers, for example, may insist that Grandma is coming back or that she's simply in another place, perhaps living underground, where she was buried.

- Don't argue with these interpretations.

- Listen to what the child says. You need not comment, agree, or disagree. Just listen.

- If the child specifically asks if Grandma is coming back, tell her the truth—gently and calmly: "No. She isn't."

Preschoolers have not reached the stage of cognitive development at which they understand death as a concept. Don't be concerned if the child does not understand. At this age, the lack of understanding of the concept of death is natural. However, you do not have to reinforce or play along with this absence of understanding. Explain quietly. Listen attentively. Do not argue or debate.

School-age children may have a very literal-minded response to death. In contrast to preschoolers, they may be fascinated with the physical facts of death and may closely question you about what happens to the body after death. They may dwell on decay and other things that most of us find disturbing. Disturbing or not, however, we should not evade the questions. Instead, answer them as honestly and positively as possible:

Child: Will Grandma rot in the ground?

You: Her body is sealed in a special coffin, so I think it will stay preserved for a long time. But, you know, she can't feel what happens to her body now. So it doesn't matter to her.

More urgently, school-age children will worry about themselves and their families.

Child: Your mommy died, Dad. What if my mommy dies?

You cannot deny the reality of death. Everyone dies. But reality isn't only about white, black, yes, no, and other absolutes. It's also about degree and probability:

You: Sally, Grandma was 78 and she had been sick for a long time. Mommy is only 34, and she is very healthy. Everyone dies someday, but most people live a long time. Your mother and I are young—and you are even younger!

Religion and Understanding Death

For some adults, religious belief is all that is needed to explain death and to make it acceptable. For children, especially young children, it is not sufficient. If religion plays an important role in your family, it should also figure importantly in how you explain death to your child; however, do not expect religious or spiritual belief to satisfy the child as it may satisfy you.

As adults, *we* may take comfort in explaining that "God called Grandma to heaven to be with Him." Because such an explanation gives us comfort, we may assume that it does the same for the child. This, however, is not necessarily the case.

- The child may resent God for taking his Grandma away. God may seem mean and selfish.

- If God can take Grandma whenever He wants, what's to stop Him from taking Daddy or Mommy or even the child himself? Instead of providing comfort, the religious explanation may increase anxiety.

The best approach, especially with preschool and early school-age children, is to combine the physical explanation of death with any religious beliefs you may have—in the expectation, however, that the child will not fully comprehend the religious explanation:

> Danny, Grandma was very, very old, and her body stopped working. But, in our family, we believe that there is a part inside Grandma, the part that made her happy and that made her love us, that we call the spirit. And even though Grandma's body stopped working and is now in the ground, her spirit is in heaven with God. I don't know if you understand how that works, but I can tell you that you'll understand more about it when you get older.

GOAL 2: MOURNING

Achieving Goal 1, Understanding, does not prevent the painful feelings associated with death or loss. Such feelings are normal and natural. In fact, experiencing them—mourning—is a second goal of dealing with death or other loss. We need to recognize this not only in our children, but in ourselves.

A death in the family will produce mourning and grief not only in your child, but in you. Do not feel that you need to put up a "strong front" and hide your grief from your child. On the contrary, it is important for your child to see that you are sad—but that, sad as you are, you will continue to care for your child and will in no way abandon her. Showing and sharing your grief is also important as an example to your child. She needs to know that it is okay to feel sad about the loss. If you hide your grief, she may well get the message that her feelings are somehow bad, and this will short-circuit the emotional processes by which she deals with death.

Showing your grief does not mean moping about in silence. Talk about how you feel:

> Pam, I'm feeling sad about Grandma. Thinking about her makes me cry sometimes. I'll feel better soon, but right now I feel sad. How do you feel?

Beyond sharing their own grief, adults need to recognize that children often feel—and show—their grief differently from adults. Preschoolers and early school-age children do not simply feel sad when someone close to them dies, they feel anxious, even frightened.

Young children thrive on the security of certain routines, and the mere fact of change—let alone change brought about by death—is enough to create a profound disturbance. The response to this may not be an obvious demonstration of sadness, but, rather, what we consider misbehavior—disruptive behavior, angry actions, unruliness. Such a response can be especially trying during a time when the parents' energies are at an especially low ebb. It takes a special effort to understand that this disruptiveness is the child's way of expressing grief. There is no magic way of communicating with the child during times like this, but communication is important:

- Share your grief.
- Check in with the child. Ask her how she feels.
- Offer extra love and comforting. You may not feel like embracing an obstreperous child, but now is the time to do just that.

Few experiences in life are more painful than witnessing the pain of a child. Our natural impulse is to try to hasten the grieving process. Alas, nothing we do will shorten this process, which may last for weeks, months, even years. We *can* do the following, however:

- We can share our own grief.
- We can give the child the message that what he's feeling is normal and okay.
- We can listen to the child.
- We can offer realistic assurance of our continued love.
- We can tell the child that, as time goes by, he will feel better.

GOAL 3: REMEMBERING

Remembering and commemorating the dead is an activity common to every culture. It is almost certainly a basic human need. In our culture, remembering the dead is done in both formal, highly ritualized ways, and in informal ways.

Funerals

Think of the first funeral you attended. If you were a child, chances are that the memory is hardly a pleasant one. For most children, especially preschool and early school-age children, funerals combine anxiety with boredom, and both of these feelings are born of bewilderment.

Should children attend funerals? Better put the question this way: Should *your child* attend a funeral? For there is no generally "correct" answer. You should decide based on the child's relationship to the dead person, the circumstances of the death, and the child's age and his ability to understand the rituals he'll be a part of. Often neglected entirely is this very important criterion: The child's own willingness and desire to attend.

If you decide that the child should attend the funeral, you can make the experience less anxiety provoking and more meaningful if you discuss beforehand what will happen and what you want the child to do:

- To the best of your ability, outline the proceedings.
- Define unfamiliar terms, such as *casket, wake, shiva, coffin, funeral home*, and so on.
- If the body will be displayed, explain this.
- Encourage questions.

Do not give the child detailed instructions concerning behavior, but do explain that she will meet a lot of people who are sorry Grandma died and who want to spend some time with all of us to remember Grandma. Let your child know that she may see people talking and even crying, and that this is all normal and okay.

Never try to coerce the child into being on his "best behavior." Many children, especially those of school age, feel anxious about how they should behave during the funeral, and threats, even gentle threats, will only serve to increase anxiety.

Formal funeral rituals are important. They are more important to some people and families than they are to others. But the formal commemoration is only one way in which most families remember the dead. We remember loved ones personally, and there is great pleasure, comfort, and relief in sharing those memories. Children should be counted in on these informal commemorations. Let them participate in conversations. Invite them to share a memory:

Parent:　Honey, what did you like about going to Grandma's house?

Child:　I liked the chocolate cake she gave me.

Parent:　That *was* good, wasn't it? She always had delicious chocolate cake for you. That was fun, wasn't it?

GOAL 4: CONTINUING

Do not rush or deny the process of grieving, but it is helpful, from time to time, to share with children two important truths:

* The pain of loss—the sadness—diminishes with time. You *will* feel less sad.

* Your grandma, your father, your sister, your friend may die, but the people we love remain in our memories.

The fourth goal of coping with death is, simply, carrying on, continuing with life. From time to time, your child will bring up the subject of the dead person. These are important occasions, and you should always make time to listen, and to listen sympathetically. To the degree that you can, share feelings on these occasions:

Child:　*(three years after her brother died)* I was eating a Hershey bar, and I remembered how Howie loved Hershey bars, and I almost cried.

Mother:　Sarah, sometimes, when I make hamburgers I remember how much Howie loved to drown the hamburger in ketchup, and I remember how much fun we had with him. I miss him. Do you miss him?

Child:　Yes, I do.

Mother:　But I'm also so very glad and grateful I have you and we have each other!

Divorce

In many ways, talking with a child about divorce resembles talking with him about death. For the child, death and divorce are both losses. Both are a kind of death in—and of—the family. In some respects, divorce may be an even crueler loss than death:

- Whereas death is final, divorce tends to feed children's fantasies about eventual reunion. This makes it harder for the child to accept the finality of divorce.

- Whereas death may be blamed on accident, illness, or age, divorce is blamed on the parents.

Communication during a divorce may be made more difficult by mother's and father's feelings about themselves and about each other. Because of the complexity and intensity of the emotions involved, it is all too easy to get confused and to give out confused and confusing messages. Such confusion increases children's anxieties. The best course is to keep your messages as simple as possible:

- In simple language, explain what's happening. In particular, explain what will happen with living arrangements and with school. Emphasize what will change *as well as what will* not *change*.

- Make it crystal clear that both mom and dad love their children, and that the kids will be taken care of. Nothing bad will happen to them.

One of the great, grave, and often unspoken fears of children whose parents are divorcing is that they, the kids, are somehow at fault. Perhaps they weren't well-enough behaved. Perhaps if their schoolwork had been better, Mom and Dad would have stayed together.

- Make it clear that the children in no way caused the divorce. Repeat this. Repeat this often.

- Make it clear that your love for your children has not changed and never will change.

Communicating during a divorce is not a one-way process. Keep your children informed, but don't forget to listen to them. Encourage them to express their feelings. This sounds easier than it is, because the feelings you may hear expressed are not always pleasant, and your children's expression of their emotions may make you feel guilty, offended, hurt, angry, and depressed. However painful, take the heat. Listen to them. Never preempt or deny their feelings.

Sidestepping the Pitfalls

In helping your child cope with loss, whether death or divorce, it is difficult to go far wrong if you listen to your children and respond honestly to what they tell you. On the other hand, the most destructive course is failure to listen and the denial of feelings.

- Do not tell your children how they should feel.
- Do not tell your children to "snap out of it."
- Do not criticize feelings.
- Do not lie. In the case of death, do not encourage fantasies of return. Do not tell your child that "Grandma is sleeping now." In the case of divorce, do not encourage false hopes of a reconciliation.

25 Words and Phrases to Use

always love you	fun times	sad
cry	good times	scary
dead	help	share
death	life	spirit
divorce	love	take care of you
everyone	memory	talk
explain	normal	tell
feelings	not alone	
frightening	remember	

25 Words and Phrases to Avoid

act grown up	blame
act like a big boy/girl	don't want to hear you say that
asleep	don't think about it
bad	don't be sad
better behave yourself	don't cry

don't disappoint me

fault

gone to sleep

gone away

hate to hear you talk that way

have to be quiet

it's not so bad

must behave

passed away

passed on

snap out of it

taken away

taken from us

you don't mean that

you'll feel better soon

16

Drugs and Alcohol

$\mathcal{T}$he most recent (2000) federally approved statistic is this: 16 percent of boys and girls, ages 12 to 17, use drugs. The most generally accepted statistic on underage drinking is that more than 50 percent of high school seniors drink alcohol more than once a month.

Most people find statistics boring. So stop thinking about numbers. Instead, close your eyes. In your imagination, line up a hundred kids. Throw your own children into that line. Now, mentally herd 16 of the hundred to one side, and ask 50 at random to step forward. The chances are pretty good that your kid—or kids—are among the 16 who use drugs, the 50 who drink, or even belong to both groups.

The next step is neither to panic nor to shake your head and do nothing. The next step is to talk to your kids about drugs and alcohol.

Finding the Heartline

Talk to your kids. That's a good idea, but the advice is incomplete. Talk freely *and* really listen. The object is to create a dialogue, not to deliver a monologue. The single most important thing you can do to protect your child against drug use and alcohol abuse is to know what's going on in your child's world. The way to gain this information is not by spying or prying, but by talking and *listening*.

Begin, then, by opening up a two-way channel of communication. When it is your turn to talk, keep the conversation free of threats and drama. Rely on facts:

- Let your child know that you love him and that, because you love him, you want him to be happy and healthy. The focus of the conversation should be on the child, not on you, and not even on the "rules."

- Tell your child that you find alcohol and illegal drugs unacceptable. Astoundingly, many parents never make this simple statement. To a surprising degree, kids are willing to abide by the house and family rules—provided they know what those rules are.

Let's pause a moment. Illegal drugs are illegal and should have no place in the family. The use of alcohol, however, has a long tradition in our culture. Can you tell your children that you find alcohol unacceptable if you, in fact, drink? The answer is yes—you find it unacceptable for anyone who is not an adult to drink alcohol. Make this clear: The decision to drink is an adult decision, period.

- Explain the health risks of drug and alcohol abuse. You need not go into clinical detail, and you need not exaggerate. Do mention, however, the great danger of contracting AIDS and other blood-borne infections from shared needles in the use of injectable drugs; slowed growth caused by drugs and alcohol; brain damage; impaired judgment; impaired coordination; impaired thinking; impaired memory; learning difficulties; the greatly increased likelihood of accidents; emotional problems; the problems of addiction; organ damage; death.

- Explain the legal issues. Conviction for a drug offense can result in jail time and a criminal record. Driving under the influence of alcohol can result in jail time. At the least, convictions for drug use or drinking while driving may cause you to lose a job, a driver's license, a college loan.

- Explain the dangers of association. The drug world is a world intimately connected to criminality. Criminals are dangerous people. People get killed dealing in drugs, including buying them.

- Explain the moral issues. This does not mean preaching that drugs are "wrong," but do point out that the purchase and use of drugs supports criminals, people who hurt and kill other people.

- Set clear limits. "In this family, we don't do drugs—and we do not spend time around people who do drugs."

What you say, then, can be quite straightforward. How you express yourself is as important as what you say. Fortunately, it is not difficult to speak effectively about drugs:

- Keep the conversation calm and soft. There is no need to exaggerate. Let the facts do the persuading.

- Don't just hand your child a pamphlet or two. Speak to him face to face.

- Invite response. Listen. Don't preach.

- Use TV shows, news stories, and the like as occasions to discuss drug use.

- Don't make "The Speech" and then drop the subject. Talking about drugs and alcohol is a perennial part of parenting. It is ongoing, a conversation that continues over a period of years. A good rule of thumb is to spend a half hour each month discussing the subject.

- Set an example. You cannot dodge this issue with the *do-as-I-say-not-as-I-do* ploy. Do not use illegal drugs. If you have a substance abuse problem, get help. If you drink socially, be sure that you drink responsibly. This includes never drinking and driving.

Help Your Kids Say No

As parents, speaking from the heart includes establishing rules, setting limits, and giving instruction. It also requires communicating in ways that *help* our children obey those rules, respect those limits, and follow those instructions.

- Do something practical: Make it easy for your child to leave a party where drugs or alcohol are being used. Discuss with her how you will come to pick her up if she feels uncomfortable—for *any* reason. Do not put your child in a position of dependency on other kids for transportation.

- Encourage sound decision making and good choices. Reinforce your child's positive choices. Tell her that you're proud that she chose to go out for the school band or get on the swim team. Build her confidence in decision making. Help her make difficult decisions. Talk about how to weigh the pros and cons of a given decision.

● Try role playing: "You're going over to Dave's after school. Dave digs a beer out of his parents' refrigerator. Kids don't drink alcohol in our family, right? What do you say to Dave?"

Listen to your child's response. Play Dave: "Oh, come on. Your folks will never know!"

If your child can't come up with effective responses, suggest some: "No, thanks. I don't drink. I want to stay in shape for the swim team." Or: "No, I don't want any beer. Let's play Nintendo instead."

In general, communicate in ways that build your child's self-esteem. Kids who feel good about themselves are much less likely to abuse drugs and alcohol than kids with low self-esteem, who feel the need for illegal substances to make them feel good.

● Take every opportunity to offer lavish praise for jobs and chores that are well done.

● Spend "quality time" with your child. Listen to him.

● Give your child chores and assignments that he can do and do well. Praise him when he does them.

● When you need to criticize your child, focus on actions and issues, not on the child. Looking over your kid's math homework, you find a lot of mistakes in addition. Instead of saying what you may be feeling—"You've got to stop being so lazy about your homework!"—focus on the *immediate* issue: "There are a number of mistakes in addition here. Check your work and try again."

What to Watch Out For

Be alert to your child, your child's world, her friends, and her activities. Be especially alert for the following indicators of drug use or alcohol abuse:

- Mood changes, especially irritability, secretiveness, sudden withdrawal, inappropriate outbursts of anger, euphoria

- Irresponsible behavior, including lateness coming home or getting to class

- Lying

- A significant change in friends or lifestyle

- Unexplained influx of cash

- Physical changes, especially difficulty in concentration, loss of coordination, unexplained weight loss, unhealthy appearance

- Decline in grades, loss of interest in school or extracurricular activities

Sidestepping the Pitfalls

This is an area of parenting and communication in which the stakes are the highest imaginable. It is natural to feel uneasy over talking to your children about drugs. What if you make a mistake? What if you say the wrong thing?

The *real* danger lies in saying nothing—saying nothing, and failing to listen to what your kids say. For the truth is that almost *any* communication about drugs and alcohol is better than none. Nevertheless, try to avoid the following:

- Preaching and lecturing. Drug and alcohol conversations should be *conversations*, not parental rants.

- Failing to listen.

- Delivering "The Speech," then turning away. Remember: Speaking from the heart about drugs and alcohol abuse is a continual process. Make it your business to devote at least a half an hour each month to the topic.

- Failing to set the desired example. Words are only one vehicle by which we communicate to our children. Our actions also convey a message—the most powerful of all. If you use illegal drugs or abuse alcohol, you can expect your child to do likewise.

25 Words and Phrases to Use

addiction

alternatives

choice

confidence

crime

criminals

danger

decision

facts

harm

health

help

hurt

information

love

love you

no

prison

rely on you

sickness

success

talk to me

think

trust

want you to be happy and
    healthy

15 Words and Phrases to Avoid

ashamed of you

can't help you

disappoint me

disown you

don't bother me

don't come to me about it

fail

I don't want to know about it

I'll talk, you listen

ignorant

it's your business

lazy

must

shame

worst thing you can do

17

Manners

$\mathcal{M}$anners are a gift. They are a gift you give your children, and, when your children possess good manners, they are a gift they give to you. For the child, good manners open many doors:

- Manners are as important to getting along in a civilized world as motor oil is to the functioning of your car. Manners aren't the fuel that drives society, but they are the lubricant that keeps it from breaking down on a daily basis.

- Good manners are essential to coping day to day.

- Good manners give the child confidence that he can get along in the world.

- Good manners help the child get what she wants. Ask an adult for something *politely*, and you're far more likely to get it than if you shouted, whined, and demanded.

For the parent—and other adults—good manners in children come as a delightful surprise.

- They make our lives easier on a day-to-day basis.

- They contribute to our serenity.

- They give us confidence in our children. Children who know how to ask for things and how to behave in the world are far less help-less and vulnerable than children who are ill at ease and bewil-dered.

- Good manners in our children reflect well on us. They show that we care about our kids—and about the rest of the world.

Talking to your child about manners is saying it from the heart, because manners are not just the superficial trappings of behavior. Nor—despite what many people think—are they designed to hide our true feelings. They are positive expressions of how we feel about ourselves and others. Help your child learn such positive expressions, and she will be happier, you will be happier, and the circle of adults and other children around her will be happier.

Finding the Heartline

Manners are taught. In large part, they are taught through clear explanation. In even larger part, however, they are taught through modeling—through your own example. This makes the acquisition of manners a long-term project.

- Act as you would like your child to act. Explain your actions.

- Treat your children as courteously as you would like them to treat you and others.

- Introduce new habits gradually and at the appropriate time. Dinnertime is the right time to introduce table manners.

- Explain in a loving voice. Don't bark out instructions.

- Praise your child's demonstration of good manners. When your child finally starts saying "please," praise her: "Thank you for saying 'please.' It makes me feel good to hear that word."

- Talk about how certain behavior makes you feel. Rude behavior is painful, whereas courteous behavior produces pleasing feelings.

- Be consistent. If, for example, you want your child to ask for things politely, always remind him to say please. Don't let it slide with certain groups, only to demand it with others.

- Prompt—courteously—the behavior you want. "Please remember to hold the door for mommy. Thank you."

Sidestepping the Pitfalls

Teaching manners should be a gentle process. Too often, however, it is strident and filled with stern threats and name calling. In short, it exhibts anything but good manners. *Request good manners.* Don't demand them. Provide instruction so that your request can be met.

You will also find it difficult to teach the behavior you want if you do not model such behavior yourself. If you shout, make imperious demands, and use foul language, these are the modes of behavior your child will learn—your verbal instructions to the contrary notwithstanding. Actions always speak louder than words.

Remember that teaching manners is a long-term process, which should span much of childhood. Don't expect overnight miracles. Do look for small, incremental victories and modest successes. Reward these with praise.

Meeting People

Even very young children—preschoolers—can and should be instructed in the basics of what to do when they are introduced to adults. Most basic of all is teaching the child to acknowledge others.

- With very young children, it is enough to remind them to say hello or hi. The idea is for the child to acknowledge the other person verbally.

- Ask older children to attach a name to the "hello": "Hello, Mrs. Smith."

- Teach older children to introduce others: "John, when we meet one of your friends, tell me his name—like this, 'Mom, this is Gary.'"

- Conversely, teach older children to introduce you to their friends: "Dad, this is Ben. Ben, this is my dad." If you like, you may ask your child to do it this way: "Ben, this is my dad, Mr. Roberts."

Early on, children should be made aware of the nonverbal as well as the verbal components of meeting people. From an early age, encourage your child to look the other person in the eye. This is a habit that serves lifelong. Looking another person in the eye communicates warmth, sincerity, and trustworthiness. Also from an early age, teach the child the mutual pleasure of a firm (but not crushing) handshake.

At the Table

Here is the venue in which manners are most critically on display. A surprising number of families can hardly bear to eat together because of fidgeting children, impatience, and short tempers. Before you begin to instruct your child in good table manners, take steps to ensure that the family dining table is an enjoyable place:

- Tell your children how much you enjoy and value their company at dinner.

- Make dining pleasant by encouraging interesting discussions, swapping news about family members' experiences during the day, and absolutely avoiding any heavy discussions, debates, or criticism.

- Focus on the present activity. Don't betray impatience. Don't convey the impression that you'd rather be somewhere else or doing something else—such as watching TV.

The family dining experience should be a daily haven.

Having done what you can to create a pleasant, positive dinner-time climate, begin with the basics, which even young children can understand:

- Explain to children that they are to sit during meals and remain seated. This single rule will make dining more pleasant for everyone. Enforce it not with threats and punishment, but with natural consequences: "Billy, if you leave the table, you will not be permitted to return—which means that you'll miss dessert tonight."

- Most people consider it important to refrain from eating until all have been served; therefore, this is a good habit to instill in your child. With very young children, such restraint may be difficult to enforce. You might have fruit or raw vegetables available on the table for children to nibble on before the main meal is served.

- Another hallmark of good table manners is chewing with the mouth closed. The only way to instill this habit is by repeated, gentle reminders. Watch your tone of voice. Keep it kind, soft, and gentle. But be consistent and persistent.

- Related to chewing with the mouth closed is refraining from talking with the mouth full. This is a habit that must be modeled by the adults in the house, and that may be difficult for many of us. As with chewing with the mouth closed, gentle and repeated reminders are effective. Add an element of cause and effect: "Chew and swallow before you speak, sweetie. I can't understand what you're saying."

- Utensil manners require a good bit of parental judgment. Small children have to learn how to use utensils, and that takes practice. In the meantime, fingers help. When you think the child is ready, gently encourage the use of the appropriate utensil: "Why don't you try using your fork on that piece, the way Daddy does?" Gradually, patiently initiate the child into the world of adult table manners. When he uses a utensil, praise him, emphasizing how grown up he is acting: "You handled that just like a grown-up!"

- Most adults have a short fuse when it comes to "playing with food." Play is a natural and healthy part of childhood, of course, but you do want to communicate that there is a time and a place to play and a time and a place to get down to business. Don't lash out at the child, but do quietly ask him not to play with the food. If you discover that the child has a favorite food for playing with, try omitting that from the table next time. Explain: "Cathy, you'll notice there are no carrot sticks tonight. If you'd like them back on the table, you'll have to promise to stop using them as swords."

- Thank the chef. Model this behavior by praising and thanking the cook. "Sam, you made marvelous fried chicken tonight. I really enjoyed it. Thanks!" Then prompt the child: "Did you like the chicken, Eddie?" If the answer is yes, suggest that Eddie thank mom or dad for preparing it. "Everyone feels good when they're thanked. It's nice to make other people feel good."

- Discourage expressions of disgust. Present a child with broccoli, and you may get a simple "Yuck!" or an elaborate improvisation on the sounds of gagging, retching, and puking. Don't laugh. This reinforces the behavior. Don't scold. Instead, instill a quiet take-it-or-leave-it attitude: "Tom, you don't have to eat that if you don't like it, but I don't want to hear those noises."

• Use your napkin, not your clothing. When the child sits, instruct her to put the napkin on her lap. "That way, it catches any food you might drop, and it's always ready when you need it. If your fingers feel sticky, just wipe them on the napkin. Don't wipe them on anything else." You can also, at intervals, prompt the child to wipe his mouth: "John, dear, wipe your mouth with your napkin."

• Ask to be excused. In our culture, dining is a highly social event. It is very rude and disturbing to get up suddenly from the table and leave. Make it a rule that the child must ask before getting up from the table. Teach her the magic words: "May I please be excused?" To reinforce this behavior, grant the request. You want the child to learn that asking permission in this case almost always produces the desired response. If you feel that the request is premature, explain: "Honey, we haven't had dessert yet." If the child stays at the table, fine. If she is insistent—"But I don't want any more"—give her permission to leave, but add: "Okay. But dinner is over for you. You can't come back to the table."

• When you feel that your child is old enough to carry his plate and utensils from the table to the sink or counter, instruct him to clear his place at the end of dinner. Be sure that the adults and older children model this behavior. "Pete, please clear your place. Carry your plate and utensils to the sink. It's a big help to me."

As your child gets older, you can work on refining her table manners. Approach this task as a favor you do for your child. It will help her get along with others and, ultimately, increase popularity.

Speaking Manners

Today's parents may sometimes long for the days in which the common wisdom was "children should be seen and not heard"; however, few parents seriously believe this really is a good approach to child rearing. They understand that children should be encouraged to use words, to express themselves, and to develop sophisticated communication skills. Therefore, any rules you make concerning talking should be made in a context that, above all, encourages communication and expression. You do not want to bully your child into silence.

Early on, you can begin to instill an awareness of the basic rhythm of conversation. Don't interrupt. Wait for the other person to finish before speaking. This is not so difficult a habit to instill as you may think. Children rapidly become accustomed to the idea of taking turns. This concept becomes a cornerstone of their perception of fairness. "Everyone gets their turn. Please wait for your sister to finish speaking before you say what you want to say."

Don't be foolishly rigid. Of course, there are times when interruption is necessary. Talk to your child about when this may be appropriate—somebody is at the door, say, or the bathtub is about to overflow—and give him the magic formula for interrupting: "Excuse me."

Instill the habit of "please" and "thank you." This is also easier than it sounds, especially if you model the behavior. Explain that these words make people feel good.

Preschoolers begin to appreciate the power of words, especially when they see the impact of certain "bathroom words." The most effective way to curb the use of objectionable words is to avoid reacting emotionally to them. Don't get angry. Don't act surprised. Above all, don't laugh. If the language persists, consider this action: "Sheila, those are bathroom words. Please go to the bathroom to use those words."

Older children can be taught greater sophistication of speech. Rules you might consider include:

- No whispering. People don't like to feel they're being talked about behind their backs.

- Respond when spoken to. Explain the pain you cause by ignoring people. Make it clear that you don't always have to have the right answer to a question, but you should at least acknowledge the question. Q: "Do you know what time it is?" A: "No, I'm sorry. I left my watch at home."

- Don't be a smart mouth. When your child responds sarcastically, try to restrain your own urge to lash out in return. Instead, *without emotion*, point out that "nobody likes a smart aleck."

25 Words and Phrases to Use

acknowledge	get what you want
apologize	hurtful
attitude	may I
best way	May I be excused?
better way	nice
communicate	pleasant
courtesy	please
delightful	pleasure
don't like	polite
enjoy	shake hands
eye contact	sorry
feel good	thank you
fun	

15 Words and Phrases to Avoid

ashamed of yourself	little monster
bad boy/girl	nasty
be quiet	people won't like you
brat	punishment
disgraceful	shut your mouth
Do as I say, not as I do.	shut up
go away	Who cares?
keep your mouth closed	

18

Sex

$\mathcal{I}$t would be hard to find a parent who'll tell you that the "Big Talk"—birds and bees, the facts of life, sex—isn't important. It's even harder to find a parent who will tell you that the Big Talk is easy. In fact, it's so difficult that most parents put it off or hand the child a book ("Here, read this."). Some parents simply avoid the topic altogether. If you are one of these parents, you're hardly in the minority.

- Most of us are more or less inhibited when it comes to talking with our children about sex.

- We lack a clear idea of what we should say.

- We aren't really sure how we ourselves feel about sex and about how we would like our children to feel about it.

The first problem can be dealt with straightforwardly: Just accept the fact that you may feel somewhat embarrassed about the subject. Parents make a great many sacrifices and endure any number of uncomfortable situations for the sake of their children. If the subject of sex makes you uncomfortable, well, just chalk it up to one more trial of parenthood.

The second two problems require more work to solve.

It is beyond the scope of this book to tell you how you should feel about sex and how you should guide your children toward feeling about sex. Arguably, it is beyond the scope of any book to attempt these things. What this book *can* do, however, is tell you that effective communication requires, first and foremost, knowing what you want to say. Based on this, you can create a plan for saying it. Saying it from the heart requires knowing what is in your heart.

207

Step one, the step you take before you speak with your child, is to explore your own feelings and beliefs about sex, and how these relate to what you would like for your child. Without going into detail that may be either impertinent or irrelevant to your particular cultural, spiritual, and personal attitude, suffice it to say that you will probably want to focus your thought and planning on the objective of conveying sex in a way that is positive, exciting, joyful, and inextricably linked to family, to commitment, and to love. Along with this sense of the power and joy of sex, you will want to provide information and guidance that will enhance the child's capacity to protect himself from the physical as well as emotional dangers of sex.

Finding the Heartline

First, then, decide how you feel and what you would *like* to convey. If you cannot decide, you may wish to speak with your child's pediatrician or you may wish to consult any of a vast number of books either devoted to the subject or containing chapters on the subject. This, however, is a bewildering array. Worth seeking out is Linda and Richard Eyre's *How to Talk to Your Child about Sex* (Golden Books, 1998). If you have a close relationship with a clergyman or clergywoman, you may wish to talk to him or her. Your own parents are yet another possible source. Ultimately, you will have to make your own decisions about what to say, but don't be hesitant about looking for guidance.

Once you feel prepared to speak, you need to consider the matter of timing. When is the right time to talk to a child about sex? How old should he or she be? How much can he or she understand? Can you tell too much?

Many experts believe that children are ready to talk about sex by about eight years old—certainly between the ages of eight and twelve. In this age range, the focus of the talk is on *knowing*. Beyond this age range, the focus begins to shift to behavior, from *knowing* to *doing*.

Probably the best idea of all is to make talk about sexually related matters a part of regular communication with a child, even before he is eight. This does *not* mean getting down to the nitty gritty of sex and sexuality, but, rather, talking about such issues as the following:

- The body
- "Modesty"—based on respect
- Family commitment
- Loyalty and friendship
- Love

Talking about such issues with your child from an early age—say three or four—creates a context of positive, loving understanding that makes talking later more specifically about sex that much easier and more effective.

Getting Into It

When you decide the time is right for a talk more specifically focused on sexuality, the most natural approach is the time-honored discussion of where babies come from. You might begin the discussion by asking your child a question:

> Where do you think babies come from?

Answers vary. Often, the response is "from the hospital." In this case, ask another question:

> True, but how do they get there?

This may be met with bewilderment or such answers as "a little seed," "from God," or even "from mommy's tummy."

At some point, you may be tempted just to start a lecture. Instead, consider asking more questions. Don't do so in the manner of a school marm or a police interrogator. Put some joy and excitement into your voice. Make these sound like questions about things that really fascinate you. This should not come across to your child sounding like a test.

> Mommy's tummy? Wow! Good answer. But how did that little baby get in there?

It is likely that the child's responses will become much more vague at this point. Let them become vague. As they do, let go of the subject and shift the focus:

Who should have babies? What kind of parents should have babies?

Steer the response to something like this: *People who like kids and who like taking care of kids. People who love children.* The idea is to put the physical explanation of procreation on hold while you introduce the more familiar concept of love. Go ahead and discuss love and caring. After you've discussed this subject for a time, ask your child how people show one another love. Responses will probably include doing nice things for each other, buying presents, doing favors. Perhaps the child will also talk about hugging and kissing. Great! If not, prompt her:

How do people show love with their bodies? What do you do with your arms and lips?

Then open your arms so that you and your child can hug. Now continue the discussion:

Do you know what? There is a bigger kind of hug that a husband and wife do. This kind of hug feels wonderful, and it is the kind of hug that starts a baby growing inside the mom.

From this point, you need to decide how much detail you want to explore. In large part, take your cue from your child's curiosity. This is a good time to share an age-appropriate illustrated book with your child. Don't just offer the book to read on his or her own. Go through it with the child. Some good books for children aged about eight include the following:

* Peter Mayle, *Where Did I Come From?*
* Sheila Kutzinger, *Being Born*
* Lennart Nilsson and Lena Swanberg, *How Was I Born?*

Following Up

Depending on the age and interest of the child, the follow-up discussion of sex may be part of a first "real" talk about the "facts of life" or you may discuss the following matters as and when you feel they are necessary.

One thing you should do as you discuss sex with your child is touch base with her to assess what she's already heard. You can ask,

"What have you heard about sex?" Then listen. Don't concentrate on correcting particular misconceptions, but do put yourself in the fore-front of information providers about sexual matters:

> A lot of kids don't learn much about sex from their parents. They talk to their friends or they hear stuff on TV. They joke about it. That's because they don't know the whole story. After the talk we just had, you probably know more about sex than most of your friends. But if you want to know more—or if you hear something that you don't understand or that interests you or that bothers you—come to me. Okay?

An effective way to get into a follow-up discussion about sex, after you've had the basic discussion about the "special hug," is to ask your child another question:

> How old do you think a person has to be to have sex?

Listen to the response, then explain what puberty is: "a time when people's bodies get ready to have babies."

> It is a time when girls start to become women and boys start to become men. You know, a fourteen- or fifteen-year-old boy and girl might be old enough to make a baby. Did you know that? Just because they can make a baby, should they?

Most likely, the response from your child will be no. Ask why not, and the reply will probably be remarkably sensible:

> They are too young to take care of the baby. Too young to be a good mom and dad.

Reinforce such a response:

> That's right! You have to be all grown up before you can really take care of a baby. But, before you're grown up, you're going to hear a lot about sex and even about having babies. A lot of what you hear is going to be pretty strange and confusing and mixed up. Remember, not everybody's parents talk to their kids about what we've been talking about. When you're confused, come to me or Mom.

"Dirty" Talk

The June 15, 1998 issue of *Time* magazine reported the results of a poll in which 7 percent of children said they learn about sex mostly from their parents. The remainder—93 percent—said they get their information from the media and from other kids. Perhaps the greatest gulf that separates what that 7 percent hears from what that 93 percent hears is language, the words associated with sex and the sex act. Parents can't ignore the "dirty words" floating around out there. Most of us don't want our children using such language, of course. It is rude, and it reflects badly on your child and you. But the fallout from dirty talk is even more serious, because it confuses the child, not just intellectually, but emotionally. At some point, talking to your kid about sex should probably address "dirty" talk:

> Remember when we talked about the "special hug" between a husband and wife? People have made up a lot of names for it. My favorite is "making love," because that's really what it is all about: love, loving each other. Some people just call it "having sex." But I've heard a lot of other words for it, some of them stupid and silly and some pretty nasty. Do you know what I mean?

Your child may reply that he does, and he may come up with a number of words you didn't dream he had learned. If he doesn't, prompt him.

> Well, there's "screwing," and there's the "f" word—a word so unpleasant that we just call it the "f" word, because we don't like to repeat it. Can I tell you something? People who like to use these words probably don't know much about "making love." They think the words make them sound grown up. But they're just faking it. People who use these words don't know as much as you do. I bet their parents haven't talked to them the way I've talked with you.
>
> So, anyway, don't let these nasty words bother you. People who use them aren't really thinking about what the words mean. Or maybe they don't even know what they mean.

Responsibility

Talking about "dirty words" can be a good lead-in to the subject of responsibility. When you are ready for this discussion, point out that "making love" or "having sex" doesn't always produce a baby, but it always should show how much a man and woman love each other.

> When they are old enough, people make love to show that they are committed to each other, that they really care about each other, and that they will be loyal to each other. We've talked about some nasty words, well, what about some really great words? What do you think "committed" means? What does it mean to "care about" another person? What do we mean by being "loyal"?

A discussion focused on key words can be the solid foundation of valuable talks about responsibility and self-control.

> Making love should be special, something that adults can do when they feel loyal and committed and loving to one another. People who have sex with just anyone—without feeling loyalty or love or commitment—spoil the great feelings that go along with making love.
>
> And there are other important reasons why people shouldn't just go around having sex with just anybody. You've heard a lot about HIV, right? AIDS? . . .

At this point, you can explain whatever you feel is appropriate about AIDS and other sexually transmitted diseases. Don't frighten your child, however. Emphasize that people can learn to protect themselves from diseases, especially if they keep sex special, something shared between two people who love each other and who feel loyalty toward one another and who are caring about one another.

Talking Puberty

The discussions we've just outlined are intended to take place between parents and preadolescent children. With the onset of puberty, the discussion becomes both more objective and more personal. It becomes more objective because your responsibility as a parent is to share more information—facts—with your child. It becomes more personal, because you now must reinforce whatever values you and your family decides to uphold.

The facts can be acquired from books; the values are drawn from your own experience, upbringing, spiritual background, feelings, and beliefs.

Facts that you will probably want to cover for children just entering puberty (approximately ages nine to twelve) include:

- what "puberty" is
- body changes
- new feelings
- acne
- menstruation
- wet dreams
- masturbation

As puberty progresses, you will also want to cover some harder topics. These might include:

- abortion
- rape
- abuse
- prostitution
- homosexuality
- sexually transmitted diseases
- pornography

Part of your discussion of topics such as these needs to be purely factual and unemotional. The discussion will lead into issues that grow out of your own system of belief and morality. This is as it should be. The important thing to remember is to provide reliable information without an edge of threat, panic, or hysteria.

Where to From Here?

What we have presented here is a starting point for discussing sexuality with your child in an informative as well as loving way. Where you take the discussion from here depends on many things, including:

- Your child's needs
- Your child's questions
- Your own beliefs and values

It is also a good idea to become thoroughly familiar with any sex education curriculum your child's school offers. Programs vary widely. If you are fortunate, your school will have a sensitive program that dovetails well with your own beliefs and values. If you are less lucky, you may find the school's program poor or even objectionable. Just what you discuss with your child may well be influenced by material learned in school.

Sidestepping the Pitfalls

Most of us find it difficult to talk to our children about sex. Even if we aren't embarrassed by the subject, we fear that we'll say the wrong things. These feelings and fears are normal.

To avoid saying the wrong things, take the time and effort to get your facts straight. Then take additional time and effort to decide what values you want to impart to your children. Sexual behavior, after all, like other aspects of behavior, is in large part an expression of the values we hold. Those values are ours to give our children.

The deepest and most dangerous pitfall is also the most common. It is the mistake of never speaking to your child about sex. No one avoids sex. (Even a choice to remain celibate is a sexual choice, a choice made in response to sex.) And the world around us does not lack for models of sexual behavior. Do we, as parents, want our children to choose whatever model is presented most appealingly on TV or in films, or by a friend, a boyfriend, or a girlfriend? Or do *we* want to guide our children? Absent parental communication about sex, we relinquish our children to whatever models of behavior happen along at the "right" time and place.

About Words to Use and Words to Avoid

Most of the chapters in this book conclude with a list of words and phrases to use and words and phrases to avoid in saying it from the heart. Talking to your kids about sex is not a topic that lends itself to such word lists. Instead, here are some rules of thumb for finding language appropriate to this subject:

- *Use the real words.* It is best—least confusing—to call things by their real names. A penis is a penis, a vagina a vagina. However, for young children, you may have family or "private" names for sex organs. If so, there is no reason to reject these, but you might point out that the "grown-up name for pee-pee is penis."

- *Don't use vulgar terms or four-letter words.* If your child asks you about one of these terms, do *not* punish, criticize, or admonish him! Instead, reply with gratitude: "Tim, I'm glad you asked me about that word. It's not a word we use in this family, because it is a word used by people who don't think about what it means. It's not a word most people like to hear."

- *Avoid hushed tones.* Speak about sexuality in a normal, open voice.

- *Be prepared to define terms.* Pause frequently to ask your child if she understands what you are saying. If not, be sure to avoid any hint of frustration on your part. Talking about new things takes patience.

Approach your conversations with your child not as a difficult duty, but as a pleasure and a joy. *This is an opportunity to teach and to share.*

Part 4

The Languages of Love

*H*eartfelt and crystal clear communication builds, enhances, and preserves romance and relationships with those we love.

19

Getting Acquainted

*W*ho isn't interested in love? Grounded in the species' drive to survive, love also rises to spiritual heights that tower far above basic biology. Love is the engine that drives much of what we do, it is the focus of much music, art, and literature, and most movies. It surrounds us. A universal presence, it is free to all. Love, and all that leads up to it, is the most natural thing in the world—thoughtlessly easy.

Not!

For many of us, love, with all its pleasures and urgencies, is complicated, frustrating, even bewildering. It should be as effortless as breathing, but, instead, when it arrives, it hits most of us like a crisis— a crisis we crave, but a crisis nonetheless.

Whatever else we feel and excitedly anticipate when we meet what the cheesy greeting cards call "that special someone," we are, most of us, also profoundly puzzled:

- What should I say?
- How should I say what I should say?
- When should I say what I should say?

However positive we feel at the moment, somewhere at the back of our minds are worries about saying the wrong things, things that will hurt us, hurt the other person, and blast the budding relationship.

Turn to a friend to ask advice about these feelings and fears, and, most likely, the reply will be something like "Oh, don't be silly!" Or: "Don't worry about it!" Or: "Just let nature take its course."

Well-meaning though such responses may be, helpful they are not. They are non-responses. They are evasions. And what they evade is not a set of imaginary problems, but very realistic concerns that are central to the commencement and continuance of any loving relationship. Look at those questions again:

- What should I say?
- How should I say what I should say?
- When should I say what I should say?

What they have in common is the word *say*. It is no coincidence that these three central questions concern communication.

In matters of love, communication is central. In matters of love, communication is driven by the heart, but it is guided by the head. Don't yield to your friends' well-meaning advice to "let nature take its course" or to just "act naturally." All this really means is that you should stop thinking. Now, when you have found what just may be "that special someone," is definitely *not* the time to stop thinking, to abandon will, to just give up and drift. This occasion, this moment of contact is too important. Effective communication at this point in your life can mean the difference between—

- Getting together or not getting together
- A love that grows or love that never has a chance
- A satisfying, enriching relationship or a disappointing one
- A relationship built on and enhanced by shared feelings and values or one that is hollow and incomplete

Any successfully married couple will tell you, whether after a year or after fifty years, marriage is about communication. So is the failure of marriage. Or, rather, it is about the failure of communication. Often, that failure is a gradual process, but it generally begins with the very first encounter. Fail to communicate successfully early on, and the relationship may simply end—or it may go on, failing a little more with each passing day and month and year. Launch the relationship with a full, positive communication from the heart, and the chances for a fulfilling experience, perhaps of lifelong duration, are increased exponentially.

Finding the Heartline

In love, as in every other important aspect of our lives, communication consists of two elements:

* Speaking

* Listening

The first element, speaking, is built on the second, listening. Where love is concerned, finding the heartline depends on careful, sensitive listening, which allows you to respond in a meaningful way. How you listen determines what you say, but you, of course, shape your speech. For now, the one rule you need to know about speaking to someone you love—or feel you may love—is to shape that speech in positive terms. Find positive, affirmative things to say. For example, a man or woman who interests you says, "It's a beautiful day!" Your choice of replies is broad:

* Yes, it is.

* I love days like this.

* I love days like this, with the air so crisp and clear.

* I love days like this, with the air so crisp and clear. They make me want to get up and *do* something.

* A bit cold, if you ask me.

* I prefer it warmer.

* Well, it's fall. The beautiful summer will soon be over, and the lousy winter is just around the corner.

* Do you really think so?

* Actually, I like rainy, gloomy weather.

* It won't last.

All of these responses are triggered by listening. The first four are positive. The others are, in varying degrees, negative. Put yourself in the place of the person who remarked, "It's a beautiful day!" How is he or she likely to think about each of these responses?

- *Yes, it is.* (Pretty noncommital. Perhaps I should say something else.)

- *I love days like this.* (Wow! We seem to be on the same wavelength!)

- *I love days like this, with the air so crisp and clear.* (Great! This is someone who feels the way I do!)

- *I love days like this, with the air so crisp and clear. They make me want to get up and do something.* (Well, well! I guess I should suggest that we go out and do something!)

- *A bit cold, if you ask me.* (Oh. To each his own, I guess.)

- *I prefer it warmer.* (Mmm. A fussy one.)

- *Well, it's fall. The beautiful summer will soon be over, and the lousy winter is just around the corner.* (I don't like pessimists.)

- *Do you really think so?* (I'd better be careful what I say around him/her.)

- *Actually, I like rainy, gloomy weather.* (That's kind of creepy. She/he probably thinks that's sophisticated.)

- *It won't last.* (Why not just shoot yourself now and get it over with?)

The point is this: Most of us respond positively to positive communication. Positive language launches things. Negative language stops things.

Sidestepping the Pitfalls

Okay, so you are already acquainted with one major pitfall in the language of love: negativity. How do you avoid it? Focus on the positive as much as possible.

In just a moment, we'll go on to talk more about listening. The other major pitfalls in communicating with someone you want to get to know all involve problems with listening.

· This is the principal pitfall: *You hear, but you do not listen.* It is a pitfall that comes in several varieties:

- You don't give the other person a chance to be heard. Perhaps you monopolize the conversation, delivering a monologue instead of engaging in a dialogue. Or perhaps you rush through the conversation, without inviting meaningful reply: "You like fall days? Great! So do I. Gotta go now!"

- You draw conclusions and make assumptions—without really listening. You attribute motives or feelings or attitudes to the other person that he or she may not have. She was fifteen minutes late meeting you. "I don't care what her excuse is, she just doesn't care enough about me to be on time."

- You read between the lines. The other person says, "I like American automobiles." You conclude that what he is *really* saying is that he doesn't plan to spend a lot of money on this date, because he's telling you he can't afford an expensive import.

- You are quick to come to negative conclusions. She was fifteen minutes late meeting you. "Well, she's a person who just can't get it together. Obviously totally disorganized."

- You play amateur shrink. She was fifteen minutes late meeting you. "She's afraid of men and subconsciously wants to avoid them."

Communicating with Your Ears

The really serious pitfalls in communicating interest in another person can all be avoided by careful, sensitive listening. Eloquence depends less on a good set of vocal cords than on a good pair of ears—with plenty in between them.

Effective listening is *not* a passive process. You have to work at it.

- You have to focus on the other person, on what he/she needs, feels, wants.

- You have to set as your goal understanding what the other person is saying.

- You have to suspend your own opinions, interpretations, and judgments while the other person is speaking. On a temporary basis, you need to become selfless.

- You have to stop thinking about what you're going to say.

- You have to stop thinking about your own opinions.

- You have to resist being overtaken by anger or other negative emotions, even if you don't like what you are hearing.

- You have to resist preparing a rebuttal while listening.

- You have to get rid of the attitude of waiting for the other person to stop talking so that you can say what you want to say.

Most of these objectives are accomplished internally, inside your mind. They are a form of *self*-discipline. However, you can aid the process of active listening by deliberately reflecting what the other person says.

- From time to time as you listen, pause, and repeat to the person the nub or essence of what he or she has said.

- A good time to pause and reflect is when you have heard just about all you can remember.

- Don't elaborate or "correct" what the other person has said. Distill, paraphrase what was said.

- Confirm your understanding. After reflecting what the other person has said, ask: "Do I understand you?" If the answer is yes, great! You *have* understood. What is more, you have demonstrated to the other person that you are indeed focused on him or her. If the answer is no, then ask the other person to repeat what he or she has said.

Active listening can serve as the foundation of a strong relationship right from the very first encounter, and it can continue to serve the relationship lifelong.

Making the Connection

We've begun by talking about the foundation of effective communication so that you'll be ready to get a potential relationship started in the best way possible. But before you can get a relationship started, you have to meet someone who interests you—and you need to make a connection. You don't have to become a denizen of singles bars or take out an ad in the local newspaper's personals pages to meet others. Take a look at the opportunities that abound around you—and make the most of them.

ON THE JOB

Most people meet girlfriends, boyfriends, and future spouses at work or in the context of work. This is not an astounding revelation. Let's say you work an 8-hour day (probably even longer!). That is one-third of your day. Another third is occupied in sleep. So the time you spend at work, at least five days out of the week, represents at least half the time you have available for meeting people. You can enhance the opportunities for such meetings by considering any of the following:

- Join volunteer or service groups that may be sponsored or organized by your firm.
- Make small talk in the hall, in the elevator, at the water cooler, at the fax machine.
- Ask people out to lunch.
- Participate in any after-work social activities that appeal to you.
- Attend office parties.
- Attend industry or trade functions.
- Carpool.

AROUND THE HOUSE

A well-worn song from the 1930s tells us:

> You'll find your happiness lies
> Right under your eyes,
> Back in your own backyard.

Make yourself visible and accessible around the neighborhood:

- Read a book on your front porch.
- If your apartment complex has a pool, use it.
- Do yard work and talk to folks.
- Wash your car and talk to folks.
- Throw a party. Invite singles, or ask couples to bring single people along with them.

AROUND TOWN

Running errands and going shopping are fine activities for meeting people.

- Ask for advice on a purchase.
- Offer advice on a purchase.
- Hang out in the local bookstore café.
- Frequent coffee bars and the like.
- In line—at the bank, at the cleaners, at the motor vehicle bureau, wherever—strike up a conversation.

RECREATIONAL ACTIVITIES

Consider some of the following:

- Join a health/fitness club.
- Join a bowling league.
- Take dance classes.
- Go to concerts, sporting events, theatrical performances.
- Go to pleasant city parks.

OTHER ACTIVITIES

Expand your horizons and your opportunities by considering some of the following:

- Take adult education classes or craft classes.
- Join a worthwhile, stimulating organization, such as the Sierra Club, Habitat for Humanity, or a political organization. Get involved in community work.
- Volunteer to support a political candidate.
- Join a church, mosque, or synagogue.

SINGLES-FOCUSED ACTIVITIES

Selectively choose from among the wealth of singles-focused activities available in many places, especially in larger towns and cities. For example:

- Singles tours or cruises

- Music clubs

- Religious, social, and charity events oriented toward singles

Of course, it is one thing to put yourself out there and yet another to spark conversation. You may have to devote some conscious effort to opening yourself up to the possibilities of conversation with a stranger:

- *Smile.* A smile invites response. All other facial expressions discourage response.

- *Slow down.* Allow yourself time to meet others.

- *Look up and look around.* Take in the people around you.

- *Expect contact.* Be optimistic. Most people do not live out their lives in solitary confinement. There is a natural urge to meet others, to get together, and even to fall in love.

Remember this: You're not in it alone. Not only do others want to meet you, but you have friends and acquaintances who can help you expand your network of potential mates. If you are looking for a man or woman to date, tell your friends. Talk about it. People love bringing other people together.

The Inertia of Fear

Okay. Let's say you are aware—or become aware—of the many possibilities out there for making contact. What do you do now?

Nothing.

Why nothing?

You are afraid.

In some situations, such as finding yourself in a burning building, fear prompts you to run for your life. This is healthy self-preservation. In such instances, fear is a most valuable emotion. In other cases, however, fear merely creates inaction. You don't run away from the person who catches your eye, but you don't approach him or her, either.

What are you afraid of?

The catalogue of things to fear is endless, but, for most of us, the overriding fear, the one that creates the strongest inertia, is fear of rejection.

This is a book about communication, not a hefty tome on psychology. For you, there may be no quick fix for fear of rejection. Maybe it's something you need to work on long term. On the other hand, perhaps there *is* a quick fix. Consider the following propositions:

- Fear of rejection is natural. You don't have a monopoly on it. Fear of rejection, doubtless, is born in infancy, when rejection means death. If our parents fail to care for us, fail to feed us, fail to shelter us, we don't survive. It's a fact of biology. Therefore, we crave nurture, and, at some level of our being, we harbor a fear that this nurture will be denied. In infancy, such fears have a very real basis, but they are irrational—that is, not the product of rational thought. Irrational though they are, these fears become part of the psychological baggage most of us carry into adulthood. Some of us travel light—just a carry-on bag, perhaps—others of us are burdened with lumpy suit bags, bulging suitcases, and massive steamer trunks.

- Since fear of rejection is natural, accept your feelings. Fear of rejection is not a brick wall topped with razor wire. It's a feeling. Accept the feeling and try to work around it.

- Try to adopt an adult perspective. Remember, feelings of rejection are rooted in infancy. You are now an adult. You have much more power now than you had as an infant, a child, or even a teenager.

- Spend some time inventorying your assets. Think about what you have to offer, what makes you attractive. Go ahead, draw up a list.

A major premise of this book is that you can use your feelings and emotions to make communication more effective, to say what you want to say and to say it from the heart. As powerful as this concept is, it does have limits. Although effective communication can greatly enhance any relationship, from the very beginning and throughout life, attraction is by no means 100 percent conscious, deliberate, and rational. That is, while poor communication can torpedo almost any relationship, effective communication does not guarantee a successful relationship. Nor is it a foolproof means of sparking attraction. We are attracted to others for a variety of reasons, including many that are beyond our conscious control. In short, sometimes the flame is there, and sometimes it is not.

‖ Sometimes you feel the flame, but the other person's pilot light is out.

Such instances can be very frustrating, even heartbreaking. You may blame yourself, you may blame the other person, you may blame both, or you may not know who to blame. The fact is that no one's to blame. Do you blame yourself for not having been born with blue eyes? There would be no point to that. Your eye color is a fact of nature. Many factors behind attraction are also rooted in facts of nature—or aspects of upbringing or personal history. They are beyond your control, and beyond that of the other person.

This realization does set a limit to what you can consciously achieve in romance, but it is also liberating. Once you accept that attraction is not always mutual—*and* that nothing you can do will *make* it mutual—you no longer need to drag along so much fear of rejection baggage or fear of failure baggage. You are free to go on to the next potential partner.

Here is another possibility:

‖ Someone may be attracted to you, but is incapable of igniting your flame.

You need feel no guilt. Even if you recognize that this other person is a fine human being, beautiful or handsome, kind, successful, you need not conclude that something is "wrong" with you—even if your well-meaning friends suggest that there is. ("What's wrong with you? Are you crazy? He drives a BMW!")

Openers

Poke around any bookstore or leaf through any number of magazines, and you will find books and articles offering lists of "surefire" opening lines.

If it were only that easy! You could just memorize a few lines and get a good shot at pairing up with whomever you set your sights on.

Why doesn't this approach work in real life?

For one thing, we communicate with a lot more than words. In the next chapter, we'll talk about the importance of body language, especially in the first encounter. But even more important than body language is the fact that what you say is less significant than what is *behind* what you say. Get in touch with your feelings and your positive emotional and intellectual attributes. Get in touch with these and speak from them. They will energize your opening line. Get in touch with or develop:

- A positive attitude
- Warmth
- Interest in others
- A gentle sense of humor
- A sense of general well-being

Get in touch, too, with your life experiences. Be ready to share them.

Okay. Good. Fine. But *what* do you *say* to someone you want to meet and get to know?

It's ridiculously simple, really. Here it is—

Hello, my name is Alice.

There's your opening line. Of course, you'll want to substitute your own name. But simply walking up to someone and simply introducing yourself is the single most powerful thing you can do to express your interest in that other person.

Now, where to from here?

There are two schools of thought on this. Both are based on the very sound assumption that what most interests people is themselves. Therefore, one school of thought teaches that you should ask questions that focus on the other person:

She: Hello, my name is Alice. You are?

He: Ted.

She: Nice to meet you, Ted. Do you come to these conventions every year?

He: No. This is my first one.

She: Is that so! What firm are you with?

And so on. This can generate a conversation. After all, no rhythm of dialogue is more natural than the pattern of question and answer. But this approach can also lead to an early breakdown of the conversation.

- What if the other person doesn't want to answer one of your questions? Where do you go from there?

- What if the other person feels that you are prying?

- What if some of the answers are unpleasant? ("What firm do you work for?" "Oh, I've just been fired . . .")

The second school of thought, still founded on the assumption that people are interested in themselves, makes the questions implicit rather than explicit. Begin by introducing yourself:

She: Hello, my name is Alice.

Then stop. Make eye contact, hold it, and be silent. Silence is one of the most powerful tools of communication. It is both an invitation and a spur. Few people will allow a silence to endure for long. The response you'll get, most likely, is something like this:

He: Hi, Alice. My name is Ted.

You might get even more. The important thing is that Ted is not responding to your explicit question, but to the question your silence implies. This is a much less mechanical and rigid pattern of conversation. It allows for more spontaneity.

You might continue:

She: Very nice to meet you, Ted. Let me tell you something about me. I just *love* this city.

Make it a statement about yourself—nothing deliberately provocative or controversial. And don't ask a question, such as, "I just *love* this city. Don't you?" Instead, stop talking. Let the silence lie there for a time, if necessary. Very soon, you'll get a response—one that involves a piece of personal information:

He: Well, I like it, too. I am a city person, I guess. This place is nice, but I really love New York. That's my home town.

And so on. One statement prompts another, yet neither of you is locked into a question-and-answer format, which is vulnerable to breakdown. Moreover, the conversation you're now having is spontaneous and natural. The result may or may not be the development of mutual attraction. Sometimes this happens immediately, sometimes it develops over time. What *will* develop is a rapport that allows the two of you to feel whatever feelings being together may produce.

The next chapter will explore nonverbal communication in matters of meeting and developing romance, and the chapter after that will delve into the world of dating.

20

The Body Language of Love

$\mathcal{I}$n Chapter 2, we mentioned the results of a 1971 study conducted by the psychologist Albert Mehrabian. He wanted to explore the mechanics of persuasion. What makes one speaker persuasive and another less so? As you may recall, Mehrabian discovered that when listeners judge the emotional content of a speech, they give the most weight to the speaker's facial expressions and body movement—that is, "body language."

How much weight?

55 percent.

That is, substantially more than half the power of a speaker to persuade us depends on visual rather than verbal cues.

You approach another person. Even before you utter a word, you begin to communicate. You begin to communicate powerfully and, for better or worse, persuasively. This is body language.

And there is more.

Even after you begin talking, a parallel communication proceeds in your gestures, your glance, your stance. In truly effective communication, this nonverbal component enhances, emphasizes, underscores, and, if you will, *sells* the verbal component. In less effective communication, the body language does little or nothing to sell the verbal message. In downright ineffective communication, it may actually conflict with and work against the verbal component: "Are you telling me the truth?" the parent asks her misbehaving little boy. "Yes, Mommy, I am," the kid replies—while shaking his head from side to side!

233

The Eyes Have It

Take a piece of paper and make a quick list of what is most important about a person's appearance. Chances are that your list includes some or all of the following:

Height

Body shape

Weight

Fitness

Hairstyle

Fashion sense—clothing, shoes, accessories

General facial features

All of these things are important, but most important of all is the face. That is usually what we look at first, and it is certainly what we focus on most intently. Within the facial focus is an even more intense focus: the eyes.

Through the eyes you send important messages:

- About how you feel

- About your energy level

- About your emotional state—happy, sad, and so on

- About your level of interest in the other person

The single most important nonverbal message you can send is interest, and the most powerful way of sending this is by making eye contact. Some people find this easy and natural, while others must make a self-conscious effort to keep their eyes from drifting aside.

- Eye contact always signals interest.

- Failure to make or maintain eye contact suggests avoidance, lack of interest, or even evasiveness—an absence of trustworthiness and sincerity.

While simply making and maintaining eye contact is a powerful signal, you can speak even more eloquently with your eyes.

- Men convey power by making eye contact with a woman and then holding their gaze longer than what feels like "normal." This may be given added power by slightly narrowing the eyes.

- Women may engage in "flirty" eye contact. They incline the entire head slightly downward, then look up at the other person, using only the eyes—not moving the head.

When you are on the receiving end of eye contact, look for the following signals of interest: Pupils slightly dilated, and eyebrows slightly lifted.

We want to *see* the person to whom we are attracted, so, involuntarily, the pupils dilate and the eyes widen to admit more light. This provides a clearer picture of the other person.

Facing Reality

As to the rest of the face, express interest and openness with gestures such as these:

- Smiling. Nothing is simpler to do, and nothing is more inviting, reassuring, and encouraging.

- Nodding the head.

- Tilting the head slightly to one side from time to time.

- Turning the face toward the other person attentively.

Taking a Stance

It is no accident that we talk about "taking a stand" on some issue or asking a politician about "her stance on" such and such a topic. This metaphor embodies the intuitive understanding that how we feel about things is reflected in the physical postures we adopt. Talk to a dyed-in-the-wool Republican about the latest Democratic taxation proposal and, chances are, you'll be speaking to a man whose arms are folded across his chest. Without having to say a word, his stance has made his "stance" clear. He's opposed.

When you meet another person for the first time, your posture reveals your "stance" toward that other person. Consider the following:

- Crossed arms indicate closedness, defensiveness, a desire not to be approached. *Stay away*, this says.

- Open gestures are inviting. Arms loosely hanging at one's sides or elevated slightly in a gesture with the palms up and outward suggest interest, openness. The same is true of hands behind the back.

- Arms akimbo is a provocative gesture. This may suggest either boldness or defiance. Most people find this stance intimidating.

- The trunk turned away from the other person conveys an absence of interest.

- The trunk turned toward the other person suggests interest.

- Leaning slightly toward someone is a strong signal of interest.

- Generally focusing on the person in front of you to the exclusion of others in the room signals interest.

- Standing *a little* closer than what feels "normal" or "natural" strongly signals interest. Standing *too* close, however, makes most people quite uncomfortable and may even brand you as creepy.

Touch

We readily label some people as "touchy feely." They like to clap others on the back, they embrace readily, they like to touch. Many people are put off by "touchy feely" folk. Touch is a very potent signal of interest, but like all powerful agents, it needs to be applied with delicacy and care during initial encounters. Touching should never come across as groping or grabbing.

- Punctuating the initial conversation with a touch on the forearm of the other person is a very strong signal of interest.

- During a handshake, holding the other person's hand a little longer than what feels "normal" is another potent signal. While shaking hands (and do so gently, but not limply), make and hold eye contact, say your greeting ("Hi, my name is Elmo."), then hold the other person's hand for just a beat or two *after* you have stopped speaking. That is, the physical handshake should last a second or two longer than the spoken greeting.

- Consider a two-handed handshake. Beginning with the right hand, then bringing the left up to gently clasp the other person's hand.

15 Signals to Give

1. Make and hold eye contact.
2. Open your eyes wide.
3. Smile.
4. Nod to communicate interest and understanding.
5. Keep your head turned toward the other person.
6. Focus on the person in front of you. Don't let your glance stray to others in the room.
7. Turn your entire body toward the other person.
8. Lean slightly toward the other person.
9. Stand a little closer than "normal."
10. Use open gestures.
11. Gesture with palms up.
12. Keep your arms generally at your sides.
13. Shake hands gently.
14. Hold your handshake a little longer than "normal"; don't release the other person's hand until *after* you have spoken your initial greeting. Consider a two-handed handshake.
15. At some point during the conversation, touch the other person gently on the forearm.

10 Signals to Avoid

1. Averted eyes
2. Frowning

3. Crossed arms

4. Eyes scanning the room

5. Face turned away

6. Body turned away

7. Fidgeting behavior

8. If seated, nervously pumping your leg or legs, or shuffling your feet (These signal a desire to get up and run away.)

9. Putting your hand across or near your mouth (This signals insincerity or evasion.)

10. Rubbing your brow, temples, or the back of your neck (These are strong signals of discomfort, displeasure, and frustration.)

21

Ungaming the Dating Game

$\mathcal{T}$he Date: Some manage to approach it easily, even casually. For others, however, it is an event shrouded in mystery, charged with powerful significance, and a source of great anxiety. It is foolish to deny that a date could—as the Steve Allen lyric goes—be the start of something big. But it is also true that even the most casual encounter, a glance, the exchange of a friendly word, can also be the start of something big. Dating has no monopoly on opportunity.

Perhaps the most realistic—and least anxiety-provoking—way to look at a date is to see it as an extension of that casual encounter or friendly word, to see it as an elaboration of an interesting, exciting, and pleasing conversation. It is not a mysterious and momentous event, but the development of an everyday exchange or series of exchanges. This doesn't mean it's not important, but it does mean that the date is no act of extraordinary genius or heroism. It is normal. It is ordinary. And it is no less wonderful for being that.

Finding the Heartline

Nothing kills romance faster than cynicism. So, don't get me wrong when I make what is bound to sound like a cynical statement. Here goes: Getting a date means making a sale.

The "merchandise"?
Your company and time.
The price asked?
The other person's company and time.

Experienced, effective sales professionals follow a time-tested formula for approaching and engaging a prospect and then closing the sale. This formula is often expressed in an acronym, AIDA.

- A—Attention. The first step in making the sale is to get the prospect's attention.
- I—Interest. The next step is to develop his or her interest.
- D—Desire. Now is the time to escalate interest into desire for the merchandise.
- A—Action. The sale is closed by moving the prospect to action.

ATTENTION

Let's see how AIDA translates into getting a date. First the A, *Attention*. This is largely addressed in chapters 19 and 20. Someone commands your attention, and you respond by taking steps to get his or her attention. This is the purpose of conversation.

INTEREST

The conversation may develop from attention into I, *Interest*. To promote this development, try guiding the conversation with some open-ended questions or statements that invite comment. Any successful sales professional knows the value of questions. They involve the prospect in the merchandise. They prompt the prospect to invest time in considering a purchase.

You can get your "prospect" to invest time in you by asking questions—or making statements—that call for more than a simple yes or no answer. Ask someone, "Do you like movies?" and you do not set up the conditions that create conversation. The question calls for nothing more elaborate than a yes or no—a minimal investment, indeed. An open-ended question requires a larger investment: "What kind of movies do you like?"

This is similar to the difference between the dopey true-or-false exams you were given in high school and the more challenging, engaging, and creative essay exams handed out in college. Open-ended questions invite creativity, thought, and engagement with the subject *and with you*. They open up whole areas of discussion.

Most closed-ended, yes-or-no questions can easily be transformed into open-ended "essay" questions:

- Not: "Do you like Japanese food?" But: "What's your favorite Japanese restaurant in town?"
- Not: "Do you like jazz?" But: "What kind of music do you like?"
- Not: "I haven't seen you here before. Is this the first time you've come to this club?" But: "How did you find out about this place?"

When you are on the receiving end of a question, give as full and conversational an answer as you can:

Her: What kind of music do you like?

Him: I enjoy all kinds, but I really love jazz, especially Swing and Be-bop. I can't get enough of Charlie Parker. What musicians are you passionate about?

Notice that the "close" to this answer is open ended. It invites more conversation.

There is another way to open up your questions. Begin with a personal revelation, *then* go on to the question:

I have a confession to make. I'm *really* into jazz—and all kinds of other music, too. What kind of music do you like?

DESIRE

"Desire" in the romantic sense may or may not be driving you—or the other person—at this point, but the "desire" you *do* need to develop now is the desire to continue the conversation. At this point, it is probably premature to ask for a date. Instead, set up nothing more than the potential for a date. This is as simple as an exchange of phone numbers:

I have really enjoyed talking to you. Can we continue this later? Let me give you my phone number—and, if you're comfortable with the idea, would you give me your number?

SAYING NO

If you are on the receiving end of the dating "sales pitch," and you don't want to go further, you can decline abruptly or gracefully.

The abrupt approach. This is appropriate if you are quite certain that you have no interest in the other person. Use body language (Chapter 20) to exhibit your lack of interest. If this fails to clue the other person in, do not respond openly to his or her open-ended questions. Deliver curt, monosyllabic answers. If this fails, just say "I don't want to talk," and walk away. It is important that you move on, make an exit, or at least walk away. You want to communicate that no means no.

The graceful approach. This is appropriate if you have been enjoyably conversing, but you do not wish to continue the conversation elsewhere, much less go out on a date. When the other person asks if he/she can continue the conversation later or asks you out for coffee, reply politely, but honestly: "Thanks for the invitation, but I'm not available to go out." You do not need to launch into an explanation.

ACTION

Assuming that you have exchanged phone numbers, the next step is to make a date. For quite some time now, it has been socially acceptable for women as well as men to do the asking; however, even today, women are more often on the receiving end.

* When to ask? Ideally, you should ask the other person out two or three days after the exchange of phone numbers. This is not a hard and fast rule, of course, but if you wait longer than a week, the other person may have assumed you aren't interested and may now be lukewarm to your invitation. If you ask sooner, you probably haven't given him or her sufficient time to think about his or her level of interest in you.

* Sales professionals learn that once you've made the sale, it's time to shut your mouth. The invitation to a date is not the time to carry on a get-to-know-you conversation. This is material for the date itself. Keep the conversation brief . . .

* . . . but not *too* brief! Don't just pop the question. Make a little light small talk first. Ask about the other person's day. Reminisce briefly about the circumstances of your meeting.

* Keep the conversation positive. Don't complain about your day, your job, your life.

* Be aware that this is a call to *action*. Sales professionals know that closing a sale requires providing the prospect with a specific course of action—for example, exactly how to order the merchandise.

Following this analogy, be certain to call with a specific invitation, not just a "we really should get together sometime." You might suggest something like this: "I'd like to meet you for lunch, any day next week. Noon would be nice. I'm thinking about Fredo's, that Italian place on 10th and Market." Obviously, you need to be flexible. If he or she can't make it at a certain time, be open to an alternative.

CAN—*SHOULD*—THIS "SALE" BE SAVED?

Flexibility is one thing, but what if the response to your proposed plans is something like "Oh, I just don't know. I'm not sure what my plans are for next week."

There are several possible reasons for such a response:

- He/she really *is* unsure of his/her plans.
- He/she is uncertain about whether to accept your invitation.
- He/she doesn't want to accept, but has a hard time saying no.

None of these reasons bodes very well for getting a date. If the person were really interested, but unsure of his/her schedule, the reply would be something like: "Oh, look. I'd love to go, but I'm not sure of my plans for next week. Can I call you back tomorrow?" As for the other possible reasons, you are faced with either trying to save the "sale" or deciding that it is not worth doing.

One advantage to the uncertain or put-off response is that it gives you an opportunity to assess just how enthusiastic *you* are about the prospect of a date. If a lukewarm or cool response quickly dashes your interest, then you are best off dropping the invitation. If, however, you find that you are still interested, you may choose one of two courses:

1. Propose an alternative time to call. "Kathy, what if I call you again at the end of the week?"

2. Find out what's *really* going on. "Kathy, I want to be sure that I'm not being a pain. Are you really interested in going out? Or would you rather not? I'd love to go out with you, but if you don't want to, I'll understand. The last thing I want is to make you uncomfortable." Be certain to deliver this speech gently and without a trace of sarcasm or bitterness. Don't *dare* the other person to say no, but do give him or her permission to do so.

ACCEPTING NO

If the answer to your invitation is no, accept the answer with grace.

- It's the right, decent, and mature thing to do.
- He or she may have friends. You want to leave a favorable impression on him/her and his/her circle of friends.
- Minds do change. Don't slam the door as you leave.

One thing is critically important. Take no as no. If he or she is playing a mind game, saying no only to invite pursuit, that is not *your* problem. Dishonest games are never a good foundation for a relationship.

How do you keep the possibilities open for the future? Accept the no gracefully and as positively as possible:

> Ed, thanks for your honesty. I understand that you're involved just now.

Then invite future reconsideration:

> If things change for you or you change your mind, why not give me a call? I'd love to hear from you.

On the Receiving End

When you're asked out—and you want to reply with a yes—do so!

- Reply honestly and with enthusiasm. Don't play hard to get.
- Don't protract the acceptance. The invitation call is not the time to get into a long heart-to-heart. You can do that during the date itself.
- Keep the conversation positive. Don't start complaining about your hard day or your hard life.
- If you like, set limits when you accept. If you are invited to what is obviously intended as a romantic dinner and you are not ready for that on a first date, suggest an alternative: "I'd love to meet you. But I'd really like to get to know you better before we do the whole dinner thing. Can we get together for a cup of coffee later in the week?"

Should you move heaven and earth to accept a date that conflicts with other plans? That's up to you. Nothing wrong with taking a raincheck, however, just as long as you make it clear that you truly are interested in going out.

- Express your disappointment.
- Explain the conflict—briefly.
- Offer or invite an alternative time.

> John, I would love to see you again. But next week I'm going downstate to visit my folks. I'll be back on the 23rd. Can we set something up for that week?

Sidestepping the Pitfalls

The pitfalls of dating are many, but, really, they are all variations on one major error: Thinking of dating as a kind of game, the object of which is to outwit your opponent. Many of us are brought up to believe that acting coy or cool on the one hand and trying hard to be impressive on the other are what is expected on a date. The antidote advice to this, to "just be yourself," is well intended, but not very helpful.

Avoid the major pitfalls by thinking of the events leading up to a date and the date itself as an occasion for saying it from the heart. This requires, first and foremost, listening from the heart, hearing the other person and responding to what you hear. A great date is one of life's most wonderful self-indulgences. Paradoxically, however, the more *selflessly* you approach the date, the more gratifying you will find it. Focus on the other person.

The Conversation Begins

Remember the lesson of Chapter 19: The greatest secret of eloquence lies in your ears. Listening is the most important component of effective communication, especially when the knowledge you are trying to arrive at is knowledge of the heart.

A knowledge of the heart, the understanding of your own feelings and those of another, is what the dating ritual is really all about. It is communication on a most tender and important level.

This book can't tell you what to say on *your* date, but there are rules of thumb that can guide the dating dialogue and make it more satisfying:

- Listen, so that you can focus on the needs, wants, desires, and anxieties of the other person.

- Although you should respond to the feelings the other person expresses, never speak for him/her. You can avoid this by censoring yourself when you feel yourself about to begin a sentence with *you*. This usually means you are about to project a feeling or motive or intention on the other person. Ultimately, such projections erode a relationship. Speak for yourself. Address the feelings of the other person, but speak from your own feelings.

- Own your feelings. The other person will trigger in you feelings both pleasant and painful. Remember that they are *your* feelings. Talk about your feelings, but don't attribute them to the other person. That is, avoid sentences beginning with "You make me feel . . ."

- Focus on the present. There is nothing wrong with pleasant reminiscence, but blame and complaints for bygone affronts and injuries kill relationships.

- Accent the positive. Resolve to focus on the positive pleasures, not negative complaints.

- Focus on one another, not others. Avoid comparing your behavior or that of the other person to anyone else or to other couples.

- Use words. Express your feelings rather than act them out.

25 Words and Phrases to Use

accept	cannot accept	express
alternative plan	eager	feelings
appreciate	excited	fun
ask	explain	grateful

great	look forward to	would love to
happy	no	would love to, but
I have plans	pleasure	yes
interesting	thank you	
invitation	wonderful time	

15 Words and Phrases to Avoid

blame	maybe, maybe not
boring	never forgive
can't stand	no (when yes is meant)
depressed	yes (when no is meant)
don't like	you always do . . .
fault	you make me feel
feel bad	your fault
hate	

22

The Romance
of the Love Letter

$\mathcal{I}$n the late 1970s and early 1980s, with the advent and early development of personal computers, technology gurus everywhere predicted the coming of a "paperless world." With digital electronic communication, they said, paper would be rendered all but obsolete.

Wrong!

At the dawn of the 21st century, with the digital revolution over and won, somebody estimated that American business was actually using far more paper than ever before in history: 775 billion pages of paper per year, enough to make a stack 48,900 miles high.

Yet in this avalanche of paper, how many *personal* letters do you get each week? Each month? Each year?

If the answer makes you feel lonely, well, you're not alone. Although our mailboxes are jammed with more paper than ever, fewer of those envelopes contain personal messages.

The most personal message of all is, of course, the love letter. If you write one in this day and age, does that mean you're bucking the trend?

Decidedly.

Does it mean you're hopelessly romantic and old fashioned?

Let's hope so.

In an age of phone calls, e-mailed notes, and junk mail, a love letter, on paper, in an envelope, with a stamp, is greeted as something rare and valuable, precious as a lovely antique. It is a very powerful medium for saying it from the heart when saying it from the heart matters more than anything else.

Finding the Heartline

"Love," that song lyric from the 1960s goes, "makes the world go 'round." Certainly, it powers prodigies of achievement. For love, the Trojan War was fought. For love, the Taj Mahal was built. For love, men and women risk and sacrifice their lives for one another. And so the force of love should make our words not just flow, but gush in a torrent of eloquence.

Right?

Not for most of us. Most of us find it highly daunting to express love in writing.

* We feel inadequate to the task.
* The emotions of love are pleasant to feel, but don't always look "right" on paper.
* Love seems to engage the part of the brain that is least verbal.
* We're afraid of sounding corny.
* We're afraid of causing or experiencing embarrassment.

These are all real and legitimate obstacles, but they come from the fundamental error of expecting too much of a love letter. Remember this: The very fact that you have taken the time and necessary thoughtfulness to *write* a letter in the first place is a powerful statement of love in and of itself. Whatever you may actually say in the letter simply amplifies the gesture.

* Anyone qualifies to write a love letter. You do not have to be a poet or novelist.
* Try to write what you feel.
* Share memories of experiences the two of you have had.
* Don't reach for high-flown rhetoric and flowery language. Use simple words.
* Picture the other person in front of you. *Talk* to him or her. Make your writing conversational.
* Keep it real. Don't talk about abstract ideas. Focus on real events and real things.

The last point is especially important when saying it from the heart. Human beings are capable of very elaborate abstract thought, but they respond most vividly and intensely to concrete, physical reality. Think about the last novel you read and enjoyed. Did it speculate about *ideas* of pain and pleasure and adventure? Or did it present *scenes* and *stories* of pain and pleasure and adventure? If the answer to the first question were yes, there would be little market for fiction. The fact is that novels are appealing because they appeal to the senses, to our *sense* of reality. Good letters—especially letters to someone you love—also appeal to reality.

- Instead of "You're so sweet," think of *why* he/she is this way— then write about it: "I love the way you took my side when I told you about that argument I had with my boss."

- Instead of "You're so thoughtful," try: "I am amazed that you remembered how much I love *white* roses. They were so lovely."

Sidestepping the Pitfalls

The great pitfall in writing love letters is intimidation. You may feel inadequate to the task of expressing the depth and breadth of your love. You may feel that your letter will somehow undercut or belittle your feelings. The result of this intimidation? You don't ever get around to writing the love letter, or you adopt a stilted, high-flown language that is not your own. The more you think of the love letter as a conversation, the easier it will be to avoid intimidation.

In the Beginning

Here are two ideas for the first love letters of a relationship:

Dear Cindy,

I *said* it to you yesterday, and now I want to set it down on paper: *I love you!*

There it is, in black and white—for me to see, for you to see, for everyone to see. Because it's the wonderful truth. And because it is the truth and so wonderful, I intend to say it and write it repeatedly to you now and forever.

I love you,

Ned

Dear Alex,

The concert last night was wonderful—but even more wonderful was what I felt after I left your house. I felt—simultaneously—complete and incomplete. I felt complete because I had been with you, and incomplete because I was not with you at the moment. That's when I realized that you are part of my life. The phrase sounds a little cold to me. But it's what I mean: You are *part of my life* now.

I want to share with you whatever I do and whatever I feel. That makes me feel complete.

I love you, Alex—

Wanda

Sharing

Dearest Joan,

The concert last night was fantastic!

I know, you're about to say I'm crazy, because, last night, you were raving about how great the concert was, and I was complaining about the songs as well as the band.

But that is the fantastic part. You and I are so much alike in so many ways. I mean, we're both fanatics about the environment, we're both stubborn as—what?—whatever animal is really, *really* stubborn, we both love the poetry of John Donne and W. B. Yeats, and we sure do feel the same way about sunsets—as well as sunrises. But we're also very different. Last night was an example. You loved the concert, and I did not. And here's the fantastic part: It is okay.

We love being alike, and we love being different.

No matter how bad that concert was (to me), I loved it because I heard it with you. I was there with you. I also love the fact that you so enjoyed the concert and that you could tell me how much you enjoyed it, and I could tell you how much I didn't enjoy it, and we *still* love each other!

I love being free together—so alike and so different.

Love a million times over,

Benny

Dear Mike,

We walked in the woods for hours—I don't know how many—but I wished the walk would go on and on. It was so very, very lovely.

The trees, the colors of the fall leaves, the smell of the moist earth, the pines, the crisp cool of the autumn air—all of this was multiplied, amplified by your being there to breathe it all in with me.

Mike, this is what love must be! Think about it. It's seeing, hearing, feeling, *breathing* the world differently because you're with the person who means most to you and makes everything else mean more than it ever meant before. I feel as if I never really looked at a wildflower before, now that I've seen it with you beside me.

I love you very much,

Sally

Missing You

Dear Nadia,

So here I am in Santa Fe at the medical conference. Yesterday evening, I attended a cocktail reception out in the desert, at a place overlooking the Sangre de Christo Mountains. The sunset paints the peaks a salmon red, a glowing red. You must think it was very beautiful. I'm sure it *was* beautiful. Half listening to a conversation, I stared at the glowing mountains, and all I could think was *This must be beautiful*. But I couldn't really feel the beauty of it.

That's when I realized how much I miss you.

Without you here to see this with me, the best I can do is know that there is beauty here, but *feel* it, really *feel* it? No.

Without you, the world is incomplete. It's that simple. Thank goodness this conference will be over in two more days, and I'll be on my way back home to you.

Love,

Stan

Dear Tom,

I look at myself in the mirror, and I'm the same woman. Same face, same eyes, same hair. I walk down the same stairs I walked down yesterday and last week and last year. I go to the office I've been going to for three years now. Same job, same nice people.

But it's all so much better because I am in love with you. The feeling I carry around with me makes everything brighter. Yet, with you gone for the rest of the summer, the world also seems emptier, unfinished, waiting to be completed. Tom, I miss you very much, and I count the days until we'll be back together again.

Love,

Frieda

25 Words and Phrases to Use

adore	I miss you	see you again
better	I love you	share
delight	intense	together
dream	kiss	understand
embrace	love	us
experience	my life	we
fantastic	my world	wonderful
feeling	our	
great	realize	

Words and Phrases to Avoid

The vocabulary of love is virtually without limit. Avoid words that do not feel like your own.

23

You Have Mail

E-mail may lack the old-fashioned charm of the envelope-and-paper love letter, but it does have the advantage of spontaneous immediacy and a casual quality that is both friendly and intimate. The e-mail love note is not a substitute for the snail-mail letter, but, these days, it is a natural supplement to it and can be a great way to stay connected.

The Heartline Online

The same general principles that govern love letters (see Chapter 22) also apply to e-mail notes. But be aware that the digital medium invites spontaneity, an off-the-cuff approach, and is also best suited to brevity. There is nothing to stop you from writing a long letter and sending it via e-mail, but most people don't like to read extended amounts of text on a computer screen. It is also true that an envelope-and-paper letter generally delivers richer emotion. It is perceived as more romantic, more substantial, if you will, more *real*—and less virtual. This being the case, you may not want to "waste" your more fully developed thoughts and sentiments on a digital transmission when you can commit them to paper instead.

We said in the previous chapter that the best love letters are conversational, written as if the addressee were sitting beside the writer. If anything, this is even more true of e-mail. E-mail invites a conversational tone. When you sit down to write, imagine the other person there before you. Don't be afraid to speak aloud as you type.

Sidestepping the Pitfalls

E-mail offers some unique—and uniquely serious—pitfalls.

As of the beginning of the 21st century, at least one of every two households owns a personal computer. If the number of PCs has exploded, even more explosive is the growth of Internet access. A majority of home computers is now connected to the Internet, and these ranks swell daily, hourly, and even by the minute. Many people regularly use e-mail to communicate with one another, from one home to another. Of course, e-mail made its first inroads in corporate settings, as business communication, and one would be hard pressed these days to find a business that does not use e-mail communication at least to some extent. In many firms, e-mail is the chief form of communication, outstripping the telephone and even face-to-face meetings. This said, please consider the following advice carefully:

> E-mailing love notes should be a home-PC-to-home-PC activity. It is very, very risky to send personal correspondence of any kind via corporate e-mail systems!

Recent court cases have repeatedly upheld the principle that e-mailed messages sent via corporate e-mail systems are the property of the corporation. This means that your employer has the right to read all of the e-mail you send—or that is sent *to* you—via the employer's e-mail system, network, and computers. You have no right to privacy when you transmit or receive e-mail via the company's network.

At the very least, then, intercepted love notes can be embarrassing, but there is even greater risk. Your employer may—

- disapprove of your using the company's equipment and time to send and receive personal messages

- consider sending personal messages unprofessional

- interpret personal messages as forms of inappropriate sexual behavior or even harassment

The result of this may be censure or other disciplinary action, up to and including dismissal.

The moral of the tale is this: E-mail invites casual communication and has the aura of intimacy, but, in a corporate setting, e-mail is public and fully open to scrutiny by any number of people. Corporate e-mail systems are not appropriate vehicles for transmitting or receiving personal communications.

Developing Digital Style

It is truly remarkable how quickly e-mail has become a part of our lives. Most of us now use it as naturally as we do the telephone; however, some of us take to the keyboard *more* naturally than others.

- For some, typing out an e-mail is a very conversational activity. The language is casual and natural.

- For some, typing out an e-mail is a careless activity. The writing is so casual that it is difficult to read.

- For some, the digital style is a kind of shorthand. Incomplete sentences are dashed off. Fragments. Words. Abbreviations. Capitalization and punctuation are abandoned.

- For some, the digital style is less like a conversation between two people facing one another in comfortable surroundings than it is like walkie-talkie communication from one besieged foxhole to another.

For personal communication, the best approach to e-mail is conversational. This is made easier if you are an adept typist. If you plan to use e-mail extensively for day-to-day correspondence, and you are not comfortable at the keyboard, you might invest in one of the several typing instructional software packages currently on the market. It is by creating a conversational style that your personality will come across most vividly in digital form.

In the early days of e-mail communication (which means only a few years ago), correspondents had nothing at their disposal beyond words. To enliven e-mail communication and broaden its emotional range, e-mailers developed a set of symbols called *emoticons*.

The idea behind emoticons was to bring to e-mail communication something of the physical immediacy of face-to-face conversation. When you talk face to face, you gesture, smile, frown—in short, express emotion. Since e-mail is often recruited to stand in for such conversation, a visual vocabulary for adding emotional expression to e-mail messages may be of some use. Hence the *emoticon*. Combining "emotion" with "icon," *emoticon* describes a symbol developed as shorthand to express via e-mail the emotions that are otherwise conveyed face to face. Reflecting the technology of early e-mail systems, emoticons use nothing more than the basic, so-called ASCII characters found on your keyboard. No fancy graphics are required. The chief limitation of the emoticons is that the "emotions" they express must be interpreted by viewing the icons at a 90-degree angle—that is, sideways. Just tilt your head to the side and start reading:

:-)	Humor (smile face)
:-) :-) :-)	Ha, ha, ha!
:/)	Not funny
'-)	Wink
(@ @)	You're kidding!
:-"	Pursed lips
:-V	Shouting
:-W	Sticking tongue out
:-p	Smirking
:-O	Eeeeeeeek!
:-*	Oops! (Covering mouth with hand)
:-T	Keeping a straight face
:-D	Said with a smile
=|:-)=	Uncle Sam
:-#	Censored (or Expletive deleted)
:-x	Kiss, kiss
:-(	Unhappy
:-c	Very unhappy
:-	Desperately unhappy
(:-(	Even sadder
:-C	Jaw dropped in disbelief
:-|	Disgusted
:-?	Licking your lips
:-J	Tongue in cheek remark

:-8	Speaking out of both sides of your mouth
(:-&	Angry
| |*(	Handshake offered . . .
| |*)	. . . and accepted
(-_-)	Secretly smiling
@%&$%&	Curses!

Emoticons can perk up your e-mail message—though like any other good thing, they can be overused. Take care not to transform a light, witty message into something cutesy and childish.

In any case, most e-mailers no longer need to work exclusively within the confines of ASCII text. Most e-mail systems today allow you to attach pictures, sounds, and even video clips to your messages. Are you far from your loved one? Why not send him/her a photo of yourself, or a recording of your voice, or even a video clip? Nor are you limited to sound or graphic material you create yourself. The Internet is filled with Web sites that feature interesting pictures, sounds, music, and video clips you might like to share. You are limited only by your imagination. But the point is this:

- Face to face is generally the best way to communicate.

- A love letter usually offers more emotional value than an e-mail or even a phone call.

- Despite these first two points, e-mail does offer certain advantages: It is convenient and immediate. Transmitted from *personal* computer to *personal* computer, it is, in a word, *personal*. Nowadays, e-mails can carry more than just typewritten words; they may also convey pictures, videos, and sound.

Editing Yourself

Spontaneity is the name of the game with e-mail. What could be wrong with this? The trouble is that composing and sending an e-mail is so easy that we are tempted to do it with little thought. The typical approach is *ready! shoot! aim!* We dash off the message, click on the send button—and *then* we happen to read over what we have just irretrievably committed to the digital ether. Invariably, we find it riddled with dumb mistakes, typos, spelling errors, and, much worse, a couple or three things we regret having said.

Just because e-mail invites spontaneity and enables haste, you are not obligated to be totally spontaneous and hasty. You can compose messages that have the feel of spontaneous conversation, but, since you aren't communicating in real time, you *do* have the opportunity to review your work, to edit yourself.

Pause a moment before clicking on "send." Reread the message, correct glaring errors, and make certain that what you've said is what you want to say, because once you do click, the message is no longer yours.

6 Digital Love Letters

The following are examples of love "letters" tuned appropriately to the digital vehicle. Remember: Personal e-mails should be sent from *home* PC to *home* PC and *not* on your employer's computer over your company's network. Nor should you send, from your home, a personal message to someone at work. Once an e-mail enters a corporate network, it becomes the property of that corporation.

FIRST NOTE

Hi, Rhonda—

I sat down at my computer to catch up on some work at home, but all I can think about is you or, to tell the truth, *us*. I've never felt so happy, excited, and comfortable—all at the same time—with anyone else. You are wonderful.

I love you—

Pete

Dear Tod,

The flowers you sent just arrived. I woke up this morning thinking *roses*. You sent *roses*. This *must* mean something—and it must be something pretty great!

If you truly can read my mind, Tod, I guess I don't have to tell you that I love you.

Sarah

SHARING MOMENTS

Terri—

I was out the door on my way to work, then I looked up at the sky, and at the big crepe myrtle in blossom at the front door. A beautiful morning, I thought, and, thinking of beauty, I thought of you. So I rushed back inside the house, turned on the computer, and wrote you this note, my love.

Sam

Bill, Dear—

They just showed *Casablanca* on TV, and I watched it for the millionth time, give or take. But, this time, I thought: Bogart and Bergman don't have a tenth of the romance in their lives that we've found in ours.

I can't wait to see you again Friday.

Beth

MISS YOU

Hello, Dear Nora—

This convention is dull, dull, dull. But I could be in a tropical paradise, on the beach, and, without you, it, too, would be dull, dull, dull. Anyplace I go, anything I do is the poorer for our not being there together. I will be very happy when I am back in good old Anytown with you.

Love,

Marv

Dear Daryl,

I'm sitting at my little brother's computer. Mom is about to call us all in for Thanksgiving dinner. I love being home for the holiday, but I'm also learning an important thing: I miss you. I wish you were with me here.

Got to go, dear. See you soon—Claire

25 Words and Phrases to Use

a few words

adore you

be with you again

blissful

can't wait to see you again

dash off a few words

embrace you

fun

hug you

I love you

in love with you

joy

love

marvelous

miss you

need you

quick note for you

reach out to you

romance

romantic

share a few minutes

thrill

together

wish we were together

wonderful

Words and Phrases to Avoid

The vocabulary of love is virtually without limit. Avoid words that do not feel like your own. Always be sensitive to the fact that others may have access to your correspondent's computer.

Understanding Misunderstanding

"*M*isunderstanding" is among the most misunderstood words in our common vocabulary. We often use it as a euphemism, a polite, emotionally neutral way of describing any argument, dispute, or even break-up. It is a fact that many arguments, disputes, and break-ups are the product of genuine misunderstanding. Person A says something that means something to him, and Person B hears it, but interprets it as meaning something else. It is also a fact, however, that some so-called misunderstandings are really arguments, disputes, and break-ups caused not by faulty understanding, but by all too accurate understanding. Person A says what he means, and Person B doesn't like it.

Relationships are full of arguments and disputes—sometimes leading to break-up. These are sometimes the product of serious, critical issues that each member of the couple understands, but cannot reconcile or resolve. Honest, open, sensitive communication generally provides the best chance of resolving these problems, but there is no guarantee that saying it from the heart will patch up all the wounds and cure all the ills. What honest, open, sensitive communication *can*—almost always—fix is genuine misunderstanding: arguments and disputes that are triggered by and perhaps exacerbated by Person A failing to make himself clear to Person B or expressing himself in such a way as to aggravate a situation instead of clarifying it so that it can be addressed and worked through.

Finding the Heartline

Communicating to avoid misunderstanding requires, first and foremost, disciplined listening. This is listening that is governed by three broad principles:

1. *Assume honesty and no hidden agenda.* Enter into the communication in good faith, with the intention of being honest and the assumption that the other person is also being honest.

2. *Hold your tongue—and your judgment.* Remember that your first objective is to listen and hear. You cannot do this while shouting. Give the other person the time, space, and silence he/she needs to say what needs to be said.

3. *Keep an open mind.* Before a trial, lawyers spend a good deal of time questioning prospective jurors to ensure that they are not sitting in judgment with their minds already made up. Listen with your mind open. Leave your agenda at the door.

When it is your turn to speak, the path of the heartline goes through the following points:

* Respect—for yourself and for the other person.

* Rules of engagement: Resolve not to allow the discussion to escalate to harsh words, name calling, or violence of any kind.

* Refusal to project: Recognize that it is potentially destructive to assume that the other person sees and feels the situation the same way that you do.

* Refusal to blame or accuse: Don't deny your feelings, but don't automatically blame them on the other person. Instead of "You make me angry," try "I feel angry with you."

* Separating behavior from the person: Instead of criticizing the other person for being bad or stupid or insensitive, criticize a specific action for being bad or stupid or insensitive. Not "You're just an insensitive person," but "Bringing up that old issue was insensitive."

Sidestepping the Pitfalls

The great pitfall that creates misunderstanding is the failure to pass conversation through the points just outlined. This failure often comes from an initial loss of perspective. When a conversation becomes a confrontation, it is very easy to lose sight of the desirable outcome of the encounter: a resolution that satisfies both people and that strengthens the relationship. Instead, you may see the only desirable outcome as your emerging the winner—no matter who gets hurt. And remember, if you get hurt, you get hurt; if the other person in the relationship gets hurt, you also get hurt. Give up the need to win for the sake of winning. Give up the need to be "right" even when being "right" makes you feel wrong. Instead, work—struggle—to retain your focus on the truly desirable outcome.

How to Stay in It Together

While effective, positive habits of communication cannot guarantee a loving, enduring, and rewarding relationship, you can be pretty certain that poor communication habits will contribute to the degradation and even the destruction of any relationship. The good habits tend to bridge the distances between individuals, while the bad habits tend to emphasize or even widen these distances.

THE SELF CONVERSATION

Conversing with yourself: The two of you are together, but you are talking to yourself. What could be less constructive than this? And yet it happens all the time. You assume and insist that you know what the other person is thinking and feeling. The result is that you carry on a conversation with yourself: "You say you want to go to the concert with me, but you'd rather be playing cards with the boys." Pretty soon, the other person ceases to exist. There is only you and *your* impression, your version of the other person.

Avoid the self-conversation. By all means, express your feelings and your fears to the other person, but then let him/her respond to them. Stop talking. Listen.

EXPECTING MIRACULOUS UNDERSTANDING

The flipside of the self conversation is the expectation that the other person in the relationship must know what you are feeling and thinking. Why? Because he/she loves you, of course, and people who love each other can read each other's mind.

There is a grain of truth in this myth. People who have lived together twenty, thirty years or more would have to be dense indeed if they did not pick up on one another's habits and habits of thought. But love does not confer the power of mental telepathy, and it is a big mistake to assume that it does and an even bigger error to assume that a failure of mind reading indicates the absence of love. It is *your* responsibility to express *your* feelings, *your* needs, and *your* desires.

PASSIVE AGGRESSION

This alternative to communication is an all too common feature of many relationships. Failing to express feelings does not magically make the feelings go away. If the unexpressed feelings are sufficiently significant to you, you're likely to express them in some nonverbal way.

"Sure, I'll drop those off at the cleaners. I *know* it's important for tomorrow."

Tomorrow comes, and . . .

"Hon, did you get my suit back from the cleaners?"
"What suit?"

Don't leave important issues undiscussed.

STONEWALLING

Feeling low, you may benefit most from a good talk. But, feeling low, you may not want to talk. The same is true when something your partner has done upsets or offends you. This is precisely the time when communication is most important, but it is also when you may feel least like talking.

Stonewalling invites the other person to carry on a self-conversation, to project his/her feelings onto you. The result, at the very least, is misunderstanding and a consequent failure to resolve whatever issue is troublesome. In the worst case, the result is that your partner magnifies whatever it is that is bothering you, making it seem—or just plain making it—worse than it is.

NAME CALLING AND RIDICULE

Not much to say about this, except don't do it. It is very hurtful, particularly because it denies adult-level dignity to both partners. Be aware that ridicule is often disguised, thinly, as "kidding": "Can't you take a joke?" Far from lightening the tone of a put-down, the fiction that it is all in good fun just adds insult to injury.

LYING

Lying tears down any relationship. The same goes for simply withholding the truth. You have to figure out a constructive way to tell the truth so that it can be dealt with.

Anger

Anger is not bad for relationships. Anger is not good for relationships. Anger is simply a part of relationships, because it is a part of emotional life. Deal with it.

- Identify the real source of anger. Anger is a threat, so we often displace it. You're in a difficult position with your boss at work. He makes you angry, but you can't afford to lash out at him. You need the job. You go home and yell at your wife instead. This is displaced anger.

- You get angry when you get hurt. By getting angry at the person who hurt you, you defend yourself against further injury.

- You get angry when you are frustrated—including frustrated by your own failures or perceived failures. This leads you to lash out at others, often with blame and accusation.

You can't ignore or simply get rid of anger, but you can recognize it in its many forms and disguises, and you can take steps to deal with it in a healthy way.

Begin by recognizing that anger is not a thing, but a feeling and that the only person responsible for your feelings is you. If you are responsible for your feelings, you are also responsible for managing them. If you feel overwhelmed by your feelings, manage them before talking to the other person about them:

- Take a walk around the block—or maybe a run.
- Count to ten. Breathe deeply.

Commit yourself to absolutely avoiding violence—to yourself or to anyone else.

If you still feel that you cannot talk about the anger without making the situation worse, consider writing down your thoughts. You might even compose a letter to the other person in the relationship. Put the letter away for at least a day, then look at it. Decide what parts of the letter you still feel like talking about.

When you are finally ready to talk, make sure that you do not relinquish responsibility for your feelings. Instead of saying "You make me furious," explain: "When you discussed our personal finances with Joe Williams, it made me very angry." This may still be a hard pill for the other person to swallow, but at least it does the following:

- It retains ownership of the anger.
- It does not directly attack the other person, but instead focuses on a particular action.
- It defines precisely the source of the anger, fixing it in time and attaching it to a particular event.

This last point is especially important, because it offers real, practical hope for a solution to the problem. If you simply tell someone that he/she makes you angry, few desirable solutions present themselves: Either the person must somehow "fix" himself/herself—or leave. If, however, you focus on a particular behavior, action, or event, you have identified something much easier to fix than a person. Try to choose a time when you can talk—*really* talk, without interruption.

Apology

Apologizing is not just saying you're sorry or expressing regret over an incident or an outburst, but is an act of accepting responsibility for the action.

The first step in a meaningful apology is not speaking, however, but listening.

- Listen without preconception or prejudice.

- Use positive body language to show that you are receptive to whatever complaints or criticisms your partner expresses.

- Express your understanding of what the other person is saying, even if you don't agree with it. It is perfectly possible to understand a point or a concept without agreeing to its truth or accuracy: "I can understand why you feel the way that you do."

- Reflect the other person's words. "You're saying that I don't respect your opinions about financial matters. Am I understanding you so far?"

- Exercise as much restraint as possible to ensure that the other person gets to talk first and express herself/himself fully. Try not to interrupt. Do not break in to defend yourself.

Once you begin to speak, you may need to decide whether you are apologizing—accepting responsibility and expressing regret—for something you purposely did to be hurtful or something you did unconsciously, even accidentally. In either case, it is up to you to claim responsibility. That is step 1 of the apology:

- Accept responsibility.

Step 2?

- Express regret. "I'm sorry what I did hurt your feelings."

Go to step 3:

- Propose a remedy. Sometimes there is some specific action that can be taken to repair damage. Sometimes it is a promise to take steps to prevent the damage from happening again: "From now on, I'll be sure to talk over any financial decisions with you. We'll work together and make the decisions together."

Apology does not occur in a vacuum. It is completed by forgiveness. If you are on the receiving end of an apology, it is up to you to decide whether to forgive or not. The decision may be made more easily if you stop to consider what forgiveness is—and is *not*.

- Forgiveness is accepting that the other person has made a mistake, regrets it, and still deserves your love.

- Forgiveness is not the same as forgetting what happened.

- Forgiveness is not the same as saying what happened is okay.

- Forgiveness is not guaranteed for life. It is important for both people to realize that you may sincerely forgive someone today, only to become angry again tomorrow. This is *not* the same as going against your word.

Disposing of the Past

Apology does not erase error or the hurt caused by error. Forgiveness is not forgetting. Yet the past must be overcome, because it is a reality that cannot be changed or affected in any way. Against the past we are powerless. To get beyond the past, we must focus on the present and create a plan for the future. When you do something hurtful, apologize. As part of the apology, offer a remedy. But don't leave it as a unilateral solution. Have a conversation about what you will do, together, to avoid a repetition of the problem. The more specific you can be together, the better. Without a plan, you can both become prisoners of the past.

25 Words and Phrases to Use

agree	help me	quiet discussion
apologize	help you	regret
as much time as we need	hurt	sorry
ask your forgiveness	in the future	talk
feel	listen to you	together
forgive	move forward	understand
get past this	next	work it out
hear you	plan	work out a plan together
	promise	

16 Words and Phrases to Avoid

bad	forever	permanent
blame	impossible	ruined
can't change	incapable	you made me
did it on purpose	incompetent	your fault
evil	never be the same	
fault	no good	

Part 5

On the
Job

The workplace engages the head as well as the heart.
This section will help you to speak and write
more effectively on the job.

Turning Apology into Opportunity

*"S*ay you're sorry."

Remember your mother telling you this? Remember how hard it was to squeeze the words out? For many of us, it doesn't get much easier when we grow up. In fact, the stakes of adult actions are generally higher than they are for kid's stuff, so, all grown up now, it can be even more difficult, embarrassing, and painful to apologize. Nobody likes doing damage control, but we all know it's necessary sometimes. Things go wrong. Mistakes are made. Stuff happens.

Think for a moment about the last time you were on the receiving end of somebody's error.

You're a do-it-yourselfer, a real tool freak. Down at the home improvement store your eyes went wide when you saw that fancy cordless drill. You bought it. You brought it home. You took it ever so gently out of the box, waited hours for its first charge-up, then, at long last, you put it to work.

No sooner did the bit bite into the wood than it ground down, slowed down, and stopped dead.

Steeped in chagrin, you are steamed. Certainly, you don't feel very good right now about Drill-O-Matic, Inc.

But the story's not over.

You get on the phone and call Drill-O-Matic's customer service department. The call is answered promptly, and somebody in charge apologizes to you and promises you that the company will stand behind the product and will ship you out a new Drill-O-Matic immediately and at no cost to you.

How do you feel now?

Chances are that you are still disappointed, but at least you're feeling better about Drill-O-Matic. Those people haven't abandoned you. They've taken responsibility. They are determined to help you.

In the world of business, errors, failures, and disappointments are not good things, and they never will be. But an effective apology can take these disasters and turn them into opportunities for creating a positive relationship between customer and company. No matter what your business, you don't just sell a product, you also sell yourself and your firm. If a particular product should happen to fail or a service fall short, you still have an opportunity to sell yourself and your firm by sending the message that you will make things right. You can turn damage control into relationship building.

Finding the Heartline

The heartline, the quickest route to effective communication in response to a customer complaint about your company's error, is *not* just about finding a slick way to say "We're sorry." It is about communicating a willingness to help the client or customer. Focusing on fixing things is what builds a positive relationship between you and that customer. Take it step by step:

1. Acknowledge the complaint.

2. Express sympathy for the customer and concern for his situation and his feelings. *Briefly* apologize.

3. Be sure to get all relevant facts. Do not grill or challenge the customer. Frame your questions in ways that make it clear that you need the information in order to make things right: "You say the unit isn't operating correctly. Can you tell me a little more about just what is going wrong? This will help me diagnose the problem and get you up and running again."

4. If possible, provide an immediate solution to the customer's problem. For example: "Please take the widget to the nearest authorized dealer, who will repair it at no cost to you." If you require additional information or some other action on the part of the customer, explain it here: "So that I can get this problem corrected as quickly as possible, I need to know . . ." If possible and appro-

priate, give your customer choices as to remedies and solutions. Choice confers a sense of empowerment, which makes a disappointed customer feel less like a victim—less like *your* victim.

5. After you have proposed a helping action, close with an apology. "I am sorry for this problem."

6. Offer ongoing assistance: "I'm sure that this problem won't be repeated, but if you have any questions or concerns, don't hesitate to call us at this number."

Sidestepping the Pitfalls

Whatever else goes into a business, business success is built on creating customer satisfaction. Errors, malfunctions, disappointing performance all threaten satisfaction and, therefore, threaten the basis of your business. In responding to a complaint or making an apology, you have the opportunity to restore lost satisfaction; therefore, avoid the following pitfalls:

- *Dwelling on the apology.* The customer is far less interested in hearing how sorry *you* are and how bad *you* feel than in what you will do to help *him.*

- *Bad mouthing the product, the company, or other employees.* Never respond to a complaint in ways that undermine the customer's confidence in the product or the firm.

- *Being defensive.* It is not true that the "customer is always right." What is true, in the case of a complaint, is that the customer is unhappy. You cannot argue with that. Instead, focus on doing whatever can fairly be done to make the customer happy. Do not defend the product by criticizing the customer's feelings about it.

- *Arguing.* If the customer is mistaken or misinformed, if he is misusing the product, or if he is using the product for an inappropriate application, do not argue with him. Instead, educate him. Work with him. Remember, your goal is not to defend your product or service, but to create customer satisfaction with that product or service. This may require helping your customer to use the product or service correctly or more effectively.

- *Lying.* Don't do it. And don't promise any solutions you cannot deliver.

3 Model Letters

OFFERING CHOICES

Dear Mr. Jackson:

I was very sorry to learn that the X unit on your Widget is defective. I can work with you in two ways to resolve the problem:

1. While the X unit certainly failed prematurely, it is a "wear part" that must be replaced from time to time. It is designed to be replaced by the customer. Therefore, I can send you a new unit, with instructions on how to replace it.

2. If you prefer, you may return the entire unit to us, and we will replace the part, then return the unit to you, together with reimbursement of your shipping costs.

The first alternative is faster, but if you really don't like to use a screwdriver, just pack the unit in its original carton and return it to us. Follow the warranty return instructions in your Owner's Manual.

Be assured that, whatever option you choose, we will make every effort to get you up and running with a minimum of delay. If you would like us to send a replacement X unit, just call me at 555-555-5555. You may leave a message on my voice answering system.

I apologize for the inconvenience and disappointment, and I thank you for your patience and understanding.

Sincerely,

William Johnson
Customer Service

Do not fail to thank your customer for patience and understanding. Not only is this an act of common courtesy, it strengthens the bond between you and the customer by reminding him that he has made an emotional investment in you by giving you his patience and understanding.

SPEEDY ACTION

Dear Ms. Smith:

I am very sorry that the Widget is not performing to your expectations, and I am eager to resolve the problem as quickly as possible. For that reason, I ask that you bring the unit to your nearest authorized Widget service center, which is located at 1234 East Huron Street in Brunswick. The technician there will diagnose the problem and take whatever steps are necessary to insure that it will operate to its optimum specifications. If the service center is unable to repair the problem within twenty-four hours, I have authorized that you be given a replacement unit. In either case, there will be no cost to you.

We want you to be 100 percent satisfied, and we will ensure that this is the case. Thanks for your patience and understanding.

Sincerely,

Benito Guiterrez
Customer Service Associate

GETTING THE FACTS SO YOU CAN HELP

Dear Ms. Perkins:

I was deeply concerned by your letter of October 4, in which you mention that you were very unhappy with the work of one of our sales representatives, Patty Smith.

I have discussed the matter with Ms. Smith, but before I meet with her again to discuss an appropriate course of action, I would like to have as much information as possible from you regarding the difficulty you experienced. Your comments on the following questions will help me—as well as Ms. Smith—understand the situation more fully and resolve it to your complete satisfaction:

1. In what way(s) was Ms. Smith "rude" to you?

2. Your impression was that Ms. Smith "deliberately delayed" action on your order. Can you explain what created that impression?

Ms. Perkins, I don't want to put you to the trouble of writing down formal responses to these questions. You might just jot down a few points and call me at 555-555-5555 with your comments.

We at Jones Company are proud of the level of service we offer. You can understand, then, how concerned I am that you were dissatisfied. Both Ms. Smith and I are eager to turn this situation around and create your complete satisfaction.

Sincerely,

Helen Smithers
Sales Manager

3 Model Memos

The essence of an effective memo is economy. Give all the pertinent facts and nothing more. Sell your message. Remember, many business organizations are flooded with daily memos. They come to be regarded as a species of office junk mail. Be sure that you state your point quickly and sharply, so that your communication stands out from the rest of the flood.

INCORRECT INFORMATION

Date: 00/00/00
To: Shipping Group
From: Pete Hackney
Subject: Contact numbers for George Youngblood

The phone contact numbers I gave you last week for George Youngblood were incorrect. Sorry for the error, but my database was not up to date. I am in the process of updating it now, and I expect to have the correct numbers tomorrow. Sorry for the inconvenience. You can be sure that the next batch of contact numbers will be up to date and correct.

ERRORS IN REPORT

Date: 00/00/00
To: Frank Peterson
From: Ellen Corwin
Subject: Problem with the Flash Reports

Frank, I've looked into the problems you pointed out in the Flash Reports. I'm pleased to say that I've located the source of the problems, but I'm not so pleased to tell you that the source is me.

I used figures from April instead of May, and the result was, to say the least, misleading. The good news here is that *you* caught my mistake before we put anything into action. Thanks for your vigilance—and thanks, too, for your patience and understanding.

I am currently rerunning the numbers, using figures from May. The report will be ready for you before the end of the day. I'll run it down to your office personally.

Frank, I'm really sorry for this.

WE'RE LATE

Date: 00/00/00
To: All employees
From: Hal Dean, Cafeteria Manager
Subject: Cafeteria closed for the rest of the week

I am sorry to report that the cafeteria will be closed for the remainder of this week, Wednesday through Saturday. Necessary renovations are taking longer than anticipated because of a delay in shipping some building materials. I have been assured that the work will be completed over the weekend and that we *will* be ready to serve you on Monday.

In the meantime, the cafeteria staff and I apologize for the inconvenience. We have installed two additional vending machines in the third-floor break room and another two machines on the second-floor break room. I know these are a poor substitute for the cafeteria, but I hope they'll help. The best solution for now might be good old-fashioned home cooking!

3 Model Phone Calls

Your number-one priority in responding to calls concerning problems with a product, service, billing, or delivery is to arrive at an action that resolves the issue. Just *how* you arrive at that action says a lot about you and your company.

Build rapport with the caller. You need to discover the facts of the matter. However, be careful to avoid asking for this information with words that convey command or demand. For example, do not demand "What is your account number?" but inquire: "Do you have your account number handy?" or "Do you happen to have your account number with you?" Be careful to request, rather than demand, information.

Guide the conversation so that the words "you" and "I" become "we." You could say something like, "I need to get some information from you." But it is far more effective to say, "Let's fill in some information together." If a customer has a problem, and you can fix it, you might be tempted to declare—heroically—"I can fix that for you." Still, it is better to say something like, "We can work that out together without any difficulty at all."

Remember, few customers call to *complain*. What they really want is *help*. If you can give them the help they want and need, you become a hero and your company becomes a source of satisfaction rather than failure or irritation.

SHIPPING DELAY

Hello, Bert. This is Frank Muir at Dextron. We've run into a scheduling glitch with one of our suppliers. He has manufacturing delays, which, unfortunately, will mean that we can't ship your order before the 30th.

I'm sorry that this delay is unavoidable. However, I'm putting extra people on the job at our end, so we will minimize the delay. You'll get your shipment no later than the 5th. In the meantime, is there anything you would like me to do to help you accommodate to the revised ship date?

SHIPPING ERROR

Miss Smith, hello, this is Jay Norwood at Acme Limited.

Having to apologize for a mistake isn't something I enjoy doing, but I wanted to make sure that you received a personal apology for our having shipped the wrong item to you. I know that this caused you a certain amount of inconvenience.

I wish I could come up with some spectacular excuse for the mistake. But, the fact is, we goofed. Period. So, instead of offering you an excuse, I'll make you a promise: I won't let this happen again.

Thanks for all of your understanding and patience.

DAMAGED GOODS

Ed, it's Beth Cosgrove at Murray Hill. I just heard that your Widget arrived damaged. I'm very sorry about that. I want to take care of this problem as quickly as possible and without any hassle for you. So, let me offer two good choices: Either return the damaged item to me by Unique Express, and I will immediately trans-ship a replacement and will reimburse you for freight. Or, if you prefer, I will send one of my staff out to your location with a replacement on Friday. He will also pick up the damaged unit. Which way do you want to go on this?

3 E-Mail Messages

PRODUCT FAILED

Ms. Smiley:

Thank you for e-mail concerning your experience with the Model 234 Widget. I am very sorry that the unit failed. I realize that it comforts you little to learn that such failures are very rare. We make every effort to ensure that our products are free from defects. But, sometimes, even the best efforts are not always adequate.

A replacement unit has been sent to you and should arrive at your location by the 5th. I am confident that it will give you years of trouble-free service.

Ms. Smiley, I apologize for the inconvenience you were caused, and I sincerely thank you for your patience and understanding. Please e-mail or call me at 555-555-5555 if you have any questions concerning the unit.

Peter Hawkins,
Sales Manager

REPAIR FAILED

Mr. Thomas:

We don't like to hear that one of our products does not perform as expected, but on the rare occasions when we fail to service the product adequately the first time we're called out, we are acutely aware that we have really let you down. That's why I was concerned when I learned that the service we provided on April 15 didn't take care of the problem, and it is why I sent our service supervisor to your plant to ensure that our fix would work once and for all.

Mr. Thomas, I am very sorry for any inconvenience the problems with the unit and with the subsequent servicing may have created. I am sincerely grateful for the patience and understanding you have shown. I hope that you will believe me when I assure you that such problems—both with the product and with the service—are rare indeed.

If you have any questions at all, please phone me directly at 555-555-5555 or send me an e-mail message.

Eunice Smith
Customer Service Manager

BILLING ERROR

Frank:

I'm very sorry that you had to go to the trouble of helping us to resolve an error we made in billing your account. I understand, Frank, that the problem is now resolved, and that your account has been properly and fully credited. You know that we will make every effort to prevent something like this from happening again, Thanks a lot, Frank, for your patience and understanding. We appreciate it.

Ted

25 Words and Phrases to Use

alternatives	grateful	rush
apologize	help	service
assurance	immediate	solution
assure	make good	sorry
choice	patience	thanks
excellence	prevent	understanding
explain	problem	urgent
fix	put right	
future	repair	

15 Words and Phrases to Avoid

against company policy	not our fault	to be expected
cannot be true	not our problem	you're wrong
don't count on it	nothing we can do	you've made a mistake
excuse	nothing wrong	
hands are tied	problems with our company	
no choice	stupid	

Heartfelt Appreciation and Thanks

Expressing thanks is not just an act of courtesy—although it certainly is that—it is also a means of reinforcing positive action and building a cohesive organization. Behavioral psychologists have long known that praise and thanks are more effective means of reinforcing desired action than using punishment or threats of punishment. The memo expressing thanks is a powerful vehicle of positive reinforcement.

Finding the Heartline

What spells the difference between a pro-forma, perfunctory thank you and a meaningful expression of thanks? In a word, *specificity*. State exactly what you are thanking the other person for, and be sure to say something about the positive effect that person's suggestion, action, good deed, or whatever has had on you or your organization.

Keep the communication straightforward. Instead of lavishing adjectives upon the recipient, get specific with nouns and verbs that describe positive consequences. The sincerity and effectiveness of your thanks are directly proportionate to the degree of specificity you include in the thank-you message.

Sidestepping the Pitfalls

It is hard to make a mistake when you thank someone, but the biggest mistake is putting off the thank you or, even worse, neglecting it altogether.

- Deliver your thanks as soon after the event or deed as possible.
- Do not put off delivering thanks.
- Do not fail to write that thank-you note or make that thank-you call.

Any thanks are better than no thanks at all; however, the best, most sincere-sounding thanks get specific. Devote a little time and thought to your thank-you communications. People love to see the *effect* of their good deeds. So, show 'em.

3 Model Letters

THANKS FOR YOUR BUSINESS

Dear Jane:

Just a note to thank you for your recent order and to express my appreciation for your continued confidence in us. When a customer remains loyal for more than five years, as you have done, it gives me great pride in my organization.

Jane, it is always a pleasure to serve you. And please be assured that we are well aware that there is plenty of competition out there. I promise that we will continue to work for you every day to make certain that you continue to be happy with the choice you have made.

Sincerely,

Gary Thomas
Sales Director

FOR A FAVOR

Dear Pete:

Many, many thanks for giving John Young a demonstration of the Wonder Widget System we installed in your plant. There's nothing that sells this product more effectively than seeing it in action, for real, at a real location. Let me tell you: You made the sale for us. Mr. Young called this morning to place his order.

By way of thanks, please let us perform your next scheduled maintenance for free. Just call me when you're ready for our technician to come by.

With great appreciation,

Ben Hilldreth
Sales Manager

FOR A RECOMMENDATION/REFERRAL

Dear Mary:

Absolutely the greatest feeling I get in this job is when I do my work so **well** that one of my customers recommends my services to a valued colleague.

Based on your good word, Harry Hopkins hired our firm to do his inventory. You know that we won't let him down. We'll make sure he has every reason to thank you for the recommendation.

Sincerely,

Arnold Blatz
Account Representative

3 Model Memos

THANKS FOR THE GOOD IDEA

DATE: 00/00/00
TO: Jenny Gerhardt
FROM: Joan Sullivan
RE: Your upgrade idea

Your idea about an upgrade incentive program has stimulated a lot of lively and productive discussion in our department. It looks like we will indeed introduce a high-profile program along the lines you have suggested. I also believe that this will significantly improve our bottom line.

Speaking on behalf of the department's management team, I am very grateful for your stimulating idea and for the initiative you have shown.

QUICK THINKING, TIMELY ACTION

DATE: 00/00/00
TO: Len Owens
FROM: Juan Bautista
SUBJECT: Saving our hides

You became the man of the hour when you managed to expedite shipment of the Smith order. We came very close to losing a major customer, but, thanks to your quick and skillful action, we ended up by strengthening the relationship.

You acted professionally and with great initiative. The entire sales team is proud of you—and grateful, too.

PITCHING IN

DATE: 00/00/00
TO: Ken Rolfs
FROM: Moira Murphy
SUBJECT: Working the weekend

Thanks to your extra effort, we completed the Smith job on time, delivering it this morning. Giving up your weekend, I know, was a big sacrifice for you, but it did mean the difference between totally satisfying this customer and failing to deliver on time. Your dedication is greatly appreciated. Thanks, Ken.

3 Model Phone Calls

FOR YOUR ORDER

Mr. Jackson, this is Larry Larson at Peptalk, Inc. I was calling to thank you for your order and to confirm that the full order will ship on Monday.

Your business means a lot to us, Mr. Jackson, so I want to encourage you to give us a call if you have any questions at all after you receive your order.

It's a pleasure working with you.

FOR LENDING EQUIPMENT

Dan, Ray Miller at RayCom. I want to thank you again for lending us that D-100. You were a real lifesaver. Without that piece of equipment, we would never have gotten our big order out on time—and that would have really hurt one of our major customers.

You made a big difference, Dan, and I want you to know I won't forget it. Thanks so much.

FOR A BUSINESS LEAD

Penny, this is Lee. I want to thank you for sending Mr. Sawyer our way. On your good word, I contacted him yesterday, and it looks like we'll be doing business. That makes me feel good, of course, but what really gives me a thrill is when we earn the confidence of customers like you, Penny. Your vote of confidence means the world to us. Thanks again.

3 E-Mail Messages

ATTENDING MEETING

Joe, John, Ben, and Gail:

Thanks to you all for taking the time to attend yesterday's last-minute meeting. I know short-notice events are a pain, especially on the subject of asset allocation—but you were ungrumbling, thoroughly professional, and super helpful. Thanks to your input, I was able to secure the additional funds we need to complete Project X. This will mean a lot to our firm—and to our department.

Way to go!

Carl

FAVOR

Tom,

Many thanks for picking me up at the airport yesterday. My schedule was as tight as it gets, but, thanks to you, I made the meeting on time—good thing, too, since developments with the new technology are unfolding faster than any of us thought they would.

Thanks for being there.

Jena

GOOD ADVICE

Kathy:

Your advice about the word processing software was right on. I bought the product you recommended, and it is exactly what I needed. So easy to use, too! You're always so well informed and thoughtful. Thanks for taking the time to help me out.

Sandra

25 Words and Phrases to Use

accept my thanks

appreciate

couldn't have been better

couldn't have done it without
  you

count on you

generosity

godsend

good advice

grateful

helpful

invaluable

just what I needed

lifesaver

making the effort

on target

perfect

sharing

splendid

successful

taking the time

thanks

very useful

worked out fine

you were right

your contribution

5 Words and Phrases to Avoid

did the best you could

good enough

nice try

owed it to me

thanks anyway

27

Celebration and Congratulation

$\mathcal{T}$he most shopworn of clichés have an annoying way of often being quite true. Take this one, for instance: *Nothing succeeds like success.*

Sharing congratulations is a way of celebrating success that also builds a climate of success in your business, office, or department. Such a climate is likely to produce even more success. Acknowledging and celebrating achievement builds morale and reinforces a winning attitude and approach.

Don't limit congratulations to the circle within your own organization. Congratulations transmitted to associates, colleagues, and customers in the outside world can serve as a way to acquire new business while building goodwill. Make it a habit to keep your ear to the ground in order to learn of promotions and appointments in your industry. Write letters of congratulations to promotees and new appointees. Before long, you'll find yourself with a full-fledged network.

Finding the Heartline

Congratulating achievement should be straightforward.

- Begin simply with the congratulation itself.
- Describe the achievement.
- Assess its beneficial effect on the organization.

Remember, although the immediate purpose of a congratulation is to celebrate achievement and make the recipient of the praise feel good, it also functions to "raise the bar" of achievement for the entire organization. Everyone should acknowledge the creation of a new standard.

When you send a congratulatory message outside of your organization, be certain to do the following:

- Emphasize your business relationship with your correspondent.

- Use the occasion of congratulation as a springboard to further business; for example, if you are congratulating a client on a promotion within his organization, you might briefly suggest how the services or products you offer can be of assistance in your correspondent's new position.

- Express the desire to continue a successful business alliance.

- Repeat the congratulations; this is especially important if you are introducing yourself—lest the letter seem wholly self-serving.

- Be generous. Never qualify your congratulations.

- Take the opportunity to reinforce existing business relationships and to establish new ones.

- Make it a habit to keep abreast of promotions and appointments in your industry. Congratulating a new appointee is an opportunity to enlarge your network and your customer base.

Sidestepping the Pitfalls

Congratulating others is one of the pleasures of business life. Too often, however, it is a pleasure we deny ourselves. The biggest mistake people make with regard to congratulations is never getting around to them. It is also a mistake to delay congratulations. The handshakes and pats on the back should come as soon after the event as possible. Finally, do not stint. Congratulations should never be stingy or qualified. The best congratulations are specific—they specify the achievement and its benefits—yet they are also extravagant: They are liberal with praise. This is not a time for careful evaluation, but for the most open-handed generosity.

3 Model Letters

CAREER ADVANCEMENT

Dear Sophie:

Congratulations on your promotion to district sales manager. I'm not going to tell you that you don't deserve all the credit for your great success—but, well, I'd like to think that we at Wonderful World helped by always supplying you with prompt, personal service and terrific value. I trust we helped make you look as good as you are.

I wish you all the best in your new position, and I look forward to continuing our partnership and raising it to even greater heights.

Sincerely,

Devon Phillips

SALES ACHIEVEMENT

Dear Ben:

What a year this has been for you! Nobody has moved so much product so well.

Ben, it's a lot of fun working with a winner, and I look forward to many more years of continued success as your supplier of high-quality widgets.

Congratulations and warmest personal regards,

Tony Pastor

NEWS OF A CLIENT'S ENGAGEMENT

Dear Ned:

Word is that you're about to leave the bachelor ranks and join the rest of us in married life. I extend my hand in welcome. Well done!

You know, marriage changes everything. For the better. And, Ned, you'll find that includes your professional life as well as your personal life. It gives you added focus and motivation.

I'm happy for you. Congratulations.

Best regards,

Norm Hollings

3 Model Memos

JOB WELL DONE

DATE: 00/00/00
TO: Helen
FROM: Ron
RE: Well Done!

Wow!

Your work organizing the recent convention was nothing less than miraculous. You made us all look very, very good. The display of the new line was especially effective and sparked a lot of conversation. I have no doubt that it will also bring us a good deal of new business.

I am looking forward to next year's convention. With you organizing the show, it will be another great event.

On behalf of the entire department, I congratulate and thank you.

EXCELLENCE ACHIEVED

DATE: 00/00/00
TO: Quality Team
FROM: Sarah Goodheart, Quality Assurance Manager
SUBJECT: Error-Free Achievement

Industry standard: 97.5 percent error-free average. A lofty goal for a healthy industry.

It was not good enough for us. And when we told the industry it wasn't, a lot of people shook their heads and wagged their fingers. Better than 97.5 is not possible, they said.

Your team proved otherwise.

Thanks to your great work, we now enjoy a 98.9 error-free rate. It is the best in the business. Maybe the best in *any* business.

Well done, ladies and gentlemen! You inspire us all.

BIRTH ANNOUNCEMENT

DATE: 00/00/00
TO: All
FROM: Tammi Coles
SUBJECT: New Life

On Friday, June 19, at 5:36 a.m., Philip Gray Doane, 8 pounds, 6 ounces, came into the world. He is the first son of Susie Doane, our assistant controller, and her husband, Benton Doane, who is associate sales manager for the Tompkins Group. Mother and son are doing fine.

Susie will be home from the hospital by Wednesday. Please join me in signing the attached card, which I will deliver to her personally.

3 Model Phone Calls

PROMOTION—POTENTIAL CLIENT

Hello, Mr. Benson. This is Peter Pryor at Do-It Fast. I just read in *News Now* that you've been named production head at Acme. I want to extend my congratulations. I've always admired Acme, and your new position should be both challenging and rewarding. I also wanted to let you know that my firm offers a wide variety of printing services, and I'd like to help you get off to a great start in your new position by getting together with you to explain some of what we have to offer.

PROMOTION—BUSINESS FRIEND

Gail, this is Herb. I just heard the great news! What a terrific move Gelbart made in bringing you on board the management team. You bring incredible talent to that group and real savvy. Congratulations to them—and to you, too!

As soon as you're settled in, I'd love to get together for lunch. I'll call in about a week to set something up, okay?

AWARD

Fred, it's Cole. Man, you are *too* modest. Why weren't you on the phone about the Lowman Prize? I had to read about it in *Carpet News*. This is a great achievement, and no one deserves it more than you. I really am thrilled for you. If I'm surprised by one thing, it's that it took the committee so long to wake up, do the right thing, and present you with the award. Well, better late than never. If you're half as excited as I am about this, you must be floating right now. Congratulations and well done, Fred!

3 E-Mail Messages

BIRTH IN CLIENT'S FAMILY

Roberta!

Ed told me the great news. An addition to your family! Wow!

Please accept the congratulations and very best wishes of all of us here at Acme Widgets.

Pam

SALES TARGET EXCEEDED

To: Everyone in Sales

From: Tom Woodworth, CEO

I'm not known for going easy on people. I don't encourage settling into a familiar, comfortable groove. I have always set high goals for all of us— and, time and again, all of you have not only achieved, but exceeded those goals.

Now you've done it again.

For First Quarter, we were looking to move 30,000 units. Your team has pushed through 41,000.

Your achievement is a testament to the excellence of our product—let's not forget that—but it is also a testament to your commitment to that product, to this company, and to the customers we serve. You work hard, and you work smart.

Thanks. Congratulations. This is *your* victory.

PROJECT COMPLETED

Tom, I just saw your report on Project X. Congratulations on bringing it in on deadline and under budget! What an achievement! This will mean a big jump in our bottom line. I am thrilled for you—and for all of us.

You should be very proud. I know I'm proud to be working with you.

Ben

25 Words and Phrases to Use

accomplishment	perspective
achievement	pride
acknowledge	proud
all of us	recognition
celebrate	share in your triumph
congratulations	smart
deserve	success
exceed	superb
excellence	triumph
goal	victory
great work	well done
great impact	wise
happy	

10 Words and Phrases to Avoid

at long last	good enough
best you could	it's about time
finally done	lucky
finally over	okay
glad that's behind us	pretty good

Sympathy and Condolence

$\mathcal{B}$usiness can be a hard, harsh world. Yet the world of business is also a community. You may be competitive, you may insist on keeping your business associates separate from your friends and family, but, nevertheless, you and the people you work with, both inside and outside of your company, are a community. One of the standards by which a community should be judged is how its members respond to one another in times of loss, stress, and sadness. Yet even the most intelligent and articulate people sometimes find it hard to say the right things on occasions of death, serious illness, or other loss. If this is the case when we communicate to friends and family, it is even truer when we reach out to business associates, colleagues, and even competitors. We are not accustomed to thinking of these people as fully dimensional human beings. We are not used to addressing the full range of their emotions. Difficult as it may be, humanizing those we work with serves to enhance and deepen the work experience. It is a good *business* move, and it is the right *human* move.

Finding the Heartline

Knowing the right thing to say in a sad or traumatic situation requires a deliberate exercise of the imagination. Put yourself in the other person's place. Under the current circumstances of loss or sorrow, ask yourself: What would *you* like to hear? What would help *you* most?

Now that you have put yourself in the mind and heart of another, return to yourself. As you sit down to write that note or to make that phone call, be yourself. Express what is in your heart and imagination.

Emotions can be difficult to contain. Do you need to find an appropriate form for your expression of sympathy? Think of it as having five parts:

First: Express your sorrow at hearing of the death or loss.

Second: Sympathize by acknowledging the emotional pain of loss.

Third: Say something good about the deceased. If possible, share a memory.

Fourth: It is often helpful gently to remind the other person of the healing power of time.

Fifth: To the extent possible and appropriate, offer your help and support.

Find the emotional tone appropriate to the situation. You may be writing or talking to a business associate on the death of one of her valued employees or you may be writing or talking to that person about the death of a mutual business friend. Another circumstance involves communicating condolence to the decedent's family. Pitch your tone to what you see as the nature and the level of the loss.

Sidestepping the Pitfalls

It's odd, and not a little frustrating, that at precisely those moments when others need our kind words most, we often feel least able to communicate. Death, serious illness, or other loss erects barriers. We *want* to say the "right thing," but we are fearful of intruding on another's grief, or we fear that what we say will only cause more pain. This leads us into the single most common and most serious pitfall of communicating condolence and sympathy: The failure to speak or write.

The fact is, all other things being equal, a person who has suffered a loss craves comfort and kind words. How do you get started? As just mentioned, begin by imagining what *you* would like to hear in the current situation. Think about your feelings, and try to speak or write from these.

What you write or say need not be a bouquet of flowery words or profound pronouncements on grief and faith. In fact, avoid vivid adjectives and nouns that may even magnify the loss: "your *terrible* loss," "your *horrible tragedy*," and so on. Your correspondent does not need help feeling bad. Beyond simply saying how sorry you are, you may share a memory or two with the grieving person. Perhaps you believe that bringing up a common memory will only increase the other's pain. This is not the case. Demonstrating that the deceased still lives in memory brings comfort.

Don't be afraid that what you say will somehow intensify the other person's grief. Do not deliberately attempt to trivialize or minimize the feelings of grief. You may give comfort by suggesting that the passage of time will salve the hurt, but do not imply that the person who has suffered the loss will soon forget all about it.

3 Model Letters

DEATH OF A BUSINESS ASSOCIATE

Dear Jenny,

I was very sorry to learn of the passing of your president, Hank Morton. As you know, I've done business with Hank for the past five or six years, and it was always a great pleasure. You know even better than I that Hank was a brilliant, generous, and honorable man. You'll miss him, I know, not just as a leader, but as a friend. I feel for your loss.

Jenny, if there is anything I can do to help during what will be a difficult time for you, please don't hesitate to call.

Sincerely,

Irv Schneider

DEATH OF A BUSINESS FRIEND

Dear Marcy:

You know all too well that Ben Goring was more to me than a business associate. He was a great friend, and I miss him very much. Believe me, I feel for your grief—because I feel your grief as well. For you, the loss is double: a good friend is gone, and so is a valued member of your management team.

But, Marcy, you have to believe that Ben will live on—through his legacy of leadership, a legacy entrusted to people like you. And he has also left us great memories of personal friendship.

If there is anything you need from me—any service I can render—please don't hesitate to call.

Sincerely,

John Sebastian

TO THE FAMILY OF A BUSINESS ASSOCIATE

Dear Mrs. Hawks:

I was saddened to hear of the death of your husband, Howard. As a business associate, it was impossible not to respect him and not to like him. He was a strong person. I can only imagine how wonderful a husband and father he must have been. I'm truly sorry for your loss.

Mrs. Hawks, you don't need many words from someone who's almost a stranger to you. Take heart in the knowledge that time will at least soothe your pain. And, please, if I can be of any assistance to you, don't hesitate to call me.

Sincerely,

Kathy Norton

3 Model Memos

DEATH OF A COWORKER

Date: 00/00/00
To: Billing Department staff
From: Pam Isham, Manager
Subject: Karen Spencer

Some of you have already heard the tragic news: Karen Spencer, one of our billing associates, was killed in an automobile accident over the weekend.

The accident occurred on I-10 at about 7 o'clock on Sunday evening. I understand that Karen was involved in a head-on collision. No one else was in her car, and I am told that she died instantly, so—small mercy—she did not suffer. I have no information about the driver or passengers in the other vehicle.

Folks, as soon as I have information from Karen's family concerning funeral and wake arrangements, I will distribute another memo. At that time, I will have information on how to contact Karen's family to express condolences.

We were all Karen's friends, and we will miss her kind words and energetic presence, as well as the high level of professionalism she represented.

SERIOUS ILLNESS OF A CO-WORKER

Date: 00/00/00
To: Shipping Department staff
From: Porter Waylon, Supervisor
Subject: Illness of Ben Thompson

Yesterday, at about 4 o'clock, Ben Thompson, warehouse foreman, was taken ill. An ambulance was summoned, and he was transported to Holy Cross Hospital, where he is being treated for a heart attack. The latest word on Ben is that he is in fair condition. At the moment, he is still in the cardiac intensive care unit, so he's not seeing visitors just now. I am in frequent contact with the hospital and with Ben's family, and please be assured that I will keep all of you informed of his condition, and you'll be the first to know when Ben is ready for visitors.

In the meantime, I know that you will join me in sending Ben our good thoughts and best wishes for a speedy recovery.

CATASTROPHIC MISFORTUNE

Date: 00/00/00
To: Editorial Staff
From: Otis Mack, Editor in Chief
Subject: Tornado hits home

As we all know, Harrisville was hit and hit hard by a series of tornadoes over the weekend. I am greatly relieved and happy to report that all of us here at Rex Publishing survived the catastrophe, but it gives me great pain to tell you that Edna Perkins, chief of the Proofreading Section, lost her house. It was completely destroyed. Thankfully, Edna and her family are fine—but, as you can imagine, they are reeling from their loss and struggling to pick up what pieces they can.

Edna and her family are staying with her sister and brother-in-law, Sarah and Peter Coughlin. Edna, trooper that she is, expects to be at work on Monday. In the meantime, I know that she can use help sorting through the remains of her home. If anyone wishes to lend Edna a hand, Rex Publishing can lend you the time. Please see me.

3 Model Phone Calls

DEATH OF A BUSINESS ASSOCIATE AT ANOTHER COMPANY

Caller: Hello, Pete. It's Sam. I just heard about Larry Miles. It was a shock to me, and I can only imagine what a blow it must be to you. He was not only your top manager, but a close, close friend.

Callee: Yes. It's very hard . . .

Caller: I know it doesn't seem like it at the moment, Pete, but you—you and your company—will get through this. Larry, above all things, would not want the company to falter. That's the kind of person he was. Remember when he broke his leg skiing? He was out of the hospital and behind his desk in record time. The company meant the world to him—and, if he could, he'd be telling you to get on with it.

Callee: That was Larry, all right.

Caller: You know, he's still there with you—in the company the two of you built. Remember that. And, Pete, if there is anything I can do to help right now, let me know. Don't hesitate to call.

TO THE SPOUSE OF A BUSINESS ASSOCIATE

Iris, this is Bob Kean. I just heard about Paul. I am so, so sorry. He and I did a lot of work together, and I not only enjoyed working with him, but I learned a great deal from him. I feel the loss deeply, and I can only imagine how you feel. But I know that Paul would want you to be strong for your children. So, hang in. Iris, if there is anything I can do to help you, please call me.

FOLLOWING CATASTROPHE

Len, I just heard about the fire in your building. It's a shock, I know, but I've also known you long enough to be confident that you will come out of this quickly and even stronger than before. Have no fear.

If there is anything I can do to help you out—including lend you some office space and the use of our phones—let me know. I'd like to be of help to you.

3 E-Mail Messages

DEATH OF A BUSINESS ASSOCIATE

Owen:

Gail was such a good friend to us both that I am painfully aware of how deeply you feel her loss. I also know that, hard as her passing is on me, it's even more of a trial for you, who have lost not only a dear friend, but a key member of your management team.

Owen, nothing can replace our friend, but I know how much confidence and trust she placed in you. She always spoke of you as a full partner. She relied on you. She shared her knowledge and judgment with you. Gail was savvy about people. She knew how well you could manage the company, and we all believe you will do just that, not only *carry* on, but *move* on—to even greater success.

Owen, please know that I am here to help in any way I can. Don't hesitate to call or e-mail.

Tom

BELATED CONDOLENCES

Max:

Just in from a two-week vacation and was given the sad news that Jake died last week. I wanted to send these condolences—belated though they are—as soon as possible. I feel for the loss to you and to your firm.

You know better than I do that Jake was a great pleasure to work with. He was a fine and generous man.

If there is anything I can do to be of assistance during this painful time, please don't hesitate to call.

Arnie

OTHER LOSS

Ted, I just ran across the news in *Industry Tabloid* about SmithCo going out of business. I know that this firm is one of your biggest accounts, and I'm sure its passing did not come as welcome news to you.

You have a great company, Ted, and I have no doubt that you'll weather this loss and emerge stronger than ever.

Let's get together over lunch to discuss some strategies and ideas for the future. I'd really like to see you. Why don't you give me a call?

Dan Miller

25 Words and Phrases to Use

admired

anything I can do

assist you

blow

condolences

feel for you

future

grieve with you

grieve

help

here for you

invaluable contribu-
tion

just heard

just learned

let's get together

loved

news

painful

please call

respected

serious

shock

sorry

sympathy

time will help

12 Words and Phrases to Avoid

despair

gone to a better place

hopeless

How can you go on?

never recover

not that bad

nothing I can do

passed away

shake it off

What will you do now?

worst thing that could have
happened

you'll get over it

Encouragement and Motivation

$\mathcal{A}$ll supervisors and managers agree: A key to effective leadership is the ability to motivate others to achieve excellence. Agreement quickly breaks down, however, over just how to go about the task of motivation. The truth is that few of us are comfortable either with giving pep talks when things go well or with rendering "constructive criticism" when things don't go so well. We find ourselves falling into generalities and platitudes, sounding off the way a high school sports coach might.

Why do most of us come up so lame when it's time to motivate the group?

We fail to be specific. Most motivating communication is made not from the heart, but in a vacuum, without reference to specific circumstances. Want to make an effective motivating speech or memo? Then dig into what's happening now. Dive into the present situation. Talk about a real problem or a current triumph or a genuine opportunity—something specific and immediately relevant to your "audience." Focus on what the problem, triumph, or opportunity means to that audience.

Finding the Heartline

Motivation is selling. You sell the idea of excellence and achievement. As in any other selling situation, success, making the sale, depends on your ability to shift the focus from your own needs and concerns and onto those of your "prospects"—in this case, the people you want to motivate.

Such salesmanship does not come out of context. One or two memos or pep talks isn't going to do the trick. To cultivate the best in your group requires developing and nurturing enthusiasm. This is not done in an instant, but over the long term. The inspired manager circulates among her team, infusing it with enthusiasm. She makes the following part of her daily routine:

- Talking with staff and subordinates
- Working closely with the group
- Suggesting new approaches to stubborn problems
- Expressing empathy in difficult situations
- Consulting and coaching on a continual basis

Communication is the soul of motivational management. The motivating leader tirelessly does the following:

- Shares observations.
- Reinforces positive achievements and attitudes.
- Continually corrects the team's direction and focus as required.

Praise, specific and sincere, is essential to ongoing motivation. Consider convening regular reinforcement meetings:

- Such meetings should be positive and upbeat; their objective is to reward, refresh, and, if necessary, refocus.
- Invite staffers to bring up their concerns, but defer full discussion of these to separate meetings, if they threaten the upbeat tenor of the reinforcement meeting.
- Introduce an element of pleasure into each meeting. Serve refreshments, perhaps, or share a funny story.
- Greet group members with kind and pleasant words: "You guys, as usual, look great!"
- Keep the tone of the reinforcement meeting light, warm, and friendly.
- Be specific in your positive reinforcement. Invite the staffers you single out for praise to talk about their success.

- Spend less than an hour in the meeting—enough time to cite, in detail, several positive examples. Allow ample time for questions, discussion, and clarification.

Don't depend solely on meetings to keep the motivational dialogue going. Supply vigorous and continual feedback designed to reassure subordinates that you have confidence in their skills and abilities.

- Make feedback specific.
- To the degree that it is possible to do so, stress the positive.
- Practice delivering feedback in a sincere tone.
- When you have to deliver critical feedback, always suggest alternatives. Never simply criticize an employee or reject his work.
- Put some *fun* in your instructions and directives. Don't turn them into jokes, but feel free to use imagination when you give directions, discuss ideas, or deliver feedback.

Motivation is not exclusively about praise. Excellence also requires correction and guidance—in other words, criticism. The heartline to effective criticism is to be generous in giving it. Consider the following rules of thumb:

- Communicate criticism in the manner of a mentor or a coach.
- Make it clear that you are committed not just to your department's or company's bottom line, but to the development of the employee as a long-term member of the team.
- Before you criticize, *be certain of your need to criticize.* Avoid using criticism merely to vent frustration, anger, or irritation.
- Ask permission to criticize. Asking permission to criticize will actually enhance the effectiveness of your remarks. Instead of starting out with something like, "You're not doing an effective job with so-and- so," begin with "We have a problem with so-and-so, which I would like to discuss with you. Is now a good time?"
- Be certain that the cure will not be worse than the disease. Even sensitively expressed criticism can damage a fragile ego. Use judgment to decide whether the problem or issue is worth the risk that critical words entail.

- Do not criticize subordinates in front of others. Take the person aside—subtly. "Mary, I need to speak to you about an important matter. When is a good time for us to get together for a few minutes of uninterrupted time?"

- As far as possible, quantify your criticism objectively: "Turnaround time in your area is a good 10 percent more than we need it to be."

- Maintain your perspective. You are both on the same team; therefore, approach the subordinate not just as an employee, but as a member of *your* team. Be friendly.

- Always address issues, never personalities. Resist the temptation to tell an errant employee what you think of him. Focus on the issue.

- Combine as much praise as possible with the criticism. You might observe that, in general, you are pleased with the subordinate's work, but that, as regards issue A, an improvement needs to be made.

- Limit your criticism to what can be changed. It does no good— and may do great harm—to criticize a subordinate for something over which she has little or no control.

- Address one issue at a time. Avoid bombarding the subordinate with a cluster of faults and problems.

Sidestepping the Pitfalls

The main reason motivation fails is that it fails to be clear and specific. Always outline specific problems or goals. Avoid issuing blanket criticism or generalized criticism. Cite specific issues and incidents. Also be sure to take the following steps:

- Resist the temptation to yell at people. Focus on problems and issues, not on personalities. It is far more feasible to fix things than to try to fix people.

- Censor yourself. If your remarks are not likely to improve the situation, don't make them.

- Reinforcement meetings should not be lectures. Make them interactive.

- Avoid criticism first thing in the morning or at quitting time. Criticism is not a good way to start or end the day.

3 Model Memos

DATE: 00/00/00
TO: Sales Department
FROM: Jim
SUBJECT: Attitude

So I'm in the hall yesterday, and I hear one of you complaining: "I missed the sale because EXPLETIVE DELETED John Doe didn't get me the right EXPLETIVE DELETED numbers until it was too late!"

Okay. We all get angry. But there are two things wrong with just fuming about a bad situation.

Number 1: It doesn't pay to get angry at people. Get angry at the situation. Don't try to fix people. Fix the situation.

Number 2: When you start blaming others—even when they do screw up—you can forget about achieving your goals.

Look, the fact is that any sale can be saved, even if we don't always have all the information at our fingertips. It takes extra effort, but it can be done. Don't panic. Don't swear. Just work the problem.

You have all shown me that you are not only capable, but also superb salespeople. I am proud of all that you have accomplished. But I don't want you to get the idea that it should always be so easy. Make the sale, if you can. Save the sale, if you must. By all means, lean on the team—but depend on yourself, and take responsibility for what you do and for what you fail to do.

REINFORCING SUCCESS WITH A GOOD STORY

DATE: 00/00/00
TO: Customer Support Division
FROM: Don Ibsen
SUBJECT: Above and Beyond

What makes a good news story?
Disaster.
What makes a great news story?

A disaster that didn't happen.

Last week, we shipped one of our best customers, M&N, a bad TVX circuit board. M&N called Dora Donbey, the customer service rep assigned to the account, who moved heaven and earth to get a new board out there.

Guess what? The new board failed.

You can bet there was another call to Dora. She scrambled to get yet another board. Nothing doing. The cupboard was bare.

End of story. Disaster—for the customer, and for us. Right?

Dauntless Dora got on the phone and called a list of her other customers until she was able to find one who was willing to lend a TVX unit to M&N. We picked up the tab for the loaner, and Dora personally ran the board over to M&N.

That, ladies and gentlemen, is motivation. Not just doing everything that's expected of you, but more—committing yourself to each and every customer, becoming that customer's partner, and refusing to give up, even when the "normal" options are exhausted.

Well done, Dora. You not only saved an important client, but you taught us all a valuable lesson. Thanks!

GETTING THINGS DONE

Date: 00/00/00
To: Billing Department
From: Iris Berman, Billing Manager
Subject: Procrastination

Inertia, any high school physics teacher will tell you, is the property of a body by virtue of which it opposes any agency that attempts to put it in motion or, if it is moving, to change the magnitude or direction of its velocity. In other words, inertia opposes action or change.

Physical objects have no monopoly on inertia. It is also a property of human beings. Many, many of us have trouble starting projects that need to be started. Call this procrastination, if you like, but it's inertia all the same.

As with physical inertia, mental inertia often requires the application of an outside force to get moving: A client screams; a boss threatens; your kids clamor for food, clothing, shelter, and a college education. These are all highly effective outside forces.

But you cannot always depend on the timely application of outside forces. Besides, if you're kicked hard enough, you'll bruise. The better answer to procrastination is to formulate ways in which you yourself can overcome inertia and break free of the procrastination pattern. Now, this does not mean simply telling yourself to "work harder" or to "get going." Procrastination has little or nothing to do with laziness. It's about structure—or, rather, lack of it. Without structure and direction, it is very difficult to get things started—and, conversely, very easy to find excuses to put things off.

Your most powerful weapon in the war against procrastination, then, is creating a schedule. Do you have trouble keeping to a schedule? Well, maybe that is because you don't create a daily or weekly or monthly schedule. The fact is that making and keeping schedules is vital to getting ahead and staying ahead in business.

Let's start with the most basic schedule for the typical work day. Plan what you're going to do for the day at the *beginning* of each day. Plan what you're going to accomplish during the week at the beginning of the week. Here's how to get started:

- Take out a piece of paper and write down the projects you are working on.
- Number them in priority order, starting with the most critical projects and working your way down.
- Now, take out your calendar—or fire up your desk-top computer calendar program—and begin plugging in time slots for the most important projects at the beginning of the week.
- If you prefer, divide the time for each project each day, but always give proportionately more time to the critical tasks.
- Next, set firm deadlines.

Let's pause on this last point. Remember when you were in college and you knew you were going to be tested on a chunk of material—but you didn't know when? I bet you cracked those books right away!

Sure.

The truth is that only when a firm date for the exam was set did you start to study. Let's face it, given a choice, we wander down the path of least resistance. With a firm deadline and a little discipline, however, you'd be surprised at all that you can accomplish. Set personal deadlines, write them down, and plan your work to meet them.

Procrastination begins at the start of the day. Well, you say, you're just not a morning person? You simply can't get your work going at 9 a.m. sharp? Then try getting into the office just a little earlier, say 8:45. By the time you've had you're first cup of coffee, checked your e-mail, and shot the breeze with everyone, you're ready to go—and, wonder of wonders, it's 9:00, or just a bit past the hour.

When you plan your schedule, do be realistic. Don't expect to produce in a half hour an hour-long presentation on a subject you don't know much about. And don't schedule for yourself more time to work on something you really enjoy, but that you know you could complete in a matter of minutes. Schedule according to needs, not desires.

Intelligent, thoughtful scheduling provides the framework you need to help you climb out of the pit called procrastination. I urge you to try it.

3 Model Speeches

INCREASING PRODUCTIVITY

Acme Industries is not the kind of place where you have bosses breathing down the necks of their staff or cracking the whip and bellowing for more "productivity." Here we pride ourselves on being self-starters, and if anyone is dissatisfied with the level of productivity generated, it's each of us ourselves. We self-starters are our own harshest critics. It seems that no matter how hard we work, most of the time we feel that we just don't get enough accomplished.

I think it is a mistake to talk about productivity in the abstract. It certainly doesn't help to tell yourself to "work harder." No, increasing personal productivity is a matter of working on the little things in your life to make them more convenient and efficient. It's about time management.

Let's begin at the best place to begin: the beginning. Begin by asking yourself: "Are you efficient?" Answer this question by making a private list. Divide the page in half. In the lefthand column, write tasks you ordinarily perform during a typical day. In the righthand column, assess how well you do them. For example, in the lefthand column you write: "Finishing projects on time," and in the righthand column: "I usually only finish the projects I'm interested in first, then get around to the others." That's an honest start. Now keep going. You'll end up with a snapshot of your level of efficiency.

Since, in essence, productivity is a matter of time management, work toward getting a handle on your time. Keeping time sheets or using a computer program that tracks the hours you spend on specific tasks is a concrete method of managing your time and gauging your productivity. You may discover, for example, that you've spent eight hours on a relatively trivial project that should have been done in no time, and yet, in that same month, you spent only three hours on a project that is critical both to your career and to the company. Einstein told us that time is relative. Who are we to argue with Einstein? But that eight hours spent on trivial tasks is still five hours more than you spent on the really important work. Don't just record your time; *track* it. Look for the important patterns by studying time sheets from several months.

Now let's talk about "free time."

If the concept of "free time" makes you laugh because you're constantly bringing home work, you're either just extremely busy or not being productive enough during regular working hours. Is there something wrong with you? Do you have colleagues who seem always to get their work done on time and at work rather than at home? What is it about their work habits that makes this possible? Do they get to work early? Do they take work home with them? Do they take shorter lunch breaks? Make a list of what you feel gives them the advantage. Study the list. Is there something you should be doing differently?

One thing you may do differently is to plan out your day. Start the morning by making a schedule of what you have to accomplish before leaving the office that day. Write down how long you think it should take to complete each individual task. Don't cheat! As you go through the day, mark down the start and stop times for each task. How did you do? Did some tasks take longer than expected? This is a sign that there may be a better way to get the task done. You just haven't thought of it yet. You can take a high-tech approach to this exercise by using your contact manager PC or Mac program. Set start and stop points for each task. You can set the alarm on your program to sound when it's time to start wrapping things up. Be sure to record how well you keep to your original schedule as you go through each task. Be sure to keep a record of all of your starts and stops. This will help you diagnose problem areas.

Now, we've been talking about managing time at the office. But who said travel time has to be "down time"? If you commute to work on the bus or subway, bring something work-related to read. Create a "traveling folder" in which you keep all the papers you're working on at the moment. This way, they stay in one place and are easily accessible, ready for you to grab for the commute to and from the office. You might also use the morning commute to plan your day. If you manage to grab a seat on the subway, bus, or train, open up your planner (you do have a planner, don't you?) and jot down what you need to get done today. You might also use your evening commute to take stock of what needs to be done the next day.

Now for those of you who drive to work, don't try to read while you're driving. However, you can still use driving time for more than just driving. If a great idea comes to you while you're driving, don't let it pass. As soon as you can stop—at a traffic light, say—jot down a note or two. Most auto parts and accessories stores sell paper pads that can be mounted on your dash. It is even a better idea to invest in a small hand-held microchip recorder. Speak your ideas into one of these.

While we're on the subject of the commute, give some thought to whether or not you're really taking the shortest route to work. Plan it carefully, taking into account traffic as well as distance. For a variety of good reasons, you might also consider car pooling. Now this won't save commuting time, but it may buy work time, including early-morning discussions with your colleagues and co-workers. You know, if nothing else, car-pool conversation gets out of the way a lot of the small talk that often adds to first-thing-in-the-morning office inertia.

Speaking of colleagues, you might start thinking of ways to coax others—not just yourself—to greater personal productivity. Begin by communicating your expectations clearly. For example: "I'm going to need that report by 4 p.m. tomorrow. If we don't have it ready by then, we risk losing this account. If you have any questions or concerns, please talk to me while we can still do something about them. Thanks."

In addition to open, clear communication, remember to plan the work, and work the plan. Sit down with those you work with and plan for the month, the week, or even just the day ahead. Be certain that you're all agreed on which projects have priority, what the deadlines are, and just how the tasks should be executed.

Just as you hold yourself accountable, don't be afraid to hold others accountable as well. While you shouldn't point fingers, browbeat, or terrorize, you don't have to be overly eager to express understanding and to accept excuses. React honestly and helpfully if you receive work that is just not up to par. Remember, though, address the issues of the work, *not* the personality of the worker. Separate the person from the problem. Then attack the problem, not the person.

Don't be reluctant to criticize constructively, but don't just criticize, either. Suggest solutions. As a manager or colleague, it is your responsibility to offer constructive solutions to the problems you detect.

Remember that information is the single most valuable driver of productivity. Get people to feel closer to what you are doing by empowering them with information: copies of important memos and other documents. Keep them "in the loop," even the memos that are only FYI.

Folks, these are all small things—small, real, concrete things. You can do them, and they will add up. Their sum will be greater than the parts. You *will* be more productive, and, almost even better, you will *feel* more productive.

LEADERSHIP—ADDRESS TO MANAGERS AND SUPERVISORS

As managers, you are the leaders at Acme Corporation. I want to speak with you, in practical, down-to-earth terms, about what leadership means.

If you are looking for a nutshell definition of what a manager is expected to do in our organization, it is that he or she is not expected to do anything, but, rather, to ensure that whatever needs to be done gets done.

Is a manager a leader or a boss?

Truly effective managers are leaders, not bosses. Bosses bark out orders, whereas leaders give direction—not just "directions," but direction. Bosses, naturally, are always right, whereas leaders are willing to admit that others may have good ideas. Bosses bully, but leaders motivate. Bosses intimidate, whereas leaders educate. The boss is a driver, the leader a coach. The boss stands upon the principle of authority, the leader on good will. The boss inspires fear, the leader enthusiasm. Whereas the boss commands "go," the leader says, "let's go."

That's all well and good—inspiring people, leading rather than bossing. But management is not only about inspiration. Effective management is about controlling time, money, and people. "Administrative management" is what we call the time and money part of the job. It includes budgets, policies, and procedures. The people part includes hiring, training, coaching, setting goals, motivating, counseling, and, when necessary, terminating.

Now, as a manager, you will be judged chiefly—almost exclusively—on the basis of how well your people do. An effective leader, therefore, devotes most of his or her time to developing and improving staff members. Spend at least three-quarters of your time working the "people" side of the management job and only about a quarter of your time on "administrative management." If you spend more time than that on administration, you may be managing, but you are not leading.

Now let's talk about leadership style. There's more than one right way to lead. You might pick and choose your favored methods from the following menu:

- *You may lead through example.* This means working harder than anyone else in the office and knowing more about the product line than anyone else. Leading by example is incredibly hard work. It's also one of the most consistently successful leadership styles.

- *You may lead through encouragement.* Since the early days of scientific psychology, tests and studies have repeatedly shown that people respond more favorably to positive rather than negative reinforcement. They learn faster, and they comply more willingly and readily. Learn to take genuine and generous pleasure in the accomplishments of your staff. Always have something positive to say. Stimulate and inspire.

- *You may lead through teaching.* This requires a high level of technical expertise and a tireless willingness to share your knowledge. You need to cultivate within yourself a passion for solving problems.

- *You may lead through motivation,* through tirelessly encouraging individual staff members to improve themselves, to work harder, and to work smarter. This style of leadership requires frequent and crystal-clear goal setting. Make rewards visible, tangible, and available. Cultivate top people. Groom them for promotion.

I've removed one highly popular leadership style from the menu I just offered. Many, many managers try to lead through intimidation. This isn't really leading at all. It's pushing. You lead from the front, not the rear. Your organization is like spaghetti. It is much easier to pull than it is to push!

An effective leader creates loyalty. This is a quality that cannot be bought or bullied. Loyalty must be earned, and managers who earn it generally do the following:

- They treat people fairly.

- They are always accessible.

- They listen well.

- They recognize achievement.

- They praise achievement.

- They reward achievement.

- They themselves are loyal. When appropriate, an effective manager stands up for his staff, defending them to senior management and, when necessary, to customers.

- They are helpful and expedite important matters with other areas of the company.

- They ensure that credit is given where credit is due.

- They are dependably knowledgeable.

- They are great coaches, mentors, teachers.

- They have and they communicate a clear sense of purpose.

This is the last leadership point I will leave you with: An effective leader has—and communicates—a clear sense of purpose. When all is said and done, this is the single most important aspect of leadership. On this, all the rest depends.

OPTIMISM—ADDRESS TO A MANAGERS' GROUP

On July 2, 1862, the Union army was about to lose the Battle of Gettysburg. With the loss of Gettysburg, very likely, would come an end not only to the Civil War, but to the United States as a single, unified nation. The northern United States would have a slave-holding neighbor on its southern border. All the Confederates had to do was take the high ground, and the Union forces wouldn't have had a prayer.

The end of the Union's line of troops—its flank, its most vulnerable point— was occupied by a badly weakened regiment from Maine, whose colonel, Joshua Chamberlain, had been a professor of rhetoric at Bowdoin College. The rebels charged repeatedly, but, somehow, Chamberlain and his men held firm.

Finally, there came a massive charge. Chamberlain's regiment, exhausted, was also out of ammunition. The proper thing to do was to surrender.

But Chamberlain knew that to surrender the flank would mean losing the battle and, quite probably, the war. In a desperate, depressing, no-win situation, Chamberlain, trained as a teacher and not as a military commander, chose the road of optimism.

He ordered his men to attack, to charge—using bayonets in the absence of ammunition.

The Confederates, shocked, retreated, then surrendered.

The tide of Gettysburg turned, and, on the next day, the Union won a victory that effectively sealed the doom of the Confederacy and ensured the resurrection of the Union.

By all reports, Chamberlain was a soft-spoken, scholarly man. He did not lead by terrorizing his troops, but by inspiring them with confidence and optimism. His optimism outlasted his ammunition and, in the end, was far more effective. Deeply felt, that optimism was contagious.

Most contagions, of course, are not so positive. Gloom, doubt, and defeatism are, if anything, even more contagious than optimism. If we allow these feelings to dominate us, we will create defeat. Now it is true that, just because we are driven by optimism, it doesn't necessarily follow that victory will be ours. However, it is far more likely that a defeatist attitude will spread and will bring disaster than it is that an optimistic attitude will create anything negative. With defeatism, then, we have everything to lose, whereas, with optimism, we have nothing to lose and, perhaps, much to gain.

To be sure, both defeatism and optimism are only feelings. But feelings are fuel. They do not *determine,* but they do *drive* our success—or our failure. So how do we "spread" optimism?

The answer is most definitely *not* to deny the reality of setbacks, challenges, problems, and disasters. However, we must embrace and broadcast a faith in our ability to cope with and even profit from setbacks, challenges, problems, and disasters.

When Thomas Alva Edison was laboring away at inventing the electric light, he told a newspaper reporter that he had tested some 1,600 substances as potential filaments for his lamp, all of which had failed.

"You must be very disappointed at the waste of time and labor," the reporter remarked.

"Not at all. Nothing was wasted," Edison replied. "Now I know of 1,600 things that will not work."

Edison had found a positive—and true—way of looking at his experience. This drove him, of course, to ultimate success.

Our task, as managers, is to help our employees look at their experience as positive. Is a customer calling to complain about a problem with a widget? Look at this as an opportunity to satisfy this customer by making that problem right. Cultivate this attitude in yourselves, and it will be broadcast to your staff.

25 Words to Use

advice	discuss	learn
advise	evaluate	lesson
analyze	expedite	manage
assist	formulate	navigate
consider	future	plan
control	glitch	reconsider
cope	help	rethink
counsel	invest	
determine	lead	

25 Words and Phrases to Avoid

better shape up

blame

can't do it

catastrophe

crisis

demand

destroyed

disaster

don't ask

don't come to me about it

don't want to hear it

don't worry about it

exploded

fault

figure it out yourself

force

foul-up

hell to pay

hopeless

idiotic

impossible

mess

misguided

must

snafu

30

Asking Favors

If you look forward to asking for a favor about as much as you look forward to root canal dentistry, you are decidedly in the majority. Root canal is hard to endure, and so is begging: asking for something in return for nothing.

That's the way most of us think about requesting a favor.

Want to make it easier to get what you need? Begin by rethinking your definition of *favor*. Erase the definition of it as a bid to get something for nothing, and substitute this: Asking for a favor is providing somebody with an opportunity to help you.

And this *is* an opportunity. Most people enjoy helping others. Being asked to help empowers the helper. It is a compliment and a vote of confidence. It is an opportunity to feel good about oneself. Asking for a favor provides an opportunity to make someone feel good.

And there is more. The business community is not all about cutting throats and pummeling the competition. Hard as it is to believe sometimes, business operates according to a kind of corporate karma—the belief that what goes around comes around. Doing a colleague a favor creates good will. Most of your colleagues recognize that and are eager for the opportunity to create good corporate karma.

Finding the Heartline

Get to the heartline by putting yourself in the right frame of mind. Purge from your head that outworn notion of the favor as freeloading.

319

Think of it as an offer of opportunity. Next, overcome the inertia that preceded that first difficult step: broaching the subject.

Begin by furnishing a basis for the request—"We've worked together for so long that I feel comfortable asking you for a favor." That done, state what you want:

- Be clear and specific about what you want.
- Explain how the favor will benefit you. This gives the other person a way to gauge just how much he can help.
- Express gratitude.

Remember also to express yourself in positive terms, and if you *can* offer a quid pro quo, do so—just don't try to disguise a request for a favor as a business deal.

Sidestepping the Pitfalls

The biggest mistake most people make when they ask for a favor is to apologize for doing so: "I'm sorry to ask . . ." This is the equivalent of warning the other person that you are about to make his life miserable. It also puts him on his guard, suggesting that you are about to make an unreasonable demand.

- Do not apologize.
- Do not tell the other person how he should feel about your request: "I know this is annoying . . ." Or: "I hate to ask you . . ."

Do not attempt to soften the request by minimizing it: "Joe, this will take a half-hour of your time at most." That's a fine thing to say— if it is a true assessment of the effort required. Joe will be justifiably annoyed, however, if the favor consumes two or three hours or more. Don't minimize the request. Don't lie.

Always express your gratitude, but avoid such phrases as "thanking you in advance." This implies that you take the other person's compliance for granted—and that is always offensive. It may also end by embarrassing both of you.

3 Model Letters

ASKING FOR A RECOMMENDATION

Dear Ed:

We've had such a great working relationship that I actually look forward to asking you for a favor.

I need a brief letter of recommendation to the Waldorf Company to help us secure a major contract with them.

We've been asked to bid on supplying them with widgets and widget-maintenance services. I don't have to tell you that this represents major business for us. It would be very, very helpful if, in addition to whatever else you feel inclined to comment on, you could make the following points about your experience with us as a supplier:

• We supply high value.
• We furnish a high level of client support.
• We offer three-hour emergency response.

Ed, we're working on a tight schedule to make Waldorf's tight schedule, so I would appreciate your sending out the letter before April 3. You'll be writing to:

Mr. Frank Miller
President
The Waldorf Company
444 23rd Street
Warrentown, NH 00013

Please call me if you have any questions, and, as always, I appreciate your time and attention.

Sincerely,

Sam Korn

CHANGE IN MEETING TIME

Dear Tom:

I am looking forward to meeting with you about Project X. In the past day or two, I discovered three new marketing venues relevant to the project, and it would be a benefit to both of us if I could have a little more time to explore these venues.

Specifically, I could use four more days to do some legwork. Can we push the meeting back to February 4?

Please call or fax with your response. The investment of a little extra time will pay off, I believe.

Sincerely,

Ron Sheldon

EXTEND DEADLINE

Dear Ms. Schultz:

I thought this would be a good time to give you a progress report on Project X.

We have completed the first three phases of the project, but we are finding that research for phase 4 is consuming more time than we had anticipated. I know that you do not want any corners cut on this crucially important project, especially not at this culminating stage. I ask, therefore, that you agree to extend the deadline for completion of the entire project to March 16.

I am confident that the improved results will justify the additional time invested at this point.

Please give me a call to confirm the new deadline or to discuss the proposed adjustment to the schedule.

Sincerely,

Robert Bennet
General Manager

3 Model Memos

CALL FOR VOLUNTEERS

Date: 00/00/00
To: Customer Service Staff
From: Tod Pointer, Manager
Subject: Volunteers Needed

Next weekend (September 23-24), we will be working with the Build-A-Home organization to help in the construction of affordable homes for needy families. Our department has been given the opportunity of contributing to this valuable and highly rewarding enterprise. Accordingly, I am calling for volunteers for the weekend.

No special skills are required. Volunteers will be fully supervised. What *is* required is a willingness to pitch in and make life better for a family in our community.

Those of us who pitched in last year remember this weekend not as a sacrifice, but as a fulfilling time spent with other good people. To join us, please call me at extension 123 by Thursday afternoon.

CHANGE MEETING TIME

Date: 00/00/00
To: Bill Williams and Gail Storch
From: Ted Matthews
Subject: Change Meeting Time

In view of the new technical developments bearing directly on the widget rollout, Bill and Gail, I think we should postpone the launch meeting for at least one week, which should allow us sufficient time to get a fresh report from Engineering.

I know we're under the gun in terms of deadline, but we can't afford to ignore the changes that are about to happen. If we don't wait for the new information, there is a good chance we will have to revise the rollout anyway—and lose even more time.

Can we meet on the 14th, then? Please let me know.

USE OF OFFICE

Date: 00/00/00
To: Ben Marks
From: Celia Randolph
Subject: Borrow Your Office

Jim Matthews from AccountTech is scheduled to come in for a meeting on Friday. I've just learned that the conference room is booked up that day. My office, as you know, is a cubicle. That leaves us without anyplace to sit Mr. Matthews down for a major strategy meeting. Can you bail me out with the loan of your office? We would need the space for three hours, from 9 to noon, on the 14th. You are, of course, welcome to my humble cube during that time.

Ben, if you can spare the space for that morning, it would really help me out of a jam. Just give me a buzz to let me know.

3 Model Phone Calls

REQUEST FOR REFERRAL

Caller: Hello, Jack. This is Pat Smith at R&T. I'm calling to ask a favor.

Callee: Oh? You are?

Caller: XYZ Company has just asked us to bid on an installation of a widget, which is quite similar to the kind of work we did for you last year. From our point of view, that project was a great success, and I believe you think of it the same way.

Callee: We were pleased.

Caller: I also believe that you know Sam Maxwell at XYZ. Am I right?

Callee: Yes, I know him very well.

Caller: That's what I thought. It seemed to me that you would make an ideal reference. What I'd like to ask is for you to make a quick phone call to Mr. Maxwell and tell him something about the kind of job we did for you. Could you do that?

Callee: Yes, sure.

Caller: It would be very helpful if you could stress the efficiency of the installation and the minimal impact the work had on your routine. XYZ is particularly concerned about down time. You have Mr. Maxwell's number?

Callee: I do.

Caller: Is it possible for you to make the call today?

Callee: As soon as that?

Caller: I would really appreciate it. This would be a major contract for us. It means a great deal.

Callee: Okay. I'll call this morning.

Caller: That would be wonderful. We would be very grateful for whatever kind words you could pass along. I hope you'll call on me some time to return the favor.

CHANGE IN MEETING PLANS

Mark, this is Kelly Pressler. I've a favor to ask you. Jack Green, from Youngblood & Youngblood, is going to be in town on Monday. He's an expert on the kind of work we plan to be doing with Project X. I'd really like to take advantage of his being in town. I know we want to keep our meeting low key, but could you see your way clear to make room for Jack? His perspective would be well worth having.

ALTER PAYMENT SCHEDULE

Ben, this is Murphy. I've got a problem I'm hoping you can help me with. As you know, when we set up the payment for our last order, I was counting on our schedule meshing with the one we'd worked out with our client, Singer and Son. Well, they got underway with the project three weeks late. Accordingly, for our cash flow, it would be great if we could reschedule our last two payments to you—namely from September 3 to September 20, and from December 5 to December 28. Would this work for you? It would do wonders for us.

25 Words and Phrases to Use

advantage	convenient	please
appreciate	do the same for you	rely on
ask	emergency	request
assist	favor	thank you
bail out	grateful	urgent
benefit	help	valuable
big help	last minute	volunteer
call on me	mutual friend	
comfortable	need	

15 Words and Phrases to Avoid

don't like to ask you	no problem for you
easy for you	no time at all
hate to ask	owe it to me
have to	pain in the neck
I know I can count on you	piece of cake
must	sorry to ask
my last hope	you can't turn me down
no choice	

31

Invitations that Invite

$\mathcal{I}$nvitations are acts of both asking and giving. They ask for a person's presence, participation, time, and sometimes, talent, even as they offer that person one's own time, as well as hospitality, perhaps, or, depending on the occasion, even opportunity and honor. The tone of the invitation should reflect its dual nature. The idea is to be respectful and grateful, but also to "sell" the value of what is being offered.

Finding the Heartline

Invitations, even in a business context, are intensely social documents. The emphasis should be on courtesy and sincerity.

- Make it clear that the invitee's presence or participation is genuinely desired.

- "Sell" the event. Be certain that the invitee understands what he is being asked to do and what benefit he will derive from doing it.

Underpinning these two messages is information. Whatever else an invitation is, it is a vehicle of some simple but crucially important items of information—the five *W*'s so familiar to journalists and news reports:

- *Who?* Be sure the invitation makes clear who, exactly, is being invited. Names must be double checked for accurate spelling. Are spouses included in the invitation? Others from the invitee's firm?

- *What?* What—exactly—is the event in question? What is included in the event? (Dinner? Lunch?) What, if anything, is the invitee expected to do at the event? (Give a speech? Participate in a panel discussion?)

- *When?* Date and time.

- *Where?* Place. Be sure to include directions, if it is likely the invitee is unfamiliar with the location.

- *Why?* What is the purpose of the event or occasion? Be certain that this is clear, especially if you are asking the invitee to prepare a speech or presentation.

Also essential are the names and phone numbers of people to contact if the invitee has questions or requires clarification. Specify, too, a response due date, together with an address or phone number for making the response.

Sidestepping the Pitfalls

Business invitations are plagued by two common problems:

1. *Unclear, incomplete, garbled, or erroneous information.* Make sure all five *W*'s are present in your invitation. Be certain the information is correct.

2. *Inappropriate tone.* Some business invitations sound like command performances. A more common fault is the invitation that is couched in apologetic terms: "I hate to ask you to come to another one of these rubber-chicken banquets, but I don't have much choice." If you cannot offer an enthusiastic invitation, it is best to rethink the invitee, the event, or both.

3 Model Letters

TO SPEAK AT BUSINESS MEETING

Dear Ms. Lawrence:

One of my most pleasant business memories is of the speech you made in Chicago last year. What you said was not only enlightening and lucid, it was also delightful. When I met with the Speakers' Committee yesterday to plan our annual XYZ Convention, I mentioned to the group how great it would be to get someone like Sarah Lawrence to speak.

"Hey, Mike," one of the committee members said, "why don't you just ask her?"

What an idea!

I would be doing a great service to my firm and our organization if I succeed in persuading you to speak. I've enclosed a flier describing the event and giving the time and place. You will have an opportunity to address—and to meet—the top people in the wholesale textile industry. The choice of topic is entirely up to you, although I might mention that computerizing inventory is a hot-button issue in our industry just now.

In addition to offering you access to industry leaders, we also serve a pretty good meal at the event. The speaker's honorarium is $500, plus your expenses.

Please think over this opportunity, and kindly call me at 555-555-5555 no later than September 5.

Sincerely yours,

Michael Wall
Vice President

TO JOIN A TRADE ORGANIZATION

Dear Frank Williams:

It was a great pleasure speaking with you the other day about our organization, Trade Focus Association. It is a great group of people who wield significant influence in our industry.

I was delighted to learn from you that you are interested in joining us, and I immediately discussed the matter with the membership at our most recent meeting. They enthusiastically agreed to extend this invitation to you.

We would be delighted if you would attend our next meeting on Monday, November 3, at 8 p.m., in the Wonder Room of the Grand Hotel, 1234 East Pell Street. You'll have the opportunity to sit in on one of our meetings, and you'll be given a full presentation on membership, including benefits, responsibilities, and dues.

I look forward to seeing you there. If you have any questions beforehand, please call me at 555-555-5555.

Sincerely,

Jan Baker

TO ACCEPT AN AWARD

Dear Ms. Standish:

Each year The Service Club presents its Milhous Award to individuals who have demonstrated an extraordinary commitment to community service. It is my pleasure to inform you that the Awards Committee has voted to confer this year's Milhous Award on you in recognition of your long and distinguished record of service.

We would be greatly honored if you would consent to accept the award and to attend the annual Awards Dinner, which will be held on December 3 at 8 p.m. at the Grand Hotel, 12324 Downtown Street.

I ask that you telephone me at 555-555-5555 to indicate your acceptance of the award and your availability for the dinner and presentation ceremony.

Congratulations and thanks.

Sincerely,

Peter Wald
Chairman, Awards Committee

3 Model Memos

MEETING—SHORT FORM

DATE: 00/00/00
TO: Marketing Staff
FROM: Arnold Booth, Marketing Manager
SUBJECT: Market Plan software meeting

Those of you who currently use or plan to use the new Market Plan software package will want to attend a tutorial meeting on Friday, May 3, at 3 p.m. in the third-floor conference room. A representative from the Market Plan firm will be present to answer any questions you may have about the software.

MEETING—LONG FORM

DATE: 00/00/00
TO: Marketing Staff
FROM: Arnold Booth, Marketing Manager
SUBJECT: Market Plan software meeting

We are currently evaluating a new software system, which, we hope, will allow us all to evaluate more effectively and more quickly the performance of our products in the marketplace.

This software promises to limber up the organization, making us more flexible, more responsive to the market, and, even more important, more capable of making accurate *proactive* decisions.

In short, Market Plan promises to make your lives easier and more profitable. That is, *if—*

1. You know how to use it.
2. It actually works for you.

On Friday, May 3, at 3 p.m. in the third-floor conference room, you will have an opportunity to explore the software, find out how it works and if it will work for you. A representative from Market Plan will be here to demonstrate the product and to answer all of your questions.

This could be a very important tool for us. Attending this meeting will be your opportunity to hit the ground running with this new technology.

GOING-AWAY PARTY

Date: 00/00/00
To: Accounting Staff
From: Pam Deaner, Manager
Re: Going-Away Party for Ed Meeks

As you all know, Ed Meeks is retiring after more than twenty years with Bold & Bolder. Whether you've been here for most of those years or for just a few months, you've doubtless come to admire and respect Ed and will want to give him a hearty send-off.

You'll have that opportunity on Friday, May 5, at 4 p.m. in the dining room. We'll celebrate Ed's twenty years with us and give him our thanks as well as our best wishes. Food and drink will be abundant.

Please join us.

3 Model Phone Calls

INFORMATIONAL MEETING

Caller: Good morning, Otis. This is Perry. Ben Karlson, Claire Toombs, Ed Spiro, and I are getting together to discuss implementation of the new accounting program. I know that you don't work with accounting software every day, but it occurred to me that you would find information on the software useful, since you do work with us quite a bit. Would you like to join us on Tuesday?

Callee: Yes. It sounds worthwhile.

Caller: Great! I thought you'd be interested. We're getting together on Tuesday, at 3, in my office. See you then.

LUNCH

Ken, this is Sam Weinstein at Benton and Hart. It's been quite a while since we last touched base. Certainly I haven't had the opportunity to meet with you since my company introduced its new line of widgets. I think you'll want to know about their new features, and I thought the most pleasant way to introduce the line to you would be over lunch. Can I take you? Say, 12:30 on Tuesday or Thursday of next week?

SURPRISE PARTY FOR EMPLOYEE OF THE MONTH

Caller: Larry, this is Marla. Ted Williams has just been named employee of the month. A number of us—Mike Jones, Billy Taylor, Ron Shelton, Patty Lease, and I—thought we'd make something special of it by giving Ted a surprise party. You're such a good friend of Ted's that we didn't want to throw this shindig without you.

Can you make it on Friday, at 4, in the conference room?

Callee: Sure. Sounds great.

Caller: Okay. We've got funding from petty cash, so no donations are necessary. The only requirements, then, are that you be there—4 P.M., Friday, conference room—and that you do *not* tell Ted! It *is* a surprise party. You know Ted. He'd never agree to this kind of thing if he knew about it.

Callee: Your secret's safe with me.

Caller: Great. See you then.

3 E-Mail Messages

AFTER-WORK PARTY

Jim, Jack, Jane, and Harold:

The Smith project is safely launched—after three solid weeks of 14-hour days. Won't you join me in a little celebration after work on Friday?

The Time: 5:30 sharp, May 3
The Place: Ivan's
The Purpose: Pleasure

Hit the reply button, please, and let me know if we're on.

Simon

INFORMATIONAL SEMINAR

John:

Our department is holding a seminar on the new mailing software Tuesday, March 6, at 10:30 in the main conference room. Ordinarily, it's just our department folks who attend, but since you are involved in a project that requires a mass mailing, I thought you would be interested in an overview of the software.

No need to reply. If you're interested, just drop in on Tuesday.

Parker

POWER BREAKFAST

Terri,

Ned, Frank, Earl, and I are getting together before the presentations on Tuesday to review our position on the new projects. We figured the most efficient way to do this was at breakfast. Your input would be very helpful to us, and I suspect you'd be eager for the opportunity to get your views known to us before the big meeting.

Our plan is to meet at Nelson's, the coffee shop downstairs, at 8 a.m. on the 23rd. It would be great if you could make it.

Sam

25 Words and Phrases to Use

any questions	hash out	invite
ask	help	meet
benefit	helpful	offer
brainstorm	honored	opportunity
eager	invest your time	overview
get together	investigate	participate in

plan	share	welcome
proud	valuable	worthwhile
review		

12 Words and Phrases to Avoid

boring

don't be left out

feel obligated to ask you

fight it out

have to ask you

if you really want to come

probably don't want to come, but

probably not interested, but

show up

sorry to ask

spend your time

you could come

Index